D1590224

A STUDY IN SURMISE

BY THE SAME AUTHOR

Novels

Weep for Lycidas
Spring in Tartarus
All the Trees Were Green
Vernal Equinox
What Are We Waiting For?
Battered Caravanserai
So Linked Together
Treadmill
There's Glory For You!
Long Vacation
The Dividing Stone
The Brain
A Hansom to St. James's

The "Rowcester" Novels

Higher Things
The House in Fishergate
Sinecure
The Darkened Room

Biography

Gambler's Glory *(John Law of Lauriston)*
Count Cagliostro: "Nature's Unfortunate Child . . ."
They Would Be King *(Lambert Simnel, King Theodore, Bernadotte, Henry Christophe)*
Prince of Hokum *(Peter Cheyney)*
Charles Dickens: A Sentimental Journey in Search of an Unvarnished Portrait
Rosa *(Rosa Lewis of the Cavendish Hotel)*
Lord of London *(2nd Duke of Westminster)*
Clarence *(HRH the Duke of Clarence & Avondale)*

Historical and Paranormal

Airborne at Kitty Hawk *(The Wright Brothers)*
The History of the Hat
London by Gaslight: 1861–1911
London Growing: The Development of a Metropolis
Mulberry: The Return in Triumph *(Prelude to D-Day)*
The London That Was Rome
Fanfare of Strumpets
The Roots of Witchcraft
Fire from Heaven *(Spontaneous combustion)*
Vanishings

The Sherlock Holmes Commentaries

In the Footsteps of Sherlock Holmes
The London of Sherlock Holmes
The World of Sherlock Holmes
I, Sherlock Holmes

Philately

Mauritius 1847
A New Approach to Stamp Collecting *(with Douglas B. Armstrong)*

Cuisine

Beer Cookery

Short Stories

Transit of Venus
Exploits of the Chevalier Dupin *(U.S.A. only)*
Murder in the Rue Royale, and Other Exploits of the Chevalier Dupin

Advertising

Technical and Industrial Publicity

A Study in Scarlet

Ormond Sacker – ~~from Soudan~~ from Afghanistan
Lived at 221 B Upper Baker Street

with

I Sherrinford Holmes –
The Laws of Evidence

Reserved –
Sleepy eyed young man – philosopher – Collector of rare Violins.
Chemical laboratory
An Amati –

I have four hundred a year –

I am a Consulting detective –

What rot this is" I cried – throwing the volume
: petulantly aside " I must say that I have no
patience with people who build up fine theories in their
own armchairs which can never be reduced to
practice –
Lecoq was a bungler –
Dupin was better. Dupin was decidedly smart –
His trick of following a train of thought was more
sensational than clever but still he had analytical genius.

A page from Dr. A. Conan Doyle's notebook: "Mark these skimpy notes well—they are the first blueprint of the world's most famous fictional detective."
Reproduced by special permission of the late Adrian Conan Doyle.

A STUDY IN SURMISE

THE MAKING OF SHERLOCK HOLMES

MICHAEL HARRISON

GASLIGHT PUBLICATIONS
BLOOMINGTON, INDIANA • 1984

ISBN: 0–934468–10–9

Library of Congress
Catalogue Card No. 81–82193

Printed in the United States of America

GASLIGHT PUBLICATIONS
112 East Second
Bloomington, Indiana 47401

A Cynthia Coulon-Karlweis

. . . une amie dont l'affection
et la générosité sans bornes,
mille fois démontrées, ne
sauront jamais être suffisamment
reconnues ni recompensées

nous dédions cet ouvrage

– un tribut modeste mais profondément
sincère de notre part à tous les deux.

Maryvonne et Michaël

Hove,
Angleterre
le 18 juin 1982

No detail is so small as to be neglected.

—as Sherlock Holmes would have said

Every man has the right to utter what he thinks truth, and every other man has the right to knock him down for it.

—as Samuel Johnson did say

What happens when a new work of art is created is something that happens simultaneously to all the works of art which preceded it. The existing monuments form an ideal order among themselves, which is modified by the introduction of the new (the really new) work of art among them. The existing order is complete before the new work arrives; for order to persist after the supervention of novelty, the whole existing order must be . . . altered.

—as T. S. Eliot, an admirer of Holmes, stated

Knowledge rests not upon truth alone, but upon error also.

—as C. C. Jung reflected

His methods are irregular, no doubt, like my own. The irregulars are useful sometimes, you know. *—as Holmes certainly observed*

Arguments are to be avoided. They are always vulgar, and often convincing. *—as Oscar Wilde warns us*

CONTENTS

INTRODUCTION by Ellery Queen

In the Introduction to Ellery Queen's suppressed anthology, *The Misadventures of Sherlock Holmes* (1944), we wrote: "Someone has said that more has been written *about* Sherlock Holmes than about any other character in fiction. It is further true that more has been written about Holmes *by others* than by Doyle himself." As the years pass since the first Sherlock Holmes story was published—*A Study in Scarlet* (1887)—the two statements quoted above become more and more incontestable. Indeed, many Sherlockian devotees may have wondered if *anything new* can still be written about the creation of Sherlock Holmes—hasn't *everything* already been said?

The answer is no: not all has been learned, and not all will ever be learned. The well of speculation and conjecture is bottomless, and research about Sherlock Holmes will never die, or even fade away. The interest, perhaps the fanaticism, in the creative sources of Sherlock Holmes is eternal.

And now Michael Harrison, author of *In the Footsteps of Sherlock Holmes* (1958), has engaged in some new and remarkable research, tracking down hitherto unknown and *unsuspected* origins of The Great Detective, and has come up with what we unhesitatingly describe as the most important discovery in Sherlockiana of the past decade, perhaps of the past quarter of a century. No, we'll go even further: perhaps the most important Holmesian discovery possible to have been made since the death in 1930 of Sir Arthur Conan Doyle, the only one who knew all the Sherlockian answers...

ACKNOWLEDGMENTS

WITH every book completed which is not one of pure fiction, I find myself under the necessity—I should hardly use the word "obligation" in this context—of acknowledging the help that I have received in gathering up the essential material of my book. Authorship, I hasten to say, affords no duty more pleasant; no duty more readily assumed and more cheerfully discharged.

Every author, man or woman, who even begins to assemble the material of a nonfiction book—let alone goes on to complete it—assumes, by the very decision to write this type of book, a heavy burden of gratitude. He or she may owe it to the living; more commonly, in matters of research, it is owed to the industrious, creative dead: the help of both should be promptly and fully acknowledged. The assistance that authors, living and dead, have given me I have acknowledged where necessary in the body of this book's text.

I have now to thank those who have so willingly responded to my various requests for essential information. The list below is in no order, alphabetical or otherwise; to have introduced any such order would have implied a distinction in importance among the kindnesses here most gratefully acknowledged. There may be no such distinction; each contribution to my fund of knowledge has its unique importance; mere quantity of information does not enter into my estimate of value; quality certainly does.

Here, then, are my warm thanks to:

The late Frederic Dannay ("Ellery Queen"), for kind permission to preface this book with the flattering introduction that he wrote for the original article, "A Study in Surmise," on which this book is based; and which article appeared in *Ellery Queen's Mystery Magazine,* of which Mr. Dannay, as "Ellery Queen," was then the Editor-in-Chief.

Mr. Roger Johnson, an esteemed fellow Sherlockian, for supplying me with a Xerox copy of that same article, when I found that I had mislaid my copy of the magazine containing it.

Miss Valerie Springett, of the British Museum, for many kindnesses shown in her sending me press cuttings, making enquiries in regard to needed books, and generally in every helpful way.

Mr. Clifford Jiggens, Deputy Editor of *The Western Times,* for having found me a copy of R. S. Lambert's book *The Cobbett of the West,* long out of print; for having made photocopies of all the relevant passages; and for having drawn my attention to the vitally important *early* association of Conan Doyle with the county of Devon.

Mr. P. W. Ellis, Area Librarian, Devon, for having supplied me with a copy of the report of the Oliver–Galley trial from *The Exeter Flying Post* of 1836.

The Reverend Father F. J. Turner, Librarian, Stonyhurst College, for patiently answering my many questions on Conan Doyle's schooldays, and on the nature of the studies at Stonyhurst when Doyle was a pupil there. And, too, for recalling to my mind that most apposite Sherlockian quotation with which I preface this book: "No detail is so small as to be neglected"–a caution to be observed by every writer.

Miss Valerie Bone, Secretary of the Institute of Shorthand Writers Practising in the Supreme Court of Judicature, for having courteously and effectively directed my enquiries to a valid and fruitful source of information:

Mr. A. G. M. Newman, Chairman of Marten Welsh Cherer Ltd., Legal and Conference Reporters, and inheritors, in the direct line, of the firm of shorthand-writers founded by George and Joseph Scherer (Cherer). Charles Dickens, who was employed as a shorthand-writer by the Cherer Brothers, has immortalized them in his novel *Nicholas Nickleby* as the benevolent "Cheeryble Brothers"–an important fact to which my attention was called, for the first time, by Mr. Newman. In answering the questions passed on to him by Miss Valerie Bone, and in lending me two now very rare books, Mr. Newman threw open the way to an uninterrupted search for the origins of Sherlock Holmes.

Miss E. McNeill, B.A., D.L.S., A.T.C.L., A.L.A., Librarian and Keeper of the Records, The Honourable Society of the Middle Temple, for sound advice to me in extending the range of my research.

Mr. Colin Taylor, Senior Assistant, Liaison and Processing, British Broadcasting Corporation (London), for having, with exemplary courtesy and exemplary patience, tracked down for me the title and date of a wireless programme on the subject of the Galley affair: *Which Dick Turpin? The Story of the Miscarriage of Justice of Edmund Galley,* a programme recorded on Monday, 3 May 1948. Mr. Taylor and the staff of the Programme Information Index of the BBC are to be further commended in that they traced this programme despite the fact that, misled by a faulty reference in another author's book, I had enquired about a non-existent title. To all concerned: my very warmest thanks!

Mr. F. P. Richardson, Librarian, The Law Society (London), for having kindly sent me valuable photocopied extracts relevant to the life and legal career of Sir Alexander Cockburn, Baronet, sometime Lord Chief Justice of England.

Air Commandant Dame Jean Conan Doyle, D.B.E. (Lady Bromet), for having given me much of her valuable time, taking me over the former Conan Doyle family home, "Windlesham," near Crowborough, Sussex–that still largely unspoilt part of one of Britain's lovelier counties that Dame Jean's father made familiar to all his readers in that fine novel *The Poison Belt*–and there, through the house and through its immediate surroundings, interpreting some most attractive aspects of Sir Arthur's character not yet to be found in any of the many biographies, exhaustive though several have been.

Over luncheon at a country inn, and over dinner at Sir Geoffrey and Lady Bromet's London flat, Lady Bromet–Dame Jean–continued this sympathetic interpretation of her famous father: an interpretation which enabled me, not only to write a description of that "Windlesham" visit for the privately-circulated American journal *Baker Street Miscellanea,* but also, I sincerely trust, to approach the subject of this present book with a greater understanding of the not-at-all uncomplicated character of Sir Arthur Conan Doyle.

Mr. Ralph Malbon, F.L.A., City Librarian, Miss Janet Smith, Liverpool Record Office, and all others who have helped me to recover the background of the Maybrick trial.

Mr. J. B. Darbyshire, F.L.A. and Mrs. N. Yuill, of the District Central Library, Blackburn, Lancashire, who not only answered, more fully than I had hoped, my questions about the Watsons of the Blackburn district when Conan Doyle was at Stonyhurst but added, for good measure, a brand-new theory to explain the "H." of "John H. Watson," in addition to supplying me with importantly relevant extracts from Victorian guidebooks and a contemporary drawing of the Blackburn windmill, reproduced in this book.

The Dickens Fellowship, for having supplied me with a photocopy of a "Phiz" illustration of the Cheeryble Brothers, and for having pointed out to me the existence of other claimants than the Cherers to the title of the original Cheerybles.

And once again, I have the pleasure of thanking my friends of The Atlantis Bookshop–Mrs. Kathleen Collins, her daughter Geraldine (Mrs. Beskin), and all the other well-wishing Collinses for encouragement, practical help in finding me rare and out-of-the-way books, and, above all, for their consistent friendship.

A WORD TO THE READER *This book is . . .*

a detective story. But, note, a detective story of a very special kind. It has, in the manner of the classic detective story, the aim of tracking something or someone down; and, as in all rational searches, its steps, no less than its motivations, are clearly described for the instruction of the reader.

I must make one essential fact understood from the very beginning: that this tale of the tracking down of a world-renowned personality (we may hardly describe him otherwise) is in no sense fiction. . .even though the quarry of our hunt has well-defined fictional elements in his make-up. What must distinguish this detective story from all others is that it sets out to track down the origins of a detective, who was conceived in a number of *facts* but eventually realized—"born," if you like—as the hero of a work of fiction, cheaply and somewhat obscurely published in the year of Queen Victoria's Golden Jubilee, just on a century ago.

The creator of this hero—and this book is deeply concerned with both Hero and Creator—has described for us, in some detail, the real person, Dr. Joseph Bell, Lecturer in Pathology at the University of Edinburgh Medical School, on whom, the Creator affirmed, he had based at least the principal characteristics of his Hero. As you will read in this account of my tracking down the original—indeed, the originals, for many a real person has gone into the making of Sherlock Holmes—you will see that my researches, undertaken over what has now lengthened to a period of some thirty years, have conclusively revealed that, of all the many real-life characters who have "added up" to that composite fictional character known as Sherlock Holmes, Dr. Joseph Bell has probably made the least contribution of all. (And why this should have been so, I shall explain in the course of my narrative.)

If no man be an island, then certain it is that no author yet, whether he or she write history or fiction, may concentrate on the subject to hand to the exclusion of all other interests, of all other subjects, of all other thoughts; and even this book of mine, setting forth my theory of the Making of Sherlock Holmes, had its accidental origin as I was engaged in research into the still unexplained phenomenon of Disappearance, on which, after having sold several articles and delivered several radio broadcasts, I eventually wrote a full-length book.[1]

Indeed, it is in this, at first glance, unrelated study of Disappearance that I first stumbled across—there is no other correct way of expressing it—the theory which, here, has been expanded to the limits of yet another full-length book.

I shall refer now only briefly to the quite serendipital discovery of the Sherlock Holmes theory, since I shall explain it at length in the course of my narrative; but—and I reiterate, very briefly—it happened that, in my study of Disappearance, I had read closely, in the contemporary newspapers, the details of what was called the "St. Luke's Mystery," which concerned the vanishing, from his shop in the St. Luke's district of London, of a German baker, Urban Napoleon Stanger. This was in 1881.

I had, I admit, seen the name of the private (and most unsuccessful!) detective called in to find the missing man; and I had seen it many times before its possible significance—its possible connection with Sherlock Holmes's literary fabrication—struck me. How the name of that private detective, Wendel Scherer, led me to the theory which now takes up the pages of an entire book, you may read in the leaves which follow.

It is now nearly thirty years since, after that first startled recognition of the *possibilities* of Wendel Scherer's name and—as I thought even then—of the significance of his *character*, as revealed

---

[1] Michael Harrison, *Vanishings* (London: New English Library), 1981.

in the first official enquiry into Stanger's disappearance before the magistrates at Worship Street Police Court, that I sketched out enough of my theory and what I offered as supporting facts to be able to offer a radio talk on the subject to the BBC and two articles, the first to the (London) *Daily Telegraph*, for which, with the friendly encouragement of the then managing editor, the late Sir Colin Coote, D.S.O., I wrote frequently. Sir Colin was always most receptive to my ideas, however fanciful, and my first article to introduce my Holmes-origin theory was not the only article that Sir Colin accepted which has eventually become a full-length book. Ten years after the Holmes article, Sir Colin accepted and printed the incunabular version of my theory that the plan of vanished Roman Londinium might be recovered through a study of London's surviving placenames and the names of its many churches and taverns; and the book which sprang out of this article appeared in 1971 as *The London That Was Rome.*[2]

To return to the Holmes theory: the second article that I wrote on this subject–it appeared in *London Mystery Magazine*, a publication of the group for which I was then a features editor–slightly expanded the theme, to which, again and again, my mind returned; but that I had not forgotten my interest in Disappearance is clear from the fact that I wrote an article, "Out of This World," for *Courier Magazine*, yet another of the group's publications.

I had, even though perhaps only half-consciously, to realize that there was an intimate and important connection between Disappearance and the creation of Sherlock Holmes–as the future was to prove.

All through the 'fifties, I wrote several articles on both subjects; it is only honest to record that those on Disappearance were more important than those on Holmes and his origins. But, in 1958, Messrs. Cassell & Company of London published my first full-length "Sherlockian" book, *In the Footsteps of Sherlock Holmes*, which established me as a "serious" writer on the Master and which gained me commendations, not only from the (London) Book Society and the (U.S.) Book-of-the-Month Club, but also

---

[2]Michael Harrison, *The London That Was Rome* (London: George Allen & Unwin, Ltd.), 1971.

from the mass of Sherlockians throughout the western world. I think with affection and regret of the late Anthony Boucher, who, in making *Footsteps* his *New York Times* book of the week, established the book's claim to respectful recognition as a major contribution to Sherlockian scholarship. (Since then, I have, as is well known, written three more full-length "Sherlockian" books and a small monograph–this last my only Sherlockian writing not to be published in the U.S.A. as well as in Great Britain.[3])

The search for Holmes's original had never ceased to hold my attention, and 1971, the year which saw the publication of *The London That Was Rome,* saw also the publication of what has proved to be the first draft of this present book: "A Study in Surmise," a nineteen-page article which appeared in the January (British edition: February) 1971 issue of *Ellery Queen's Mystery Magazine,* with a full-page introduction of this "major discovery in Sherlockiana" by Ellery Queen (Frederic Dannay), who needs no introduction from me! In addition, four of the world's outstanding Sherlockians–Vincent Starrett, Howard Haycraft, Rex Stout, and Dr. Julian Wolff–contributed flattering criticisms of my discovery and of the article in which I announced it.

Magazine publication is not the best means of securing permanent availability to any writing; even more so than hardcover books, magazines tend quickly to go out of print and to be accessible to the student only with the greatest difficulty–if accessible at all.

---

[3]In order of publication, they are: *In the Footsteps of Sherlock Holmes,* (original version) London: Cassell and Company, Ltd., 1958; New York: Frederick Fell, Inc., 1960; (revised version) Newton Abbot, Devon: David & Charles, 1972; New York: Drake Publishers, Inc., 1972; (paperback) New York: Berkley Publishing Corporation, 1976. *The London of Sherlock Holmes,* Newton Abbot: David & Charles, 1972; New York: Drake Publishers, Inc., 1972. *The World of Sherlock Holmes,* London: Frederick Muller, Ltd., 1973; New York: E. P. Dutton & Co., Inc., 1975; (paperback) London: New English Library/Mentor, 1975. Two additional Sherlockian publications are: *Theatrical Mr. Holmes* (limited edition monograph), London: Covent Garden Press, 1974; and *Beyond Baker Street: A Sherlockian Anthology Edited and Annotated by Michael Harrison,* Indianapolis/New York: The Bobbs-Merrill Company, Inc., 1976.

(I had an example of that this very afternoon, when I telephoned the *Daily Telegraph's* library to enquire whether or not I might have a photocopy of the Sherlock Holmes article. It was *not* available: "Oh. . .some time in the 'fifties? Oh, we don't keep files as far back as that. . ." Yet they manage in France: my wife visited the French Military Archives at Vincennes and there obtained the photocopied complete file—the full military career—of an unimportant young assistant surgeon killed at the Battle of Leipsic in 1813. . .and this despite the fact that, since 1813, France has known five wars, three major and some smaller revolutions, four occupations, and destruction on a scale that Britain has never known.)

Well, not to stray from my subject: the relevant issue of *Ellery Queen's Mystery Magazine* was long since sold out, and my article, as I have since found, did, for all that, enjoy quite a wide circulation among Sherlockians in photocopy. An American publisher of limited editions was anxious to publish the article, illustrated, in hardcover; but, as final arrangements were being made between us, he died, and nothing came of the venture.

Then, in the March of 1981, as I was in the nursing home, recovering from a major surgical operation and urgently desiring some cheering news to offset the depressing influence of all the pills which were being prescribed, I received a letter from Jack Tracy of Gaslight Publications, asking my permission to publish "A Study in Surmise" as a hardcover, but also suggesting that the book would be even more acceptable to the public were it to be expanded and to carry illustrations.

Now, I had already determined that there was still something important to discover before the whole story of Holmes's creation could be completed; I did know for what I was seeking, though at the time I had not found it. I wrote to Mr. Tracy, accepting his invitation but explaining the situation and informing him that I would communicate further as soon as I was ready to begin work on the final version.

There were obstacles: all the *established* sources were unable to help me. And then, as so often in my life as a researcher, I "struck oil"—and, since sorrows, as Shakespeare tells us, come not single spies, but in battalions, so one lucky find almost always has companions. When my luck turned, I had the happiness of realizing that my search for Sherlock was over, and that all which now remained to be done was to assemble my rich stock of material and actually get down to writing the book.

As the reader will find, this is a tale which ranges widely, not only in the realm of an author's imagination—Conan Doyle's, I mean, not my own—but in space, no less. The true tale gathers up, not the most incongruous elements, but without doubt the most diverse; and chance brought Conan Doyle, in his own research, to a pair of notable characters who had already been marked for literary immortality by no less a writer than Charles Dickens. Who these brothers were will be explained as we proceed with our narrative.

For Doyle, the creation—element by element—of that rare being, Sherlock Holmes, yielded what, in the modern jargon, may be called some valuable "fringe benefits." One of the most important came when the search for Holmes took Doyle back to the end of the eighteenth century, to a French general who was the uncle of the Scherer brothers for whom Dickens worked. The general, Barthélémy-Louis-Joseph Scherer (1747–1804), had twice commanded the French revolutionary armies in Italy, had been appointed Minister of War under the Directory, and was set, as the phrase has it, for even greater success, had he not fallen foul of the young Napoleon's ambitions. To the interest that Doyle conceived for this brilliant but unlucky man, we must justifiably attribute that broader interest on Doyle's part in many more men and happenings of Napoleonic times, and see in that interest the origins of Doyle's inimitable Brigadier Gerard, an outstanding literary creation second only, in my opinion, to Sherlock Holmes. (And, incidentally, we must owe the French element in Holmes's pedigree to Doyle's having had his attention called to the glittering world of the Directory, the Consulate, and the Empire—a world very kind to artists of every kind, including the Vernets . . .)

What didn't Doyle gather up as he moved from one hint to another—a rolling stone of research, gathering moss as he went! For nothing that Doyle ever read was permitted to go unused. His having been fascinated by the infamous poisoner, Dr. Palmer, of Rugeley, is echoed in so many ways: in the well-known Sherlockian dictum, "When a doctor does go wrong, he is the first of criminals. He has nerve and he has knowledge. Palmer and Pritchard were among the heads of their profession" [i.e., of the profession of murder!]; in references to those subjects to which, after Palmer, Doyle was led through having studied Palmer's terrible career. There is hardly a name occurring in the Palmer case, even in casual mention, which is not used at some time or other by Conan Doyle–some twenty altogether; and even the name of the mare, *Polestar,* belonging to Palmer's last victim, John Parsons Cook, was pressed into use in the title of one of Conan Doyle's best non-Sherlockian stories, "The Captain of the Polestar."

Palmer's obsession with horse-racing, which took the Rugeley doctor to the scaffold, moved Doyle on to consider the racing activities of an even more odious (though not legally criminal) character, Sir Frederick Johnstone, Baronet, who was one of the central *dramatis personae* in what must be considered the very nastiest of Victorian scandals. Doyle was led to consider Sir Frederick through the former's professional study of ophthalmology–though that is a story which must be told in another

Which Vernet . . . ? Holmes told Watson that "my grandmother was the sister of Vernet, the French artist" but did not specify which; and there were several artists in the Vernet family. Here are the two most likely candidates: on the left is Antoine-Charles-Horace, generally known as "Carle" Vernet (1785–1835); on the right, Horace (1789–1863). Both were eminently successful; both, highly decorated.

Popular as an artist on both sides of the Channel, "Carle" Vernet's work sold equally well in England and in France. Here is his lithograph of a familiar figure in Paris: the woman who made and sold sweetcakes.

place. What is, however, relevant here is that Sir Frederick, whatever his behaviour socially—and it was bad enough finally to earn him dismissal from the intimate circle of Albert Edward, Prince of Wales—was a hero to the horse-racing fraternity, an experienced and consistently winning owner whose *St. Blaise*, winner of the Derby of 1883, must be seen as the original of *Silver Blaze* (what else...?). And that Doyle, studying the racing calendar, almost certainly in his *Whitaker's Almanack*, did not confine himself to a study of Sir Frederick Johnstone's "form" is made amply clear by the introduction into the tale of *Silver Blaze* of the rightly famous *Isonomy*, "the Unbeatable," winner of the Ascot Cup, 1879 and 1880, and (all in 1879) the Goodwood Cup, the Doncaster Cup, and the Queen's Vase—four "classics" in one year.

There is an old saying: "One thing suggests another." Of no other author was this phrase more suitable in application than when applied to the browsings of Conan Doyle; even Lord Falmouth's *Silvio*, winner of both the Derby and the St. Leger in 1877 (and we shall see later why the name "Falmouth" would have instantly caught Conan Doyle's attention), and Monsieur Lupin's *Salvator*,[4] winner of the 1875 Grand Prix de Paris, had their names fused and pressed into service to provide "Count Negretto Silvius" *(The Mazarin Stone)* with his surname.

In the original and briefer version of this present study, I remarked that the two names "Holmes" and "Sherlock" so forced themselves on Conan Doyle's notice that, as I said, "the name was unavoidable." Since I wrote that, now more than ten years ago, further research has brought up other encounters with the name "Sherlock" or its echoes—all of which will be described later. Here, though, we might mention that, from 1868 to 1870,

---

[4] In a history which is haunted by coincidence, this is surely one of the most extraordinary of the many coincidences involved. For, much later than the first appearance of Sherlock Holmes in 1887, the French writer Maurice Lablanc created what was intentionally a literary rival (one might almost say a pastiche) of Sherlock Holmes in Leblanc's certainly not unsuccessful Arsène *Lupin*. And that Leblanc had intentionally based his detective hero on Holmes is clear from the fact that Leblanc actually brings them together (Sherlock Holmes as "Holmlock Shears"!) in one of his novels.

an Irish lad named Patrick Sherlock was at school with Conan Doyle (but, in all the six years that Doyle was at Stonyhurst College, there was no one named Holmes, nor any named Watson).

Here, then, is the background of my research: in the following pages, I shall describe, step by step, my follow-up of the various clues which have led me, eventually, to the analysis of that composite character Sherlock Holmes into its many but all significant elements.

A STUDY IN SURMISE

The American Bar of the Criterion Hotel ("The Cri' "), where Watson met "young Stamford," as it was in the twilight of London's–and the British Empire's–Golden Age. "The American Bar remains the same. The ceiling has been recently renovated. . . with some extra gold leaf; otherwise there is little change."

murdered in what British newspaper and novel readers of the day had no difficulty in accepting as a typical Mormonish fashion.

Jefferson Hope, the man living only for vengeance, is tracked down and arrested by Holmes, but the murderer of the two Mormons escapes the gallows by falling dead of an aortic aneurism –though not before he has confirmed the accuracy of the reasoning which enabled Holmes to identify him as the killer.

So much for the plot of *A Study in Scarlet*. Let us see now to what extent it reflects, and owes its inspiration to, the events arising from Urban Napoleon Stanger's disappearance on 12 November 1881.

2

A BAKER VANISHES

At the time of his disappearance, Urban Napoleon Stanger was thirty-six. His wife Elisabeth, also German, was a year younger. Stanger's manager, Franz Felix Stumm, who also had a shop of his own, was a year younger than Frau Stanger. Stumm, too, was of German birth, as were most of the others connected directly or remotely with the vanishing. Indeed, in a querulous "leader," *The Times* complained that the case involved nothing "but German bakers and foreigners generally," a complaint echoed by the *Daily Telegraph*, and, later, Watson in *A Study in Scarlet* was to "recall" these complaints.

I shall come later to the question of these names and to the important fact that their significance, as *words* (and not as names), would not pass unnoticed of that Conan Doyle who had studied under the Jesuits at their college in Feldkirch, Vorarlberg, Austria. Reading the various newspaper accounts, which listed the successive appearances among the *dramatis personae* of these strangely (to a German-comprehending British ear) named foreigners, Conan Doyle must also have been struck by what *might* have been the–appositeness?–of such names as Stumm, Geisel, Reiners, and Scherer–not to mention the name of Stanger, already in the list of actors in this very strange drama.

Now, as to the Stangers' financial circumstances: that Stanger was in debt seems proven; that he was in debt to Stumm, as Stumm claimed, was never conclusively proven, at least not to the satisfaction of Mr. Justice ("Hanging Judge") Hawkins and the jury at the Old Bailey.

Until 1881, Stanger had been living and doing business at 64 Cable Street, in the dockland area of the East End of London. But, for reasons now no longer to be ascertained, Stanger, in the year of his total vanishing, shifted bakery and home to the hardly more fashionable quarter of St. Luke's, a couple of miles from Cable Street.

It may well be that a strong desire to remove himself from the neighbourhood of too-pressing creditors was the reason for Stanger's having uprooted himself. In any case, his reason must have been a powerful one, since, in leaving Cable Street, Stanger left behind him compatriots who were mostly friendly–at least, they all spoke the same language; perhaps in more senses than one. He was leaving not only his old baker friend, Georg Geisel, of 23 Baker's Row, Whitechapel, but also the German landlords of several nearby taverns–such men as Ernst Scheel of "The Hoop and Grapes," Peter Schmidt of "The Blue Anchor," and Gerd Reiners of "The Magpie and Stump."

And, more, the theory that Stanger's move was an attempt to remove himself from the disturbing proximity of his creditors seems to be strengthened by the fact that, though the Post Office London Directory gives his name correctly (Urban Napoleon Stanger) when his address was 64 Cable Street, the Directory for 1882–the year after his move–gives his name now as "Urbin Stinger," of 136 Lever Street, St. Luke's. Was this a mere clerical error on the part of the Directory's compilers? Or was it a clumsy effort at name-altering for the purpose of hiding his true identity? (What is curious about the change in the name is that "to sting," in English slang, means "to overcharge," with a strong suggestion of fraud in the transaction. Had Stanger, then, a wry sense of humour?)

At any rate, whether as Stanger or as Stinger, this was the last time that the German baker was to appear in the classified sections of the Post Office London Directory. When the time came for the 1883 edition to be made ready, even the editors of the Directory knew that Stanger was no longer to be included among the active German bakers of London.

As I have said, it was at 11:55 P.M. on 12 November 1881 that Stanger was last seen alive. Christian Zintler, German, a baker employed by Stanger, was going back to his lodgings for the night. He had just left the bakery by the back door and had turned into Lever Street when he noticed that four men were gathered on the sidewalk outside his employer's shop: Stanger, his manager Stumm, and two others whom Zintler did not know.

Zintler afterwards remarked that he had taken no particular notice of the four men, nor concerned himself with speculating on the reason why they were talking outside Stanger's bakery; though he did remember that Stumm and the other two had gone off all together, leaving Stanger alone on the sidewalk. Zintler, as he later testified, then saw Stanger enter the house door adjoining the shop. (Zintler was never questioned on an apparent discrepancy in his testimony; at least, it so appears to me. He seems to have observed a great deal for a man who was just passing by. It looks as though he stopped long enough to study the quartet and watch their breaking up. Why . . . ? What was there about this gathering which attracted his attention? Did Zintler see–or suspect–more than he was later to admit? If so, the forensic questioning let him off lightly indeed.)

On the following morning, Sunday, 13 November, at 8:00 A.M., "sharp," Zintler reported for work. On his arriving at 136 Lever Street, he was met by Frau Stanger, who told him to go straightaway to Stumm's bakery at 131 St. John Street Road (about half a mile distant) and ask the manager to come at once. This Zintler did. A fortnight later, on 26 November, Frau Stanger informed Zintler, who was a young man, that, "as Herr Stanger had gone back to Germany," Zintler was in future to sleep on the premises.

On or about 12 January 1882–it was most likely Thursday, the 12th, as most people in Britain, natives or not, prefer to avoid doing business on a Friday the 13th of any month–on or about 12 January, then, Stanger's old baker friend from Baker's Row, Georg Geisel, called at Lever Street to try to collect money for some flour that Geisel had supplied to Stanger. Geisel was astonished to find Stumm alone and apparently in charge–astonished and disturbed to hear that Stanger was recuperating in the country, "having broken a blood-vessel." (Let the reader take careful note of this statement; for Conan Doyle did, as we shall see.)

A few days later, Geisel received a letter, bearing a German postmark, which letter, though purporting to have come from Stanger, was a forgery of so clumsy a type that even the simple

German baker was not deceived into his accepting the letter as genuine. Now deeply uneasy, Geisel returned to Lever Street and asked Stumm for Stanger's address. Stumm gave Geisel an address in Kreuznach, in Hesse-Cassel, Germany. Geisel wrote to Stanger at the address that Stumm had given. I cannot think that Geisel was too puzzled when the letter was returned to him, marked "ADDRESS UNKNOWN."

Now completely confirmed in his suspicions of Stumm and his evasions, Geisel looked around for a private enquiry agent to trace the missing man.

There was no dearth of such talent in the London of 1882: at least three private enquiry agents used to advertise regularly in *The Times:* Ignatius Paul Pollacky, "Correspondent to Foreign Police Gazette"; F. Field, Private Enquiry Office ("Established 1852"); Attwood's Private & Confidential Inquiry[1] Office (9 Craig's Court, Charing Cross). As Conan Doyle, with these and many other advertisers of the same kidney well in mind, makes Sherlock Holmes say in *A Study in Scarlet:* "Here in London we have lots of Government detectives and lots of private ones."

Of them all, Ignatius Paul Pollacky seems to have been one of the most active, and thus one of the most successful. A person of exotic origins, he had the advantage of speaking several languages at a time when uncontrolled immigration was making London more and more polyglot. A typical Pollacky communication, that I found in the agony column of *The Times* of Wednesday, 2 April 1879, is this:

> MONSIEUR D.L.C. . . . , who, during April and September, 1876, visited Buxton, will oblige by sending his address to Mr Pollacky, 11, Paddington-grove.

But, typically, Geisel went to none of these, nor to any of the eight others listed in the Post Office London Directory for 1881 and 1882. Instead, Geisel sought out a private detective with a German name, though Geisel was not to know that the man's family had become completely Anglicized over several generations.

---

[1]"Enquiry" or "inquiry": either spelling is permitted in standard British orthography, though modern practice favours the former style.

It was the name which had attracted Geisel: Wendel Scherer—and in the reports of the St. Luke's Mystery, it was the first time that Conan Doyle was to encounter the name, as that of a *living* person, though the name had already become familiar to Doyle as that of an important work on the German language, published in 1868 by the eminent philologist Wilhelm Scherer, which was one of the "required" works at the Jesuit College at Feldkirch when Conan Doyle was studying there. But, as regards the dead Scherers, he had met and admired them in print, as I shall explain in a later chapter; but the mention of Wendel Scherer in the newspapers of late 1882 caught his eye with a now-familiar name, and we have all had the experience of seeing an unusual name recurring, as though by some "occult" significance. In fact, this phenomenon, in Doyle's case, did have something of the mystically providential about it; for him, the name "Scherer" was to be the key to a life of almost uninterrupted success; that *auspicium melioris aevi*—that certain assurance of better things to come—that all of us hope for, and so few attain.

And Wendel Scherer certainly caught Conan Doyle's attention, as he read through the vast eight-column pages of *The Times*, the *Daily Telegraph*, and, no doubt, some lighter journals. The same name . . . yes, as that which had already become familiar to him through the gossip of his disastrous stay at Plymouth; and, Conan Doyle must have reflected, as he read of Wendel Scherer's conflict with the Worship Street magistrate, the traditional Scherer gallantry, the traditional Scherer pride, the traditional Scherer obstinacy in a good cause . . .

Geisel, reconciling himself to the fact that Scherer was German only by name, still retained the "private consulting detective" and empowered him, as a first essential step toward the tracing of Stanger, to offer a reward of £50 for any information which might lead to the finding of the missing man. But despite numerous newspaper notices of the reward, and what we may suppose were Scherer's diligent house-to-house enquiries, the reward money was never claimed, and, after a few weeks of Scherer's "detecting," Geisel, impatient with Scherer's inefficiency (or merely his bad luck?), did what he should have done in January 1882. A little late, Geisel went to the police.

That the London police of Autumn 1882 took the disappearance of Urban Napoleon Stanger so seriously—dealing with it at once on the highest (that is, the Scotland Yard) level—may be explained by pointing out again what I have already mentioned: that Britain, at that time, was being terrified by a wave of inexplicable vanishings—men, women, even children. The terror generated by these vanishings, which extended over a whole decade which ended with the "Jack the Ripper" murders, may be likened to the terror which seized Boston, Massachusetts when "The Strangler" was on the prowl.

In the very edition of *The Times* which carried the report of the St. Luke's trial at the Central Criminal Court, there were advertisements by private detectives, offering rewards for two missing girls, Elizabeth Carter and Mary Seward. Young and old—and not all women—had been caught up in this wave of disappearances. Some of the missing were later found dead—unmutilated but dead, and so all the more mysteriously horrifying for that.

Stanger, then, was one of the Disappearers in a terrifying visitation of Disappearance; and, as one of those who had seemingly vanished without a trace, the German baker's vanishing had been treated by the police as "top priority" from the moment that Geisel had reported that his friend (and debtor) was not to be found.

In their desperate anxiety to get at the pattern, the motive, the *modus operandi* of these snatchings, the men of Scotland Yard, extremely angry with Geisel that he had not called them in earlier, by-passed the local police and entrusted the investigation to one of its most senior Inspectors, as was later reported in *The Times:* "Henry Radky [*sic;* but the correct spelling was "Radike"], inspector of police, said that in April [1882] he received instructions to make enquiries. On April 28th, he saw the prisoner [Stumm], and took a statement."

Of Scotland Yard, this may be justly said: its man took the trouble to check Geisel's statements as well as those of Stumm. The fact that a letter had been returned from Kreuznach, Hesse-Cassel, was no proof that Stanger had not, in fact, gone there; and Inspector Radike, A Division (Whitehall—Scotland Yard), set out for Kreuznach to check the facts for himself. He returned to report that there was no trace of Stanger in Kreuznach, nor had the police (to whom, as in all German towns, he would have had to report on arrival) any record that he had ever visited their town. The Inspector came back to Whitehall to ask for a warrant, and, armed with this, he called on Stumm, to arrest him on 12 September 1882, "upon a charge of forging an order for the payment of £78." (Actually, the sum mentioned in the indictment was £76 15*s.*–a sum the significance of which I shall point out later.)

The "order" mentioned is simply officialese for "cheque." As *The Times* wryly pointed out, all the other cheques that Stumm was known or assumed to have signed with Stanger's name had been "lost." Only this single cheque had, unluckily for Stumm, survived to serve as evidence against him.

Still, this solitary document was sufficient to get Stumm ten years' penal servitude, despite a brilliant defense by Montague Williams, Queen's Counsel, ably assisted by his "junior," Mr. Fillan, whom Stumm rewarded by a stream of abuse from the prisoners' dock.

That Stumm was guilty of forgery seems obvious. And that he had a hand in Stanger's vanishing seems as obvious to me as it did to the average Briton of 1882. For, if Stanger were really decamping to dodge his debts, as Frau Stanger claimed that he had confided to her, why did he leave £400 in his current account at the bank–money that he left to finance the guilty "honeymoon" of his wife and her lover, Stumm? money that Stumm had to forge cheques to draw out of the bank's keeping?

At the various courts through which, in keeping with normal English legal procedure, the guilty pair went (Frau Stanger was discharged after the hearings at the Magistrates' Court, and Stumm went the rest of the journey to prison alone), they made a bad impression by their extremely unattractive conduct. Juries *do* revenge themselves, for all the fiction that they don't–or shouldn't–and a judge often signifies *his* disapproval by laying on a whacking great sentence. But ten years for a cheque of less than one hundred pounds! It seemed excessive to many at the time, but they did not realize that the sentence had to be long enough for Stanger's body to be found and a capital charge brought against his supposed murderer or murderers. But the body was never found, nor was it ever shown how Stanger had gone–or been made away with.

Suspected–though never convicted–of having done away with the German baker Urban Napoleon Stanger: Stanger's wife Elisabeth and his manager, Franz Felix Stumm, seen here in the dock at Worship Street Police Court, City of London, October 1882. The illustration from *The Penny Illustrated Paper* clearly shows that, in the year between the vanishing of Stanger and the trial of his wife and his manager, the latter had replaced Stanger's name on the shop-front with his own! No wonder this brazen pair were brought to trial!

Stumm served his sentence; and penal servitude in those days of oakum-picking, stone-breaking, and the treadmill was, in the popular phrase, no picnic. But all sentences, even of life, come at last to an end, and, when the prison gates opened to let him out, Stumm walked to freedom and, so far as official history is concerned, to oblivion.

Only as fiction has his history been preserved, if not for ever, then already for a century, and, I think, for very many years to come.

Conan Doyle, as I shall show, was deeply stirred by the St. Luke's Mystery. And the strange appositeness of the various names! he must have reflected.

Stumm: "dumb, mute, silent"; Geisel: "hostage"; Scheel: "cross-eyed, squinting, envious, jealous." And as for "Scherer": well, *scheren* meant "to cut, clip, trim," our English "shear"; but the root had acquired, in usage, a darker significance: *Schererei* . . . "trouble." And poor Wendel Scherer had certainly had more than his share of that!

But, when all is said and done, it is not Stumm's petty dishonesty, even (if he did get rid of Stanger) his murderous capacity, with which we are concerned here.

The real interest of Stanger and Stumm is the interest that this case had for young Dr. Conan Doyle, now shakily setting up his practice in the seaside town of Southsea, a suburb of the great British naval base, Portsmouth.

It is true that Doyle was deeply interested—as was all Britain at that time—in the question: What happened to Urban Napoleon Stanger?

But Doyle's interest went further, and somewhat more erratically, than that. He was even more interested in the answer to the question, that he devised and propounded for his own answering: What would have happened in the case had Georg Geisel chosen a *professionally competent* private detective, and not the well-meaning but ineffectual Wendel Scherer?

For Wendel Scherer's incompetence was now a matter of public record. The Magistrate at Worship Street Police Court, Henry Jeffreys Busby, had seen to that. It was at Worship Street Court that the preliminary evidence had been taken, and Stumm,

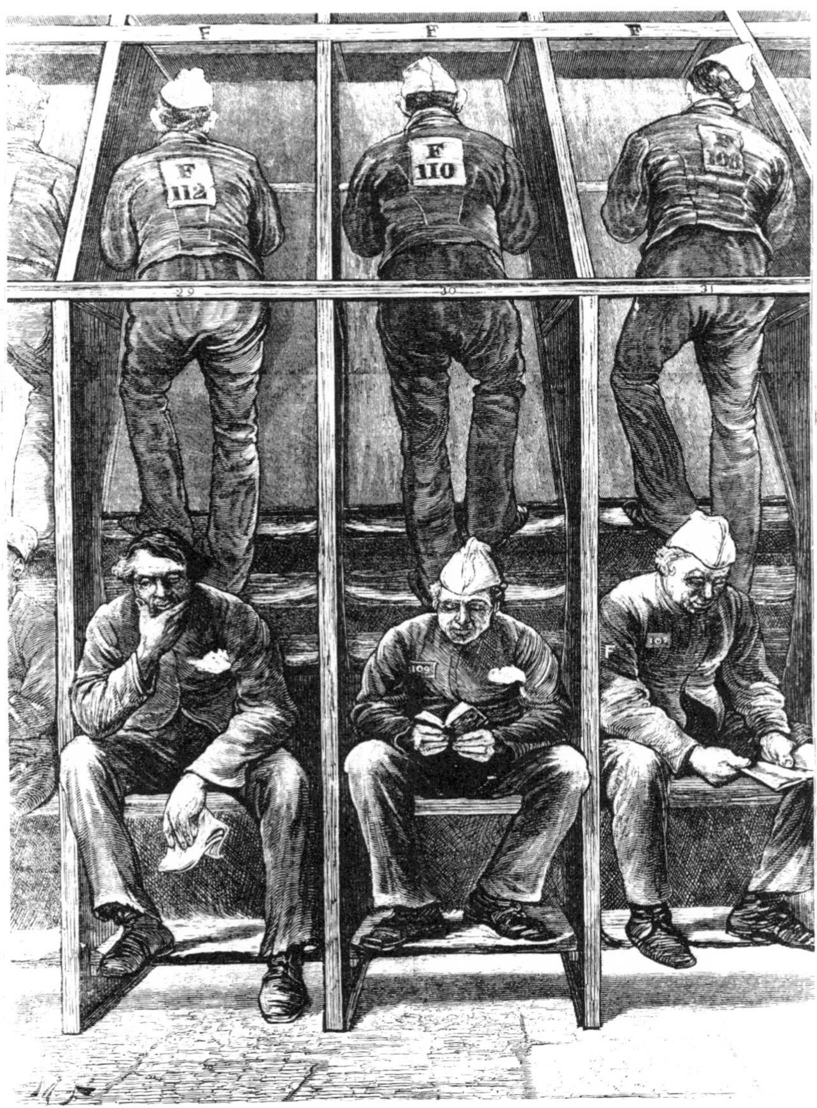

Stumm escaped hanging but got what many a tough felon considered worse: ten years of *Victorian* hard labour, which included the treadmill. Here are convicted felons working the treadmill at the Clerkenwall House of Correction, Stumm's "local chokey."

committed for trial at the Central Criminal Court, had been handed over to the custody of the court. That got rid of Stumm, but, for the time being, Mr. Busby had not done with Mr. Wendel Scherer; and it was because of the Magistrate's scathing remarks on the detective's incompetence that Scherer found himself, for a short while, the most famous detective in Britain.

Called to enter the witness box to give evidence, Scherer drew Mr. Busby's and—after the newspapers had reported—all Britain's attention to himself at this preliminary enquiry by refusing to name the person who had retained him to advertise for Stanger—even though it was that person who finally had gone to the police!

Calmly, firmly, almost arrogantly, Wendel Scherer declined to be either ordered or threatened, for all that Mr. Jeffreys Busby sneered and angrily denounced the upstart's claim to "professional status."

MR. BUSBY: You are an enquiry agent?

WITNESS: Not an enquiry agent. A detective.

MR. BUSBY: It is the same thing. "New presbyter is but old priest writ large," I suggest. Eh, sir?

WITNESS: With respect, sir, not so.

MR. BUSBY: A detective? Then you are a member of the Detective Police? They are the only detectives known to me. Mr. Radike, of Whitehall, is one. Are you under that gentleman's jurisdiction?

WITNESS: I am under the jurisdiction only of the Common Law of England. I am not a member of the Detective Police Force. I am a private detective—a private consulting detective. *(Witness stressed the word "consulting.")*

MR. BUSBY: People "consult" you, Mr. Scherer? In an office? In chambers, like some professional gentleman . . . ?

WITNESS: In an office. I *am* a professional gentleman; I am a professional consulting detective. This is why I must respectfully insist on my preserving the anonymity of my client. It would be a grave breach of professional etiquette were I to reveal his name.

MR. BUSBY: Hoity-toity, sir!—you try my patience a little too far! I should commit you for contempt! An enquiry agent, forsooth, of which half-a-dozen advertise their services every day in the newspapers—and we have these preposterous claims of yours to professional dignity, professional secrecy, and I don't know what else! Stand down, sir!—but do not leave the Court—I shall wish to speak with you later.

But Geisel, now fearful of what might happen to Scherer—and, perhaps, to himself—saved Scherer from further questioning by volunteering the information that it had been himself, Georg Geisel, who had hired the private consulting detective. ("Why could we not have had this at the beginning?" the Magistrate grumbled.)

Yet, whether or not Mr. Busby's snobbish opinion of "enquiry agents who called themselves professional gentlemen" was justified, there was one avid reader of the newspapers who altogether disagreed with the Magistrate and felt a warm sympathy with the detective. This was Dr. Conan Doyle, graduate of the Medical School of Edinburgh University, to whom Mr. Busby never would have denied the "professional status" that he had denied to Wendel Scherer, private detective.

In his ranging himself on the side of Wendel Scherer, Conan Doyle was *instinctively* displaying that sympathy which, throughout his life, he was to show to the poor, the downtrodden, the bullied, the neglected, the despised. This spontaneous, uncalculated, uncontrolled—indeed, uncontrollable—sympathy is a fundamental characteristic of the Celt, specifically of the Gaelic Celt, and Conan Doyle, for good or bad, was a most representative member of that ambivalent creation that one of their own has called "the most unhappy people" and, a little more accurately (though in quite another context), Shakespeare called the "Mars of malcontents."

In later years, Dr. (afterward, Sir) Arthur Conan Doyle was to exhibit, in the most active fashion, that same instinctive sympathy with men whom he considered to have been wrongly condemned: Beck, Slater, Edalji—and it is the measure of his sympathy's spontaneity that none of these three men, for whom Sir Arthur fought so vigorously—even, one might say, violently—was a man of attractive personality (which was why, in all probability, they had had a rough deal in the first place). St. Francis was not the only warm heart to have reserved the leper for special consideration . . .

But, as I shall show, this sympathy, and—more—a desire to translate this sympathy into effective action, had received the strongest encouragement from Conan Doyle's having read, in the year-old newspapers of Plymouth, and in listening to the still-vigorous chatter of Plymouth's inhabitants, of a Champion of Lost Causes (a sort of uncanonized St. Jude!) who, though dead, had, at last, triumphantly won a battle for the liberty and rehabilitation of a man convicted of murder nearly half a century before.

This Champion had not fought alone, and there were other stalwarts—more "important" than he—at his side; men who survived to see the reward of their long struggle in the cause of Truth and Humanitarianism. But the Champion who had set out as leader to the spearhead trio had a name that Conan Doyle recognized at once when he came across it again in reading of the St. Luke's Mystery. His name was George Scherer, and he is mentioned, with the greatest respect, by the then most famous of England's barristers, Serjeant William Ballantine, in his autobiography *Some Reminiscences of a Barrister's Life,* which appeared in the year following the long-protracted culmination of the fight for Edmund Galley's redemption.

We have learned a great deal about the character of Arthur Conan Doyle, not merely in the half-century which has elapsed since his death but in the near century-and-a-quarter which has gone since his birth. His was not, as so many commentators with a vested interest in clouding the issue make out, a greatly complicated character; of all the world's famous (that is, enduringly successful) writers, he is the least difficult to understand. And so, as we shall see, his hunt was not merely for Heroes on which to model himself; that hunt failed to satisfy him until he had, to a degree greater or lesser, as Fate would have it, not merely copied, emulated, the Hero, but, to the best of his effort, spiritually *and physically* identified himself with the Hero's thought, impulse, and action.

The fight for Edmund Galley's pardon took forty-three years; the case was not ended until forty-five years had passed since Galley's conviction. George Scherer did not live to see the vindication, not only of Galley, but also of Galley's stout champion, George Scherer—though all who survived remembered and praised Scherer's name. And this is certain: that one of the most powerful influences in Conan Doyle's life was the example of George Scherer; it is to Conan Doyle's passionate desire to emulate Scherer that, in the after-years, the unloved and unlovable Beck, Slater and Edalji owed that apparently miraculous emergence of a stalwart champion, prepared to take up their seemingly hopeless cause, make it his own, and fight the evil of those whose Bible is the official printed form.

Conan Doyle, joining the infamous Dr. Budd as "partner," had spent only a month or two in Plymouth after his unhappy experience as the *Mayumba's* doctor; but in those months he had come to learn a great deal about the fight for Galley. It had been Plymouth's, Exeter's, Falmouth's, and, indeed, all Devon's, prime subject of conversation: how three men—the late George Scherer, shorthand-writer practising in the Supreme Court of Judicature; the late Sir Alexander Cockburn, Baronet, Lord Chief Justice of England; and the still-living (God bless him!) Thomas Latimer, "The Cobbett of the West," editor of Exeter's most successful newspaper, *The Western Times*—had joined to reverse the verdict on a man convicted of a local murder and transported as a reprieved-from-the-gallows felon; and, after damned nearly half a century, managed to get the Queen's Free Pardon and—think of it!—a thousand pounds in compensation, to boot!

But to return to the second most important Scherer in Conan Doyle's life: Wendel, the snubbed champion of the private detective's claim to professional status . . .

Knowing Conan Doyle as we do—or, by now, should do—we may understand that, reading of Mr. Busby's ill-conditioned snubbing of Wendel Scherer, Conan Doyle felt emotionally moved to side with the detective, a man who, doing no harm to others (save by his hack-handed incompetence, perhaps), had simply tried to "better himself" in the rigidly caste-organized society of Queen Victoria.

And then—in what Kierkegaard calls the "qualitative jump"—came the imaginative author's brain asking itself the vital question: "But suppose that a man *justifiably* called himself a 'private consulting detective'?—a man with as tender a regard for his professional status as ever Mr. Wendel Scherer claimed; but, unlike poor Wendel Scherer, with professional *efficiency;* with true, unchallenged professional *integrity;* with true, unchallenged professional *standing;* to back up his self-esteem . . . ?"

(Sherlock Holmes had not yet come into being; but, like the babies in Maeterlinck's fantasy, he was gathering substance about himself; like those babies, he was waiting to be born. But with this essential difference: when, at last, he did emerge into being, it was into fully-developed, vigorous, almost superhuman adult life. But, for some time, Conan Doyle would merely "play about" with his conception; trying it out, one might say, for size. Holmes still needed a lot of creative work done on the *idea* of him before Doyle was ready to let him make his début. But the *concept* of Sherlock Holmes was not only implicit in the view that Doyle was taking of the despised Wendel Scherer, it was of quite assured growth, development, and ultimate perfecting.)

Now, let us follow Conan Doyle's excited thinking along these lines; imagine his wondering what would have happened had a *real* private consulting detective been pitted, in a mystery such as that of St. Luke's, against the professionals of Scotland Yard. Imagine further–as Doyle undoubtedly did–a London police-court's Magistrate's daring to question the standing of such a man; and, should the Magistrate so dare, imagine with what lordly pride, with what consummate self-assurance, would the *real* detective reject the sneers of the Magistrate; with what unruffled self-confidence would the *real* detective insist on the standing of his profession!

The young doctor, returning from his brief and eye-opening "partnership" with the noisy con man, Dr. Budd, had set up in practice for himself, as has already been mentioned. But there were no patients at first, and few indeed afterward, so that, in an endeavour to eke out the slender earnings of his unsteady medical practice (£154–then $770–was the first year's total income), he had begun to write short stories. His mind was full of stories, both long and short; but he had yet to write his first long tale.

Now, pondering not only on what he had learned and thought of the *second* Scherer in his life–we shall come to the first presently –and recalling, too, what he had learned of the first in his short stay at Plymouth, and in his few wanderings over the lovely Devon countryside (including the not-quite-so-lovely bleakness of Dartmoor, which, twenty years later, he was to evoke around the legend of an evil Baskerville), he began to busy his overactive mind still further with a mystery in which a private consulting detective should succeed brilliantly where Scotland Yard had demonstrably and lamentably failed.

This man would be, of course, a confidently self-proclaimed private consulting detective; successful where Wendel Scherer had proved unsuccessful.

Yet there would be much of Scherer in him–not the least, that courage that Scherer had displayed in the face of the Magistrate's bullying; the pride that Scherer had maintained in the face of overt sneers; that self-sacrificing loyalty to his client (in the very finest tradition, Dr. Conan Doyle noted with admiration, of the finest professions–his own included!) to which Scherer had so resolutely stuck.

This fictional detective who was emerging into vigorous, highly individual life in Conan Doyle's fertile imagination was intended, by his creator, to be all the fine things that real-life Wendel Scherer was–as well as many other fine things that poor Scherer was not.

The fictional detective was to be self-assured, arrogant always, even insolent when necessary; almost superhumanly intelligent; able to reason out a solution from clues that Scotland Yard would never see or (if seen) correctly interpret. He would be tender-hearted to the weak and defenseless; he must be, of necessity, active, ageless, learned, yet contemptuous of the "useless" academic knowledge that the ordinary man despises. He would be a master of "manly" exercises such as boxing, but no waster of his time on effete "aristocratic" sports–he was never to shoot grouse with Lord So-and-So or ride to hounds with a fashionable Hunt.

Whilst the Stanger–Stumm–Scherer case was still fresh in his memory, Dr. Conan Doyle, in one of those long waits between patients, smoothed out a leaf from his notebook and began to make some notes. What he wrote is shown, in holograph, on the frontispiece. Mark these skimpy notes well–they are the first blueprint of the world's most famous fictional detective.

But before I go on to trace the fictional Sherlock in the real-life Scherer, let me first trace the origins of *A Study in Scarlet* in the St. Luke's Mystery.

I must make an important fact clear from the start: *A Study in Scarlet* is not a fictionalized account of the St. Luke's Mystery.

We may understand well the essential differences between the real-life and fictional mysteries if we bear two points in mind:

1. So long as Urban Napoleon Stanger was missing "in suspicious circumstances," the murder charge against Stumm was not dismissed but "reserved." The case, therefore, was *sub judice*, and any fictional "solution" might well have been treated as contempt of court, and might have brought the author into conflict with the law. Important newspapers might risk a discussion of the case; an impecunious young provincial doctor dared not take such a risk.

2. The whole purpose of *A Study in Scarlet* was not to proffer a solution of the St. Luke's Mystery but to provide Conan Doyle with the opportunity of presenting *his* version of the ideal private consulting detective. It must be remembered that there had been, and were when Conan Doyle was planning Sherlock Holmes's "presentation," private consulting detectives, of whom the most famous was probably François Vidocq, the felon turned detective who founded the French Sûreté. On his retirement from the Police Judiciaire, Vidocq had entered into private practice; and if, at times, Sherlock Holmes strikes us as being just a little too competent to be entirely human, see what *The Times* of 9 June 1845 wrote in all seriousness of Vidocq, on his coming to London:

> The principal curiosity. . . will be found to be M. Vidocq himself, whose appearance is very much what might be anticipated by those who have read his memoirs or heard of his exploits. He is a remarkably well-built man, of extraordinary muscular power, and exceedingly active. He stands, when perfectly erect, 5 feet 10 inches in height, but by some strange process connected with his physical formation he has the faculty of contracting his height several inches, and in this diminished state to walk about, jump, etc. . . .

When Robert L. Fish, in one of his stories about Schlock Homes and Dr. Watney, endows his curious detective with that same power of "diminishing" himself, it is regarded as one of the late Mr. Fish's better jests—"Special shoes, Watney . . ." (Even the factual *Times* did not hesitate to depict the detective as something a little more than human.)

But we must remember, too, that no real-life private consulting detective was of the type that Conan Doyle was inventing;

and, to that degree, Doyle's private detective was an entirely novel creation; and the purpose of Doyle's first long story was, as I have said, to present his version of the ideal private consulting detective.

Now, in order to do that, his creator had to provide the fictional sleuth with opportunities of *reasoning* and *acting* denied to the real-life Wendel Scherer. Even had a fictionalized solution of the St. Luke's Mystery been permitted to Conan Doyle, it would not have served as a vehicle for the presentation of the new-type detective. Note that the "blueprint" has not a word of what "I Sherrinford Holmes"[2] *does* in a professional way–it is completely concerned with character and background; what he *is*, rather than what he *does*.

However, Conan Doyle did not wish his readers to overlook the fact that his story owed its inspiration to a mystery with which all would be familiar, so, as I shall now try to demonstrate, the real-life case is echoed again and again in Conan Doyle's *A Study in Scarlet:*

The St. Luke's Mystery	*A Study in Scarlet*
Urban Napoleon STANGER: missing–perhaps on the run.	Joseph STANGERson: missing–certainly on the run.
Issue of *The Times* reporting Stumm's conviction heads its front-page column of adverisements with a bold ad for the GUION Line.	Two tickets "from the GUION Steamship Company" found on dead Enoch Drebber.
Stumm charged with having forged a cheque for £76 15*s*.	Found on the dead Drebber: "Pocket edition of Boccaccio's *Decameron*, with name of Joseph Stangerson upon the flyleaf," and "loose money to the extent

[2] I suggested to the late Adrian Conan Doyle, when thanking him for permission to use the "blueprint" to illustrate the original version of this study, that the initial "I" (dropped in the final version of Holmes's name) was probably intended for "Innes," the name of Conan Doyle's younger brother, killed in France in the First World War as a colonel of infantry.

of seven pounds thirteen." Is it by chance—surely not!—that Conan Doyle selects a book with the element "ten" (Greek, *deka* = ten) in the title, and makes the dead man's pocket yield a sum *exactly one-tenth* of that mentioned in Stumm's indictment?

When Geisel inquires of Stumm after the missing Stanger, Stumm says that Stanger has gone to the country, "having burst a blood-vessel."

When Drebber's body is found in the empty house in Lauriston Gardens, Brixton Road, it is covered in blood. This is not Drebber's blood, but that of the avenger, Jefferson Hope, *who burst a blood vessel.* As Hope explained later: "I believe I would have had a fit of some sort if the blood had not rushed from my nose and relieved me."

Stanger, *the man who disappeared* in still unexplained circumstances.

Doyle gives Drebber, as Christian name, that of the prophet Enoch, memorable also for *having disappeared* in still unexplained circumstances: "By faith Enoch was translated that he should not see death; and was not found, because God had translated him . . ." (*Hebrews* 11:5).

Year of Stanger's vanishing: 1881.

Holmes and Watson go to the empty house in Brixton to view Drebber's body: 1881.

The Times, 12 December 1882 *(issue printing "latest" in the St. Luke's Mystery)* reports the serious illness of Lord STAMFORD—"The Earl of Stamford and Warrington remains in a critical condition."

Dr. John Watson is introduced to Sherlock Holmes by "young STAMFORD, who had been a dresser under me at Barts."

"Bart's" (St. Bartholomew's Hospital) is the local big hospital for the St. Luke's district—the heart of the St. Luke's Mystery.

Conan Doyle makes Holmes and Watson meet in the pathology laboratory at "Bart's."

Stanger's bakery in Lever Street was near the famous Eagle

Not only does "Eagle Canyon" occur in the Mormon section of

Tavern, subject of a then popular song: "Up and down the City Road, in and out the Eagle; that's the way the money goes! –And pop goes the weasel!"

"General" William Booth, founder of the Salvation Army, *bought the Eagle Tavern* but was ejected for having failed to comply with the terms of the sale: a much-publicized story which received excellent coverage from *The Times*.

A Study in Scarlet, the name "Eagle" may well have suggested the slight change of German to American emphasis in Conan Doyle's story.

At this time–and all fully reported in all the British newspapers–serious rioting broke out against the meetings of the Salvation Army in Brighton, Worthing, and Gravesend–all seaside holiday towns. Scare newspaper reports of Mormon missionaries' alleged enticement and/or abduction of "simple, ignorant servant-girls" must have suggested the Salvation Army/Latter-day Saints transposition to Conan Doyle, both sects being equally obnoxious to the late-Victorian *bourgeoisie*, and inextricably confused in many a Victorian middle-class mind.

But an entry in my late friend Eric Partridge's *A Dictionary of Slang* may well provide the reason for Conan Doyle's semantic linking of Salvation Army and Mormons. Partridge gives this: "**War-cry.** A mixture of *stout* and *mild* ale: taverns': 1882 [Note the year!]–*ca* 86. Ware[3] derives it from the *War Cry*, the periodical of the Salvation Army, which 'spoke stoutly and ever [?] used mild terms'." The "explanation" of "war-cry" fails to convince me; but that a popular tavern's drink should have come to carry the name of the Salvation Army's house journal is an historical fact. The truth–*not* involving any catachrestic play

[3] J. Redding Ware, *Passing English* (1909).

on words—is that Drink and "The Sally Army" became linked in tavern-users' minds because, then as now, "soldiers" of the "Army" used to hawk the anti-booze *War Cry* in all the taverns (though not, curiously enough, in such places of alcoholic refreshment as the American bar of "The Cri' "—a nice point for the social historian's consideration).

Salvation Army members were often attacked in the St. Luke's district by organized gangs of loafers and street arabs, who called themselves "The Skeleton Army" in unseemly ridicule of "General" Booth.

" 'It's the Baker Street division of the detective police force,' said my companion gravely; and as he spoke there rushed into the room half a dozen of the dirtiest and most ragged street Arabs that ever I clapped eyes on.

" ''Tention!' cried Holmes, in a sharp tone, and the six dirty little scoundrels stood in a line. . ." —*A Study in Scarlet.* (I shall have more to say about the "Baker Street Irregulars" later, but here I ask the reader particularly to note and to remember the words "ragged" and "Arabs" and noting, too, that Conan Doyle, always a meticulously careful proof-reader, has given the latter word a capital letter.)

The strong German element in the St. Luke's Mystery provoked this querulous comment from the leader-writer of *The Times*, a newspaper, in those days, of a never-very-liberal complexion: "Almost every one whose name occurs in the proceedings seems to be *either a German baker or a German miller*" (*The Times,* 12 December 1882).

And Conan Doyle retained this strong German element, despite the superficial "Americanization" of the background to the crimes. The author was still so conscious of the strong German element in the real-life St. Luke's Mystery that he makes the *Daily Telegraph* remark upon "the German name of the victim." Also, after Hope's nose has bled over the dead Drebber, Hope dips his finger in the blood and writes the German word *Rache*–"revenge"–on the wall of the empty room.

Here I must interpose with a comment which includes two of the facts revealed in the course of the story. The first: that the first victim, Drebber, is found to have been carrying a pocket copy of *The Decameron* belonging to his secretary, accomplice, and companion-on-the-run, Stangerson. The other fact: that Hope's haemorrhage from the nose *(epitaxis)* was attributable to an aneurism. The two facts, I suggest, are not only linked (at least in Conan Doyle's mind) but are introduced into the story as items in a sexual element that Doyle, for obvious reasons of prudence, afterward cut out of the final draft.

For the St. Luke's Mystery is not only notable for its strong German element; it is notable for its strong sexual element as well. To the public–and in that collective noun, we may confidently include the police–the facts were clear: Frau Stanger and her husband's manager, Stumm, were lovers, and, adopting an immemorial solution to remove the obstacles to their love, Elisabeth and Franz had conspired to rid themselves of the husband–and had done so with remarkable skill, so that the homicidal manager got only "ten penn'orth" instead of the rope. All the elements which went to make up the St. Luke's Mystery are reflected in *A Study in Scarlet*–all, that is, save one: the sexual element which had caused the real-life mystery to arouse such interest in the newspaper-reading public. It is true that a sexual element has been permitted to remain in the tale, but it has been well "wrapped up" for Victorian family consumption. That rape is a worse sexual crime than the most shameless adultery, even the rigid Victorians would concede; yet the rape in *A Study in Scarlet* has been so bowdlerized, by a well-known Victorian set of literary conventions, that those readers who did not wish to accept the ravishment as such were under no compulsion to do so.

What sexual elements Conan Doyle has left in the tale are like the whispered "asides" of the stage; no one need notice them, let alone try to puzzle out their meaning; and the more that I consider all the facts and, even more significantly, the implications of this seemingly simple but, in reality, very complex tale, the more I am inclined to think that there was once an original version of a strikingly different character from that published in *Beeton's* for Christmas 1887. Must we assume that, in editing out the strong sexual element from the original draft, Doyle overlooked two brief sexual "mentions" surviving from that original text?

What are these two? Well, in the first place, Boccaccio's *Decameron* was held, by Victorian opinion, to be a smutty book, out of the same stable which produced *The Heptameron*, *Gargantua*, *Pantagruel*, *Fanny Hill*, *Maria Monk*, all of which, usually flanked by *The History of the Rod* and "Aristotle's Works"–poor Aristotle! –were to be seen in the dingy windows of even dingier little bookshops in Villers Street or Holywell Street. Condemned by two Popes and by the assembled authority of the Council of Trent, *The Decameron* was not even respectablized when, treated as "classical" smut–though still, note, smut, for all that–it was published, with most of the other "classics" of like type, by the very respectable firm of George Routledge of London. But please bear in mind that, in possessing and reading *The Decameron–and* writing his name on the flyleaf–Joseph Stangerson proclaimed himself a man with a regrettable taste for the erotic (and thus, in Victorian reckoning, a Bad Man). . .

Next. Hope is a good man. That he seeks revenge does not make him a bad man (which is why Conan Doyle spares him the ignominy and physical pain of the rope). He is good because he seeks revenge under the most fearful provocation.

But. . . and this is curious indeed: he suffers from an aneurism, concerning the nature of which young Dr. Conan Doyle would have been well informed.

An aneurism occurs in an artery of which the muscular lining becomes weakened, so that the outer lining "bubbles" in balloon fashion to form a large swelling on the vessel's side. The young doctor would have known that, in as much as ninety-five per cent. of cases, the occurrence of an aneurism is attributable to syphilitic disease. There are other causes, of course: injury, strain, arteriosclerosis–and, in Hope's case, he may have owed his embolism to any of these. But why should an author, with every other disease with which to infect his para-herö, choose one with such sinister implications?

In that first, so-very-different draft, was Hope given, as the smut-reading Stangerson (and Drebber, too, who borrowed

Stangerson's book) must have been, a history of erotic indulgence? Were they *all*—Hope included—no better than they should have been? Which is why, perhaps, all three had to die, to avenge, not merely Lucy Ferrier's death, but, we may suppose, some even darker rejection of the Good.

So much, then, for the principal points of "echo" between the real-life St. Luke's Mystery and the obviously heavily-edited fictional *A Study in Scarlet*.

Let me proceed now to examine two other matters of interest: the emergence of "Baker Street" as the Holmes–Watson residence, and the origins of "Sherlock Holmes" in the real-life private consulting detective, Wendel Scherer, whose name it was, in the newspaper accounts of the St. Luke's Mystery, which caught Dr. Conan Doyle's eye *because the surname was already familiar to him*—as we shall see. It was because of the eye-catching quality of Scherer's name that Doyle was drawn to read the accounts of the case in which Scherer achieved a momentary but national fame; and Doyle's interest in the case originated in his initial interest, not so much in Wendel Scherer's behaviour, as in his surname. This should be kept well in mind, in view of what I shall narrate shortly.

But to return to "Baker Street," an address that I put into inverted commas as it became the well-known street in the Borough of Mary-le-Bone,[4] London, W.1 only after Conan Doyle, on reflection, had decided to move his hero to the more select address of Baker Street, Portman Square—for there were, and are still, other streets of the same name in less fashionable parts of Westminster.

Baker Street—by which we now mean that Baker Street which connects the Marylebone Road[5] with Portman Square—has come, within the past century, to enjoy a fame almost equal to

---

[4] Now absorbed into the newly-organized Borough of Camden.

[5] In the official name of the Borough, "Mary-le-Bone" is always spelled thus: in three parts (like Caesar's Gaul); but "Marylebone Road" is always—and officially—spelled so. I do not know why, even though I lived in the borough for many years, and worked there, too.

that of the famous sleuth who has shared rooms there with Dr. Watson since 1881. If, in Britain, we name our Sherlockian fan club after the Master (The Sherlock Holmes Society of London), the "Mother Lodge" of Sherlockiana in the United States is partly named after the street in which the Master is held to live (The Baker Street Irregulars). Why, in choosing a London residence for Sherlock Holmes, did Conan Doyle decide on "diggings" in Baker Street?

Well, if the reader will look again at the frontispiece notes for *A Study in Scarlet,* it will be to see that Conan Doyle, in this original draft, places "I Sherrinford" (not yet "Sherlock") Holmes at 221B Upper Baker Street.

When Conan Doyle sketched out his detective (rather than the tale) at some time between the beginning of 1883–after Stumm had been sent to prison–and the middle of 1886, when Messrs. Ward, Lock purchased the copyright of *A Study in Scarlet* for £25 (though, as Dame Jean Conan Doyle informed me, afterward returning the rights to the Conan Doyle Estate: a fact which ought to be more widely known), there was both a Baker Street and–separated from it by the short length of York Buildings and the width of the Marylebone Road–an Upper Baker Street (where Mrs. Sarah Siddons once lived). Today, these three streets–properly three sections of one street–have been gathered together as "Baker Street," and the identity of the Holmes–Watson residence claimed arbitrarily and quite improperly by the Abbey National Building Society, which employs a secretary whose sole task it is to answer letters addressed to Sherlock Holmes. One is given to understand that his is no sinecure.

But, at the time when Conan Doyle invented the address, "221" was a purely imaginary number for a Baker Street address; in those days, there were only eighty-four numbers in that much shorter Baker Street. But why the word "Upper"?–as well as the name "Baker Street"?

If one look at the map of east-central London, and concentrate on the St. Luke's district, it will be noticed that an important thoroughfare of that district is *Upper* Street; and I should like the reader to bear that fact in mind whilst I demonstrate how the "Baker" element is so important in the Stanger–Stumm case that the name must have forced itself inescapably on anyone as name-conscious, as susceptible to suggestion, as young Dr. Conan Doyle.

What now becomes obvious is that Conan Doyle, fascinated by the St. Luke's Mystery and the opportunity to write a new kind of detective story—or, more precisely, a detective story with a new kind of detective—not only read all the newspaper reports but also looked up the relevant reference books to which I, a century later, necessarily went. It was what Conan Doyle found in those reference books which coloured both his imagery and his choice of names when he came to set about the task of "converting" the real-life St. Luke's Mystery into the fictional *A Study in Scarlet*.

Let us examine the sources from which the "Baker" element in Conan Doyle's material came:

1. The BAKER ELEMENT in the actual proceedings:

The missing man:	Urban Napoleon Stanger, BAKER.
The anxious friend:	Georg Geisel, BAKER.
The accused:	Franz Felix Stumm, BAKER.
The gaoler:	At Worship Street Police Court, where the charges against Stumm were summarily heard, the accused was taken into custody by the gaoler, Thomas BAKER!

2. The BAKER ELEMENT from other sources:

The witnesses and friends:	As *The Times* querulously remarked (12 December 1882), all were either German BAKERS or German millers.
The friend of Dr. Doyle:	Mr. Boulnois, friend of young Dr. Conan Doyle, and member of the Portsmouth Literary and Scientific Society, was a son of one of the partners who owned the prosperous BAKER STREET BAZAAR, where the most famous tenant was Madame Tussaud's Waxwork Exhibition (which included, even then, the popular Chamber of Horrors).

There is one other curious point which ought to be mentioned here.

In turning up Baker's Row in the Post Office London Directory for 1881 or 1882, Conan Doyle may well have made the same mistake as did I: I found myself looking at a list of the inhabitants of Baker's Row, *Clerkenwall,* and not those of Baker's Row, *Whitechapel* (that I wished to see so as to check Georg Geisel's address). However, this "wrong" Baker's Row gave me a bit of a shock, for the resident of No. 1A was listed as–Richard HOLMES!

What is most important to realize in all this is that all the names, whether of persons or of trades, that Conan Doyle had first encountered in reading the newspaper reports of the St. Luke's Mystery kept cropping up again as he checked the facts in the various reference books–and, as I shall now demonstrate, the names of Holmes and Sherlock, no less than the name Baker, were obviously "forced" on Conan Doyle.

We shall never begin to appreciate the full character of Sherlock Holmes if we do not constantly keep in mind the real-life person in whom Sherlock Holmes originated. For if Sherlock Holmes be not exactly Wendel Scherer, Holmes is still Scherer as he might have been; Scherer as he ought to have been. Sherlock Holmes is Wendel Scherer idealized, and we have Conan Doyle's own letters and notes to prove that he was, at this time, deeply concerned with an idealized detective.

"I have read Gaboriau's *Lecoq the Detective,*" he wrote; "*The Gilded Clique* and *The Lerouge Case.* All very good. Wilkie Collins, but more so." There are other references to Gaboriau's books (they were, by the way, "Blood-and-Iron" Bismarck's favourite detective stories), which had just begun to appear, in the early 1880s, from the London publishing house of Vizitelly.

And when Conan Doyle at last sits down to rough out the plot of *A Study in Scarlet,* we see that he is still thinking of Lecoq, as well as of Edgar Allan Poe's Dupin, though Poe's detective is far more superhuman than Gaboriau's Lecoq. Perhaps the desire to apotheosize Wendel Scherer into something superhuman is the reason for the change in his opinion of Lecoq when Conan Doyle comes to make the notes for *A Study in Scarlet.*

The stories, one notes, about Lecoq are no longer "very good" or "Wilkie Collins, but more so." Instead, on the notebook page already shown, Conan Doyle makes "I Sherrinford Holmes" assert that "Lecoq was a bungler–Dupin was better." The omniscient, arrogant Sherlock Holmes is certainly emerging from the less-well-equipped chrysalis of the real-life Wendel Scherer (so that one might hazard a guess that the "I" of "I Sherrinford Holmes"–notice the absence of the full point after "I" on the page of notes–may not be the initial of the name "Innes" at all, but may well be what it seems at first glance to be: the dogmatic assertion of individuality–"I, Sherrinford Holmes!").

What, then, were the regular steps–semantically considered –by which Wendel Scherer "became" Sherlock Holmes? Let us, in orderly manner, trace the successive steps by which the transformation was effected in Conan Doyle's mind.

If one look at almost any stall outside almost any British second-hand bookshop, one is practically certain to find a copy of *The Autocrat of the Breakfast Table* or one of the other works (*The Professor, The Poet*) of that great American humourist-philosopher, Dr. Oliver Wendell Holmes. For decades, Wendell Holmes–with his fellow Americans, Louisa May Alcott and Kate Douglas Wiggin–was a bestseller in Britain and throughout the British Empire, and we may put speculation aside here respecting Conan Doyle's opinion of the first author: we have it on record that Conan Doyle, like so many tens of thousands of his fellow subjects, was an ardent admirer of the American writer. We hardly need to labour the suggestion that the unusual first name "Wendel" must irresistibly have brought to Conan Doyle's mind the perfect complementary name of "Holmes."

Now, before I go on to explain that "Holmes," as a name, was already familiar to Conan Doyle–and in a way which links it to the name "Stamford" ("young Stamford, who had been a dresser under me at Bart's")–I must call the reader's attention to yet another name–the first of a pair–which appears on the rough draft of *A Study in Scarlet:* "Ormond" (first half of the name originally intended for Dr. John H. Watson: "Ormond Secker"–and *not* "Sacker," as it is quite often misread).

London's most famous children's hospital–the hospital for whose support Charles Dickens did so much–is to be found, as the *Great Ormond Street Hospital,* in the Bloomsbury thoroughfare of that name, the small street flanking the side of the hospital being Powis Street, a name which afterward–in another tale–

indicates that Great Ormond Street was very much in Conan Doyle's mind, even long after he had written and published *A Study in Scarlet*.

So much, then, for the inspiration which yielded the (after-

Britain's most famous actor-manager, Sir Henry Irving, scores a spectacular triumph, both for himself and for the author, as the central character of Conan Doyle's *Waterloo* at the Lyceum Theatre, London. *Contemporary drawing from life by Balliol Salmon.*

ward dropped) name of "Ormond"–what now of Watson's original other name, "Secker"?

The second most famous children's hospital in London is *The Royal Infirmary for Children and Women* (now re-named *The Royal Waterloo Hospital,* though the original name, in glazed Victorian tiles, still adorns the pediment of the building). Its interest to us here is that, on the left-hand side of the hospital, in the 1880s, was to be found the shop of one Thomas HOLMES, whilst, on the right-hand side, STAMFORD Street runs into the Waterloo Road, and at the back of St. John's Church (across Stamford Street) we may still find short, narrow little SECKER Street. And though a connection here is with Conan Doyle's non-Sherlockian work, it is worth noting that, until a few years ago, opposite the hospital stood a large, dingy Victorian gin palace, the name of which was boldly displayed in moulded plaster-work above the cornice: "Hero of Waterloo." Those who have read Conan Doyle's tear-jerking short story of "A Straggler of '15," Corporal Gregory Brewster, or seen *A Story of Waterloo,* the splendid curtain-raiser into which that story was brilliantly dramatized, will not need to seek Doyle's inspiration further than in the name of that Waterloo Road pub. And by the side of Waterloo railway station is . . . HOLMES Row!

One may now see where that experimental and happily discarded "Sherrinford Holmes" originated, for it is clear that Conan Doyle had the Waterloo Road district well in mind (in addition to the St. Luke's–City Road–Upper Street district, of course) when he was experimenting with *A Study in Scarlet.*

I suggest, then, that in seeking a fictional name for Wendel Scherer which would disguise but recall the original, Conan Doyle had the following names running in his head:

1. Wendel SCHERER
2. STAMFORD Street
3. Earl of STAMFORD and WARRINGTON (*The Times,* 12 December 1882)
4. STANFORD and WINNINGTON–"THE BURNING OF STANFORD COURT: The fire at Stanford Court, the seat of Sir Francis Winnington, was not extinguished until Wednesday afternoon" (*The Times,* same date)

The near-likeness of two pairs of names in adjoining paragraphs is always a certain attention-catcher. It is easy to see how these pairs of names would instantly and inerasably imprint themselves on the memory of Conan Doyle.

So, as a trial essay in name-changing, we have "Sherrinford," compounded, obviously, of "Scher-ing-ford" derived from SCHERER/WARRINGTON and WINNINGTON/STANFORD and (for good measure) WINNINGTON/STAMFORD.

And so, perhaps, the name might have remained—had not Conan Doyle, that inveterate checker of facts, done what I myself did a century later: looked up the senior officers of the Metropolitan Police, as they were listed in the Post Office London Directory for 1881. Perhaps Conan Doyle was merely concerned to verify the correct spelling of the name of that Inspector that *The Times* had printed as "Radky." But whatever Conan Doyle's reason for having consulted the Directory, this is what he found:

A Division, Whitehall (Scotland Yard): Inspector Thomas HOLMES (for inspection of common lodging-houses)
B Division, Rochester Row: Chief Inspector James SHERLOCK

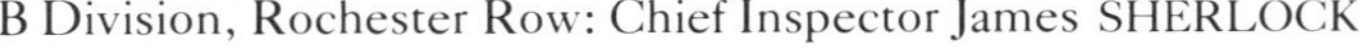

The first home of "A" Division, Metropolitan Police, popularly known as "Scotland Yard" from its proximity to the still-existing street of that name. From Whitehall Gardens (shown here and demolished in 1938), the "Yard" moved first to the Thames Embankment in 1891 and then, after World War II, to a skyscraper in Broadway, Westminster.

H Division, Whitechapel: Inspector John LE COCQ *(sic) (Stanger had moved to St. Luke's from Whitechapel, where Geisel still had his place of business)*
L Division, Lambeth: Chief Inspector William SHERLOCK
D Division, St. Marylebone: Inspector James STANFORD (of Public Carriages)

Now Conan Doyle, having attended the Jesuit College at Feldkirch, in Western Austria, understood German and knew that the German *scheren* means "to cut, clip, trim, shear"–indeed the English and the German words are but the same word slightly differentiated in spelling. But there is also a word besides the English *shearer* (which is the style now adopted by some of the Rhodesian Scherers): a slang word which belongs as much to the nursery and the children's playground as to the British Army and Royal Navy: "Shearlocks," the Service hair-cutter.

Only the other day, on my way to mail some letters, I saw some children playing in the street and, as I passed them, heard that they were singing the words of a simple old song:

Shearlocks the barber–went to shave his Farver...

Whether Conan Doyle had decided to set the scene of Drebber's death in the Brixton Road ("Lauriston Gardens") before or after he had seen the Metropolitan Police list, I do not know; but it must be noted that the Brixton Road is situated within L Division and that, in 1881, L Division was under the authority of Chief Inspector William SHERLOCK.

And, of course, Doyle had not forgotten that Patrick SHERLOCK who had joined Doyle at Stonyhurst College in 1868...

So that the name was unavoidable. The surname of the "idealized" Wendel Scherer had been "Holmes" from the very beginning of the name-changing–Oliver Wendell Holmes had made that inevitable. But now the Christian name (if that be the correct word?) was no longer "Sherrinford" or even "I Sherrinford," but "Sherlock."

Sherlock it had to be. The name not only recalled "Scherer"; it was a near-enough translation of "Scherer." Out, for good, went Sherrinford; in, for ever, came Sherlock.

Conan Doyle must, as they say, have "tried it for size." He wrote it down. He spoke it aloud. He wrote it down again . . .

Yes . . . it *sounded* right. It *looked* right.

So–for the ages–Sherlock Holmes it became. Wendel Scherer, idealized, was to endure for ever as Sherlock Holmes.

3

THE FIRST SCHERER ENCOUNTER

In September 1882, nearly a year had passed since Urban Napoleon Stanger had mysteriously passed out of the sight and knowledge of men; but, in the official phrasing, "the Police had not yet completed their enquiries," and the many and full reports of the St. Luke's Mystery–which were to bring Wendel Scherer to the notice of the public and, in particular, to that of Dr. Conan Doyle–were still to come. By the end of the year, all Britain would know all which was to be learned about the Stangers, Stumm, and Wendel Scherer; in the Autumn of that year, such knowledge was, as Poe liked to say, *mellonta tauta*–"these matters are about to be."

Now, if, as I affirmed, the year 1881 were the most important in Doyle's life–or, at any rate, in his literary career (which was, when all is said and done, his whole life)–the following year saw the redemption of that vast promise implicit in the events of 1881; events which were yet to be revealed to that true favourite of Fortune, Conan Doyle.

I have already mentioned Conan Doyle's deep interest in, if not an actual obsession with, the case of the poisoner-physician, William Palmer of Rugeley, who died, according to the Jack Ketch who "topped" him, "like a gentleman."

What there was, in either Palmer's character or in the character of his several poisonings, which caught Conan Doyle's interest, I cannot say; but that he read the full account, published by *The Times* at a penny, of the history of Palmer's crimes, the use by

Conan Doyle of the names from Palmer's background makes certain, as I have already pointed out. On reflection, a very possible reason for Conan Doyle's deep interest in Palmer may be the now generally forgotten fact that there was an exceptionally vocal body of opinion, heard noisily from the moment of Palmer's conviction, that he, like the other alleged poisoner of thirty-three years later, Mrs. Maybrick, had been a victim of a mistrial. Pamphlets and even full-length books supporting this opinion–two by barristers–appeared with most convincing arguments; and there are responsible criminologists today who state that, had the Court of Criminal Appeal been established before the present century, both Palmer and Mrs. Maybrick would have been cleared of the charge of murder. It is true that Doyle makes Holmes say to Watson: "When a doctor goes wrong, he is the first of criminals. He has nerve and he has knowledge. Palmer and Pritchard were among the heads of their profession." And I must now suspect that, as with many others, I have read too much into that statement of Holmes's, and accepted it as Conan Doyle's acceptance of Palmer's guilt *as a convicted murderer*. A more careful reading of the statement will demonstrate that Doyle (as Holmes) committed himself never so far as that. He calls Palmer a criminal. . .and so he was; but that comment of Holmes's on a doctor's "going wrong" need mean no more than that Palmer did exactly so: "went wrong" in neglecting the promise of his medical training at "Bart's," in neglecting his practice at Rugeley; in getting himself deeply into debt at the racecourse; and in trying to extricate himself from the toils of his indebtedness by shabby and, indeed, even fraudulent expedient. But though all these things were urged against him as evidence of his guilt, it does not necessarily follow that Palmer was guilty–and Conan Doyle, always eager to see the patent oppression of the innocent rather than the just conviction of the guilty, may well have swallowed, hook-line-and-sinker, the arguments for Palmer's innocence *of murder.*[1]

---

[1]If Conan Doyle had been persuaded–or even half-persuaded–of the possible innocence, in respect of the capital charge, of Palmer, the most persuasive of all the pro-Palmer literature that Doyle could have read is the brilliantly argued *The Cries of the Condemned: Proofs of the Unfair Trial of Wm. Palmer* by Thomas Wakeley, Esq. (London: C.

The case may have held a further interest for Conan Doyle, apart from anything to do with Palmer himself, in that two of the four brilliant counsel "briefed" to defend him were Irish: Mr. Serjeant[2] Shee and Dr. Kenealy. The latter afterward ruined his career by his fatuous behaviour as defender of the notorious "Tichborne Claimant," a butcher from the dockside of East London who impudently asserted that he was the missing heir to the baronetcy, granted in 1621 by James I, of the ancient pre-Norman Conquest family of Doughty-Tichborne. The Claim–its notoriety entitles it to be given a capital letter–with Arthur Orton, *alias* "Sir Roger Tichborne," as plaintiff, was presented at

---

Elliott, 1856). Wakeley was not only a barrister-at-law but also occupied the highly responsible position of Coroner for the City of London. The best *modern* presentation of the case for Palmer's innocence of murder is the eminent Robert Graves's *They Hanged My Saintly Billy* (London: Cassell and Company, Ltd., 1957).

An ironical comment on the relative honesty of prosecutor and defendant in this trial is to be found in the curious experiences of Edwin James, Queen's Counsel, one of five counsel appointed by the Crown to prosecute Palmer. James's extravagant mode of living puts Palmer's spendthrift habits quite in the shade; and when James's unpaid–and unpayable–debts reached the then handsome total of £60,000 ($300,000), the Lord Chancellor disbarred him for five years, as a penalty for his improvidence, on the sound legal principle that the best way to deal with a debtor is to deprive him of the means of clearing his indebtedness. One must live, however, and so James, no longer a practising barrister, went on to run up a further £40,000 ($200,000) of debt, on which he emigrated to New York, built the first Winter Garden in that city, and lived out the rest of his life a wealthy and highly respected *entrepreneur*.

[2]The Serjeants-at-Law, the oldest legal body in England, were abolished by the Judicature Act of 1873, which initiated widespread changes (often erroneously described as "reforms") in the English judicial system. All existing Serjeants retained their title for life. They had formerly enjoyed many important privileges, the most important being that they were not (as King's or Queen's Counsel were) subject to the control of the Crown. They wore wigs of a distinctive shape, decorated with a small black patch to represent an original monkish tonsure, and attended court, not in black, but in scarlet, robes. The rank was not abolished in Ireland until the establishment of the Free State in 1922, the famous Serjeant Sullivan being the last survivor of the Irish Serjeants-at-Law.

its first hearing by one of the most famous of all the brilliant advocates of the last century: Serjeant William Ballantine.

In the early part of 1882, Ballantine's memoirs appeared, published by Richard Bentley & Son, "Publishers in Ordinary to Her Majesty the Queen," as *Some Experiences of a Barrister's Life*. No book that I know gives a wider or a clearer view of Victorian and pre-Victorian legal and social life than these consistently interesting memoirs of an advocate who had figured in most of the important trials of more than half a century. The book deserved to become popular, and it did, running into ten editions in the course of its first year of publication. At least two references in Mr. Serjeant Ballantine's book indicate that Conan Doyle must have read it.

Ballantine is recalling his involvement in the matter of the Tichborne Claim:

> The solicitor originally retained for [Arthur Orton, claiming to be the missing Sir Roger Tichborne] was a gentleman named HOLMES, who certainly believed in him, but before he took any steps in the matter desired that [Orton] should be seen by the mother of Sir Roger, to which the Claimant readily consented, and an interview took place in an hotel in Paris where he was staying.

And further:

> When I was first consulted upon the matter by Mr. HOLMES, I felt that the disturbance of a family in an estate that they had held unchallenged for so many years [since before the Norman Conquest of A.D. 1066] was so grave a matter that I ought not to act in it without satisfying myself, as far as it was possible for me to do so, that there was reasonable ground for the claim, and before moving in it, requested an interview with Lady Tichborne, which was accorded without hesitation.

But this passage from Ballantine's memoirs was, for Conan Doyle, even more important than his encountering, once again, the surname Holmes:

> When [Sir Alexander Cockburn, Baronet, Lord Chief Justice of England] was nearly a briefless barrister, a case was tried upon the Western Circuit before Mr. Justice Williams. This was not the eminent lawyer and distinguished judge, Vaughan Williams, but the "Johnny" whose jokes I have recorded. The prisoner was convicted. The details would afford no amusement nor add any point to the anecdote that I am relating; it is sufficient to say that [the convict] was sentenced to

transportation for life, and, notwithstanding very earnest endeavours on the part of Cockburn and others who considered the evidence to be unsatisfactory, underwent a great portion of his sentence, and it was only recently that, the case being again ventilated, the late Lord Chief Justice, in the midst of his pressing avocations, renewed with unabated energies his endeavours on [the convict's] behalf, and with success. The innocence of the convict, now bowed down by years, has been recognised. He has received a free pardon, and a sufficient pension for his remaining years. It is not only in this case that the public has to recognise an enlightened change in the constitution of the Home Office. *I am glad to take the opportunity of mentioning a very dear and valued friend of mine, and [of] many others of former days. I allude to a gentleman named SCHERER, a shorthand writer,* very accomplished in his own profession, and possessing other qualities which endeared him to many friends at the bar as well as elsewhere. *He was one of the most earnest believers in the innocence of the person I have referred to, and energetic in his endeavours on his behalf. Poor Scherer's premature death did not enable him to reap the reward of his disinterested exertions, as his friend Cockburn had the satisfaction of doing.* [Emphases added]

This passage struck me—as I know now that it struck Conan Doyle—as relating to an incident so important that I could not understand the casual way in which the good-hearted Mr. Serjeant Ballantine had dismissed it, with the quite unhappy comment that "the details would afford no amusement nor add any point to the anecdote that I am relating..." What an extraordinary thing to say about a fight for justice, lasting, obviously, over many years, and culminating in a belated justice for the wrongly-accused-and-convicted, with a free pardon at the end! In English as in any other judicial system, the free pardon is and must be the rarest of all forensic decisions, since it demands that, somewhere along the chain of baseless cause and indefensible effect, some pettifogger must be shown to have erred... and who will admit such error, or, *within the system*, place the responsibility for error squarely where it belongs? Was this almost insuperable difficulty, I asked myself, why the usually honest and bluntly-spoken Ballantine was suddenly so coyly tactful, mentioning only the defenders of the wronged man and leaving out, as I was to discover, the ablest and most tenacious defender of all, and not any name of one or more who had wronged the man in the first place? It seemed to me that here, though I have always admired (and still do admire) the character and achievements of Ballantine, that he was engaged in that well-known "cover-up" activity familiar to all who have watched a group–any group: at school, at the University, in the Armed Services, in business–draw together and protect what the group perceives as its own interests against any attack–even the mildest criticism–delivered by the Outsider.

Yes. . . that, surely, was why, in Ballantine's opinion, "the details would afford no amusement nor add any point" to the account of a successful fight to right an old wrong, and to achieve that rarest reward of all: the free pardon. I decided that this was something–quite apart from the involvement of a *Scherer* in the proceedings–of such importance intrinsically that I had to uncover those suppressed details for myself.

I may say that it was not without great difficulty that I managed to do so, successful as I found myself at the end. (Rather like finding the details of the near-war between Great Britain and the United States in 1895 over the sovereignty of the uninhabited Atlantic island of Trinidad, in the Martin Vaz Group, six hundred miles east of Bahia, Brazil. Not one of the thirteen books on Anglo-American relations in the Caribbean and Central and South America as much as mentions the very serious dispute. It is not only the Great Russian Encyclopaedia which finds it convenient to fail to record the inconvenient past. . .)

At first sight, the tracing of the defended convict should have been easy: I had two limiting dates–the date of Alexander Cockburn's call to the Bar and the date (still as Lord Chief Justice) of his death. His appearance on the Western Circuit, before Mr. Justice Williams, should have given me an ascertainable date, and a look at the calendar for the Western Circuit whilst Cockburn was still "nearly a briefless barrister" should have made the identification of the eventually-pardoned convict no difficult matter. A further clue to the required dating–at the end of the affair, this time, and not at the beginning–was Ballantine's remark in his book that "*it was only recently*" that the convict received his free pardon. Well, "recently" is a relative term, and its significance is mostly a matter of personal estimate. I did, however, bear that estimate well in mind as, unsuccessfully, I tried to find some allusion to the case in, for instance, the very detailed biographical note on Sir Alexander Cockburn in the

Dictionary of National Biography and similar reference works. The "expected" libraries were not helpful, and, though formally polite, their librarians told me, in effect, to go on hunting *by myself* until I had found what I had been seeking. So that I did what I realize now that I should have done at the very beginning: gone laboriously through the index of *The Times,* working backward from the date of Sir Alexander Cockburn's death in 1879. I looked, of course, for a reference to a free pardon, and I was fortunate enough to find three references, all in 1879 and all relating to what was obviously the same case. The mentions were to be found in *The Times* for 11 April, 28 May, and 11 June. As I shall be telling the whole story of Edmund Galley in the next chapter, I need say no more at this point than that, having asked the young lady assistant at Brighton Central Reference Library to put the relevant reels of microfilm on the projector, I saw at once that I had, as they say, struck gold:

11 April 1879, page 9, column f:

A Plea for Mercy.–The *Western Times* of yesterday publishes a correspondence between the Lord Chief Justice of England and the Home Secretary in reference to the case of Edmund Galley, who was tried in 1836 and sentenced to death for the murder of a farmer named May in the county of Devon. The capital sentence was afterwards commuted into one of transportation for life, and Sir Alexander Cockburn, who, as a "young barrister on the Western Circuit," heard the trial, wrote, under date March 16, 1879, a long letter to the Home Secretary, setting forth the grounds on which he hoped that the remainder of Galley's sentence would be remitted . . .

Well, evidently I now had what I needed to find, eventually–the complete details of the case. I had an initial date, 1836; I had the name of the defendant; so that I had only to consult the national and provincial newspapers of the day in order to learn how and why the case of Edmund Galley had troubled so many over so long a period–forty-three years. Though the year, 1879, was, as I was to discover, *not* to be the year in which this extraordinary case was brought to a successful conclusion–that did not happen until the end of August 1881, so that when Conan Doyle joined the odious medical con man, Dr. Budd, as a "partner" in Budd's practice in Plymouth, Devon–the town and county were still ringing with the triumph that the aged but still vigorous editor of

The Western Times had achieved, as one of the Fighting Trio: the late George Scherer and the recently-dead Lord Chief Justice, Sir Alexander Cockburn, being the other two, though the trio was joined later by Sir John Eardley Wilmot, Baronet, the Conservative Member of Parliament for South Warwickshire.

I wrote off at once to Mr. P. W. Ellis, Area Librarian of the Central Devon Area, and, through his courtesy, I soon received ten photocopied pages from the (long defunct) *Exeter Flying Post* of 4 August 1836, reporting the trial, on the charge of the wilful murder of Jonathan May, farmer, of *Edmund Galley,* "alias *Turpin,*" and *Thomas Oliver,* "alias *Buckingham Joe,*" "by dragging [May] from his horse, throwing him on the road, and with a large stick striking him, and also kicking him while on the ground: thereby giving him divers wounds, of which he languished and died."

The account of the Galley-Oliver trial is headed, in bold 12-point "Egyptian" capitals:

TRIAL OF THE MURDERERS OF MR.
JONATHAN MAY

The *Exeter Flying Post* solemnly printed Mr. Justice Williams's warning to the jury:

> . . . [A]t 20 minutes to 7 o'clock, the Judge began to sum up. His address to the jury was one of the most elaborate description; entreating them in a case of this kind, and one in which there was much of peculiarity, to cast behind them as most treacherous and unsafe; as being injurious in the extreme;—as the most fertile source of error, all that might have been brought to their minds touching this transaction,—if any such there had been, by public rumour and to give their decision in it according to the weight they might be enabled to attach to the evidence which had been adduced . . .

We shall see later what "weight" the jury attached, not only to "the evidence which had been adduced," but also to the learned judge's warning.

I have said that I now had what I needed to find, eventually—the complete details of the case. There was, of course, more to be found; and, as is so often found in research which has met with initial obstacles, the rest of the required information came to me, as the saying goes, "like a dream."

I followed up the clue inherent in Mr. Serjeant Ballantine's alluding to "a gentleman named Scherer, a shorthand writer, very accomplished in his own profession," and, having "got nowhere," as they say, with the Law Society and some other founts of forensic wisdom and legal history, I did what common sense should have counselled me to do at the beginning: I addressed an enquiry about "a Mr. Scherer, a shorthand writer," to the Institute of Shorthand Writers Practising in the Supreme Court of Judicature at their offices at 2 New Square, Lincoln's Inn, London.

The Secretary, Miss Valerie Bone, answered me promptly and most courteously, having no information but assuring me that "I am making enquiries among my colleagues to see if we can be of any help and, if so, I will write to you further in due course."

I had not long to wait, though it was not Miss Bone but a Mr. A. G. M. Newman who next wrote to me; and with Mr. Newman's letter–which followed his telephoning me on the morning of Monday, 23 November 1981–I could no longer doubt that I now had all the information that I needed successfully to conclude my search for Sherlock Holmes.

In his letter, Mr. Newman, who is the Chairman of Marten Walsh Cherer Limited, a "Legal and Conference Reporting" firm of 36–38 Whitefriars Street, a turning off Fleet Street in the City of London, gave me invaluable information and, with exceptional generosity, enclosed two of his own books to help me in my quest.

The more important book–certainly from the point of view of its relative inaccessibility in England (it was published privately in Rhodesia)–is *The House of Cherer*,[3] which, in the author's words, tells "the story of a family which starts with General Barthélémy Louis Joseph Scherer, a French army general who fought with distinction in the Napoleonic wars, but [whose] successes were followed by failures and disappointment, which eventually led to his persecution and flight from France in the days when human

[3]R. Cherer Smith, *The House of Cherer* (Salisbury and Bulawayo, Rhodesia: R. Cherer Smith, 1972).

The monument, seen at the extreme lower right, erected in honour of the French general Barthélémy Scherer (1747–1804) in his home town of Delle, Eastern France. General Scherer was the uncle of the Scherer Brothers, employers of Charles Dickens and champions of the unjustly-convicted Edmund Galley.

life was cheap and the guillotine the inevitable end for those who fell out of favour with the rulers of that country."

(This is more than a little exaggerated, historically, since the General's having fallen out of favour with the rulers of France–the Directory–was some time after the initiators of the Terror had perished in it as its last victims. There was no guillotine for political opponents of the System after 1794.)

Certain statements in this quite (to me) invaluable book I have been unable to check; for instance, that the General's nephew, George, the hero of the fight for Edmund Galley, was a barrister. And another statement: that "A radio play was performed on the British Broadcasting Corporation programme in which George Cherer [*sic;* the name had been Anglicized from 'Scherer' by *some* members of the family, not by all] formed the central character, based on a book by Richard S. Lambert, entitled *The Innocence of Edmund Galley,*" is, in fact, most misleading, as I shall explain.

This passage, by the way, emphasizes the danger that we all risk when–oh, yes: Conan Doyle has done it, and the writer has done it, too!–when we lazily fail to check our references and rely on our all-too-fallible memories. Lambert's book was *not* entitled *The Innocence of Edmund Galley*, and, because *I* did not check the title under the author's name in the British Museum's Catalogue of Books, I had to wait several weeks to hear from Mr. Colin Taylor, Senior Assistant, Liaison & Processing, Sound Activities, British Broadcasting Corporation, London, that his department had finally traced my misnamed *The Innocence of Edmund Galley* to a radio feature titled *Which Dick Turpin?—The Story of the Miscarriage of Justice of Edmund Galley*, which was broadcast on 3 May 1948.

The second book received from Mr. Newman was of only slightly less importance; indeed, in some respects it may be held to be of greater importance than *The House of Cherer*—though not, I submit, in this present search for Sherlock Holmes. This second book is *Charles Dickens: Shorthand Writer* by William J. Carlton,[4] which makes inarguably evident that, when we find both Dickens and Conan Doyle using the same "fictional" themes, it is because both these great writers were influenced by the interests and activities of an outstandingly influential newspaper editor, whom Dickens certainly knew well and whom Conan Doyle knew by reputation, even though Doyle may not have made this editor's personal acquaintance.

In addition to his having informed me of—and kindly sent to me—the two books mentioned above, Mr. Newman gave me an item of information of what has proved to be of the first importance: that, besides George Scherer[5] and Sir Alexander Cockburn, the wrongly-convicted Edmund Galley had had another, quite as influential, not less energetic, and with greatly superior staying-power, protagonist: the famous "Cobbett of the West," Thomas Latimer, editor of *The Western Times* when the young Charles Dickens, still earning his living as a shorthand writer, took the coach from London to Exeter (£4 return: 173¾ miles in guaran-

[4] William J. Carlton, *Charles Dickens: Shorthand Writer* (London: Cecil Palmer, 1926).

[5] So Mr. Serjeant Ballantine spells his name, and so I shall continue to do.

teed nightmare discomfort) to cover the Exeter by-election; his report being printed in the *Morning Chronicle* of Saturday, 2 May 1835.

The "real" report, told in Dickens's inimitable style, is, of course, to be read as the "Eatenswill" election—but, when that was published, Dickens had become an author, and was no longer either a professional shorthand writer or a newspaper reporter.

Later, I shall point out the use, by both Dickens and Conan

Doubtless strongly based on the real-life brothers, George and Joseph Scherer (Cherer), the fictional Cheeryble Brothers are shown here, drawn by the artist "Phiz" for the first edition of Dickens's *Nicholas Nickleby*.

Charles Dickens in 1835, at the age of twenty-three, working as a reporter for the *Morning Chronicle*, a job which took him down to Exeter, where he began his long and close friendship with "The Cobbett of the West." *From a miniature by Miss Rose E. Drummond.*

Doyle, of similar themes in their writings; but Dickens's tribute to the Scherer Brothers, shorthand writers, by whom he was employed for a time, was far more generously given – at any rate, apparently so, for the almost-too-good-to-be-true "Cheeryble" Brothers in *Nicholas Nickleby* are, without doubt, his youthfully enthusiastic (though completely sincere) tribute to the brothers George and Joseph Nelson Scherer, nephews of the General. Dickens's calling his benevolent fictional brothers "Cheeryble" indicated that Dickens knew his employers as "Cherer" rather than as "Scherer." It was this double naming which, I now realize, may have hampered my research at the beginning: for what was I asking my sources to look – "Scherer" or "Cherer"?

What seems evident to me is that the family name "Scherer" was retained for private use, and that the brothers, who founded their – from the start, most respected and in every way successful – firm of shorthand writers to the judicature in about 1830 "traded under" the style of "Cherer"; a style that A. G. M. Newman's firm, Marten Walsh Cherer Limited, still retains.

After Mr. Newman had called my attention to R. S. Lambert's book *The Cobbett of the West*,[6] my next step, obviously, was to communicate with the present editor of *The Western Times*, and accordingly, on 27 November 1981, I wrote to Sidwell Street, Exeter. Once again, matters seemed to be moving in my favour:

Dear Mr. Harrison,

As fortune had it, your letter turned up on my desk (I'm the deputy editor); and I happen to be both a Holmes fan and much interested in Thomas Latimer. (My interest in Holmes dates from a visit to the 1951 Festival of Britain exhibition at 221 Baker Street, and my Holmes file includes your Ellery Queen's Mystery Magazine article. My interest in Latimer arises from research I am doing into the history of Exeter journalism.)

Well! this was luck indeed!

Mr. Clifford Jiggens, evidently a fan of mine as well as of the Master, offered to, and promptly did, photocopy the relevant pages–relevant, that is to say, to Thomas Latimer's long and ultimately successful fight to secure justice for Edmund Galley: a fight begun in 1836, ended only in 1881!

And, at the end of his letter, Mr. Jiggens wrote this:

Nothing really to do with the above, but since you mention Dickens . . . I should add that Latimer was a friend of Dickens. The latter, while a reporter for the Morning Chronicle, came to Exeter to report an important political meeting, and met Latimer then. They kept in touch over the years, and Dickens occasionally visited Latimer.

Well, I knew that Dickens had gone down to Exeter to cover the "Eatenswill" election; I did not know that the great novelist and the great editor had maintained over many years a friendship begun when Dickens was a young reporter. And that they

---

[6] R. S. Lambert, *The Cobbett of the West: A Study of Thomas Latimer and the Struggle Between Pulpit and Press at Exeter* (London: Nicholson & Watson, Ltd., 1939).

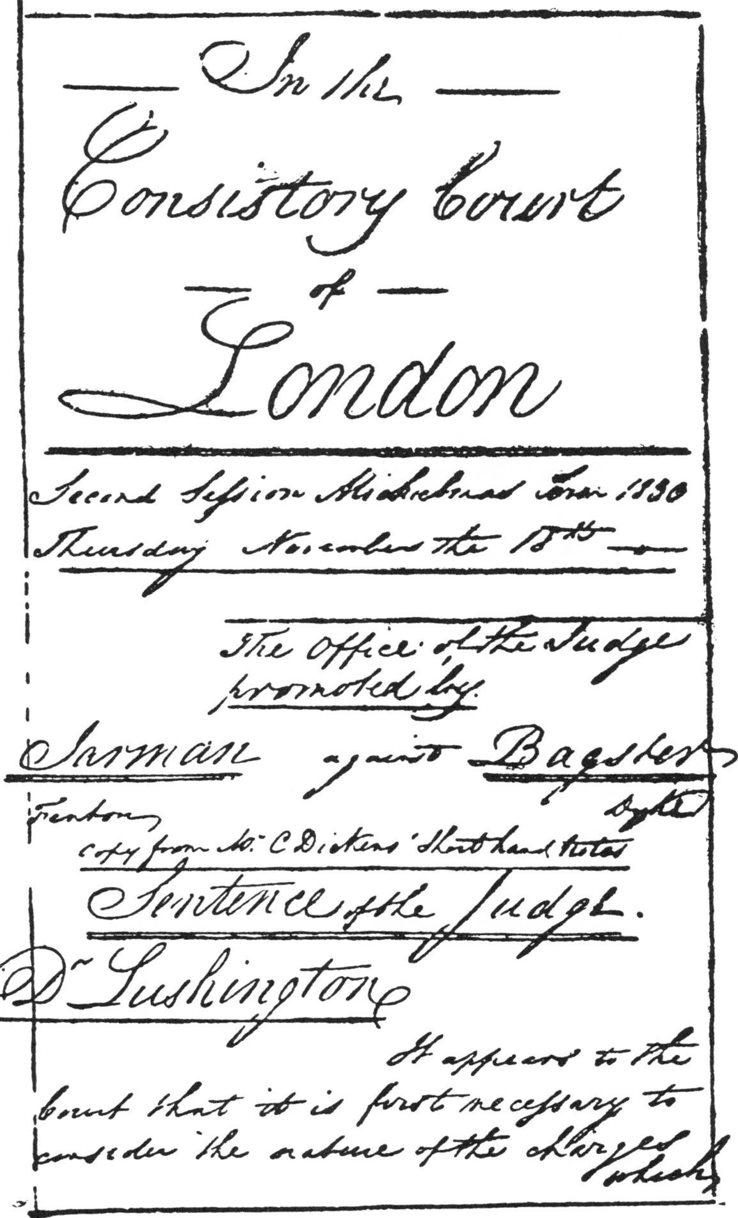

In the
Consistory Court
of
London

Second Session Michaelmas Term 1830
Thursday November the 18th

The Office of the Judge
promoted by

Jarman against Bagster

Fenton Dyke

copy from Mr. C Dickens' Short hand Notes

Sentence of the Judge.

Dr Lushington

It appears to the
Court that it is first necessary to
consider the nature of the charges
which

Dickens as a court reporter, employed by the Scherer brothers. This is the front cover of a Consistory Court judgment, taken down in shorthand by the future famous novelist when he was only eighteen and transcribed in his own neat handwriting.

even greater than the offence itself. The
expence of these proceedings when it falls on
the shoulders of those convicted under this
statute, is so heavy, as in many instances
to bear no proportion to the guilt committed,
and it would be in direct opposition to all
general rules and principles, on which
punishment is inflicted if such were to be
the case in the present instance. The legislature in providing for
offences of this description, had no other
object in view, than the interest of the public
at large, - it did so for the purpose of
preventing the commission of the like offences
in future; but if the punishment were to
be more than adequate to the offence, this
jurisdiction would in the public opinion
be considered oppressive and unjust. Therefore
considering that eight witnesses have been
examined on the part of the Promoter, not=
-withstanding my being of opinion that
some of the interrogatories which have been
addressed to them have a very remote
bearing on the question at issue, I shall
content myself with condemning the
Defendant, in the sum of £35, nomine
expensarum.

x'd
C Dickens
Shorthand Writer
5 Bell Yard
Doctors Commons

10

The last page of the Consistory Court judgment, reported and transcribed by Dickens in 1830. Note that Dickens signs himself as "Shorthand Writer" and gives his (business) address as the offices of the Scherer (Cherer) brothers, whom Dickens was to immortalize as the Cheerybles.

discussed the Edmund Galley case–with the reprieved but convicted Galley now transported to a then very distant Australia –is evident from at least two allusions, one most important, the other not so much, to Australia.

The whole plot of *Great Expectations,* one of Dickens's finest novels, springs from, and develops from, the fact that the small boy Pip aids–or tries to aid–a convict on the run: Abel Magwich. Later transported for life (as Edmund Galley had been), Magwich serves his sentence in the penal colony to which he has been sent and, as a free man–though never free to return to Great Britain–makes himself rich, able, without revealing to Pip the source of the wealth which now comes to the young man, to express the gratitude of "an old lag" who once received ungrudged kindness from a child. In the end, Magwich risks death at the hands of the law by returning to England, though the death that he eventually meets comes to him by drowning and not by hanging.

The attitude of Dickens to transportation in this fine novel is both impressive and deeply moving; but seen against the background of his sympathetic discussions with Thomas Latimer, Dickens's attack on the system of transportation acquires a very personal coloration indeed; and from being a general, though intensely emotional, denunciation of a system that the Australians themselves were to end by unilateral action against the Home Government, Dickens's sympathy for the hunted Magwich must now be interpreted as a highly personalized plea for the transported Galley–and for all others in his condition.

The less important of the two mentions may have something of Dickens's well-known facetiousness in it: the destiny allotted to the egregious Mr. Micawber at the end of *David Copperfield.* Dickens's ambivalent attitude toward the ever-hopeful Micawber is often interpreted as the novelist's attitude–half amused, half indignant; half affectionate, half embarrassed–toward his own improvident, pettily dishonest father.

Micawber's "bubble schemes," always promising the insanely optimistic projector a fortune, even whilst he is borrowing shillings to support his Walter Mittyish imaginings, come always to nothing. . .until Dickens invents for Micawber the same fortune that he invented for Magwich, though without the sinister threat which hung over Magwich. But like Magwich–though not on a convict-ship–Micawber goes to Australia, and there, just as did Magwich, becomes a rich and influential man: Magwich, in other words, without the social blemishes . . .

American readers of this book will not need to be reminded of the power which may sometimes be wielded by "out-of-town" newspaper editors; and, though distances from the Capital are much shorter in Britain than they are in the United States, these distances have been sufficient to permit the rise and flourishing of important influences outside those of London. The provincial press of the years between, say, the beginning of Victoria's reign in 1837 and the outbreak of the Great War in 1914, produced some remarkably influential newspapers or journals, all, without exception, reflecting the dominant personality of a vigorously opinionated editor. The names of the *provincial* newspapers strongly influencing national opinion are still, in Britain, respected for what they were then: such newspapers as, for example, *The Scotsman, The Yorkshire Post, The Manchester Guardian, The Liverpool Post,* and, not less respected, *The Western Times* under the sixty-year-long editorship of Thomas Latimer.

"Reigning" almost as long as the great Queen–Latimer began his campaign for Galley's pardon in the year before Victoria came to the throne "of all the Britains"–and bringing it to a triumphant conclusion as his Sovereign was coming up to her Golden Jubilee, Latimer, as with all men of strong opinions and the tireless energy needed to pursue his aims, was at times more dangerous as a friend and protagonist than he would have been as a possibly less energetic enemy. Not every cause that Latimer championed profited by that championship; the very fact that Latimer was espousing some "good cause" made Latimer's critics and enemies the critics and enemies of that cause–"good," "deserving," "for the public benefit" as even his enemies might have conceded had anyone else been that cause's upholder.

When, as the reader soon will, one hears the full story of Latimer's fight–in company with George Scherer, Alexander Cockburn, and, at the end, Sir John Eardley Wilmot–for justice for Edmund Galley, the reader may well be left, as I found that I was, with the uneasy suspicion that Galley's cause *might* have been better served had it been taken up by less forceful self-appointed guardians of the public and private weal. Lesser

Thomas Latimer, "The Cobbett of the West," for half a century editor of *The Western Times*, Exeter, a fearless critic of Authority, and an untiring champion in the cause of the Underdog. *Portrait attributed to Mogford, circâ 1846; reproduced by courtesy of Cyrus P. Crofts, Esquire.*

persons are too often inclined to see, in the rational demands of the more forceful—who are, in general, the more "important"—only what they resent as the arrogance of the demanding, rather than the justice of the demand. In the case of Galley—as in the case of the American Mrs. Maybrick[7]—the spectacle of a Lord Chief Justice fighting on behalf of a legally convicted person (Sir Alexander Cockburn even broke with all precedent in publishing a pamphlet in Galley's defense: *A Plea for Pardon*) was too tempting to those with the power to refuse justice for Galley to do otherwise than to deny that justice; not that Galley's fate interested them, one way or the other. But it was richly rewarding to be able to refuse, in the holy name of Precedent, what a Lord Chief Justice was urging. Richly rewarding, indeed.

Nor was a snubbing of Thomas Latimer, "The Cobbett of the West," to be regarded as other than rewarding. This vociferous pleader for the Democracy in general and for all the hard-done-by in particular, had long been a thorn in the flesh of the Establishment; notably as regards the inherited and often tyrannical power of the Established Church. And—though he was a very late comer on the battlefield of Justice—Sir John Eardley Wilmot was a wealthy, well-connected baronet of decidedly independent views, never disposed to fly from opposing, on a point of principle, even the leaders of his own political party. He seemed, to the more politically established, to the more pliant fawners and trimmers and place-seekers, a worthy object of snubbing. Indeed, the wonder is not that it took forty-five years to put matters right for poor Galley—nor so much that it did not take even longer—as that justice, however belated, however grudged, however meanly conceded, was secured for Galley at all.

When I wrote and published, in the pages of *Ellery Queen's Mystery Magazine*, the relatively short monograph of which this present book is the greatly expanded version, I was, as I have

---

[7]The second Lord Chief Justice, who fought as gallantly—though, alas! less successfully—for Mrs. Florence Maybrick, convicted of having poisoned her husband with arsenic, as Cockburn fought for Galley, was Sir Charles Russell, Q.C., first Baron Russell of Killowen, whose pleas for justice for the American lady convicted on servants' gossip and racial prejudice fell on the deaf ears of Home Secretaries of all shades of political opinion.

explained, ignorant of the presence of an earlier Scherer in Conan Doyle's lively consciousness; I was, too, as totally ignorant of the extraordinary importance that the Galley case was to have on the thinking and the writing of at least two world-famous authors: Charles Dickens and Arthur Conan Doyle. Both were inspired, not only to consider the character and unhappy fate of Galley alone, but also to gather in and use subjects of what the biographers like to call "related interests." The two writers were men of very different personalities, and thus, inevitably, of very different talent–having in common only the impressive quality of being storytellers of the very first rank.

If I mention here that Doyle, for all his Irish blood and Irish-Scottish upbringing, had almost no sense of the comic, with which Dickens was so richly endowed, it is by no way of introducing a trivial irrelevancy into this study but to prepare the way for my eventual introduction of what has never yet, I think, been detected by other Sherlockian exegetists: the existence and significance of those (not so defined as to be called puns, but rather) tricks of wordplay which have been given so little emphasis in Doyle's various texts–though it is with the Sherlockian that I am primarily concerned here–that they have gone quite unperceived by even the sharpest-eyed gleaner in the rich field of Sherlockian scholarship.

But, their distinctly differing gifts apart, and considering here only their shared great gift of storytelling, how similarly did Dickens and Doyle (Jung, I think, would have found a deep "synchronous" significance in the shared double-initials) respond to the stimulus of most of the many ideas that the conjoined histories of George Scherer and Edmund Galley suggested!

To take but one idea, one theme: both nobly responded to the challenge to write something memorable on either that fake "Rising of an Oppressed People" which, oddly for an ignobly conceived plot, threw up many a character as worthy as he was admirable, or on the greatest man of all to have emerged from the social action and reaction of the French Revolution. Dickens gave us *A Tale of Two Cities,* which, despite the historical inaccuracy and error-compounding class prejudice which mar the pages, is, for all its faults, still one of the world's great novels.

Social unrest attracted Dickens: there was a very dark side, as Pamela Hansford Johnson once remarked to me in a letter, to

Dickens's interests (and so, of course, to his imaginings). It is significant that he got up early in Rome to see a felon clubbed to death by the Pope's executioners, and it is surely significant that, when the defeated, dying Napoleon III trudged wearily to the headquarters of Bismarck, it was to find that the Iron Chancellor, destroyer of the Second Empire, had been reading *Little Dorritt*, in parts the darkest of all Dickens's darker tales.

The social upheaval of the French Revolution had no appeal for the more romantically-minded Conan Doyle; he was attracted to the character of the man who, born under the old régime, was swept to power and world fame by the Revolution yet mastered it, contained it, regulated it, and took what he could of virtue from it for the re-civilizing of Europe. There are no heroes—not even a single hero—of historic authenticity in *A Tale of Two Cities;* in all the "Brigadier Gérard" tales, we are never permitted by Conan Doyle to forget that, over his moderately humble hero stands that gigantic Arch-Hero in all his superhuman power and glory. To Conan Doyle, as to his creation, the gasconading cavalryman Gérard, Napoleon was what Caesar was to Cassius:

> Why, man, he doth bestride the narrow world
> Like a Colossus; and we petty men . . . peep about
> To find ourselves dishonourable graves.
> Men at some time are masters of their fates:
> The fault, dear Brutus, is not in our stars,
> But in ourselves, that we are underlings.

Compare the different treatment that comparatively recent French history has received from the pens of these two masterly writers; yet never forget that their passionate interest in two very different aspects of that history may be traced to the fact that George Scherer was the nephew of a French general of German descent, whose most promising career had withered away as the genius of the young Napoleon overtook and erased the older man.

Then—strange are the ways of the creative talent!—reflect how we owe not only Brigadier Gérard, but no less Sydney Carton and Lucie Manette to the fact that both Dickens and Doyle, their interest caught up in the strange case of Edmund Galley, learned of the French origins of the Scherers: Dickens because he worked for "the Cheeryble Brothers" as a shorthand writer at their offices in Doctors' Commons; Conan Doyle because he arrived in Plymouth whilst the triumph of Thomas Latimer and Galley's other defenders was still the subject of proud and excited gossip in Plymouth and Exeter and throughout the whole of England's West.

4

THE TRAGEDY OF EDMUND GALLEY

THE TRAGEDY of Edmund Galley began on the night of Friday, 16 July 1835, when a prosperous farmer, Jonathan May, was riding home after having visited Moretonhampstead Fair, near Exeter, in the county of Devon. Riding alone, he stopped at a wayside spring known locally as "Jacob's Well" to water his horse.

As the farmer drew up at the spring, two men–it was clear from the marks in the dusty road that there had been two men involved–leaped down from one of the high banks between which the toll road ran and attacked May by dragging him from his horse, beating him about the head and upper body so severely that the farmer lost consciousness nor ever regained it before dying of his fearful injuries on the following day.

As is so often the case in this sort of robbery, it was the riderless horse which drew attention to the fact that something grave had happened to its owner, and a search of the road beyond the toll-gate through which May had passed discovered his battered but still breathing body lying in a ditch in the shadow of a roadside hedge. He was gently picked up and carried off to the White Hart Inn, where, as I have said, he died on the following day.

We shall see that there was one who claimed to have been a witness of the crime; and if Elizabeth Harris had really been an onlooker at the murder of May, we must, when all the other facts have been taken into account, inevitably reach the conclusion that she had not been, as she claimed, an accidental, involuntary, and horrified–but completely innocent–witness. We shall have to assume that, if she saw the murder at all, it was as at least an accessory during the fact, non-participating, in the active sense, though she may have been.

There were other witnesses at a later stage of the crime; witnesses to May's condition when found; how his clothes had been singularly disarranged–" . . . the person lay on the left side of the road coming from Moreton, and nearer to Moreton town than Jacob's Well. I knew it was Mr. May as soon as the light was brought. When I came to him, he was lying on his back, with his arms by his side; his waistcoat was unbuttoned; his small clothes open; the pockets turned out; and he lay in a gore of blood."

Most of the witnesses who had seen the body lying in the road almost immediately after the attack testified to having seen that May's "small clothes" (that is, his breeches or trousers) were open and that his pockets had evidently been searched. Yet the robbers must have been disturbed, for:

John Tallamy was on the Exeter road on the night of the 16th of July: saw the body of Mr. Jonathan May; searched the pockets for such property as might be about him: found the two pockets of the small clothes, and one of the waistcoat pockets turned inside out. In a pocket on the inside of the waistcoat found two £5 notes. In the coat pockets were a handkerchief, a pair of gloves, and a small bag containing a sample of wheat. There was no pocket-book nor watch . . .

The majority of the missing objects were found, some at a considerable distance from the scene of the crime, evidently having been thrown away by the robber or robbers:

William Crocker:–I am a labourer living at Doddiscombleigh. In February last [1836], I was working for Mr. Thomas Archer:–I know the road leading from Hennock to Crocombe Bridge: I know Crammer's Brook; William Caseley was with me there last February.–I found a pocket-book lying in the hedge:–I took it up,–opened it and looked at the papers in it, and then threw it along the road. I took none of the papers; William Caseley took up some of them after I had thrown them down. It is a parish road where the pocket-book was lying,–a bye road, leading from Hennock to Teignmouth . . . I found the pocket book by the bye road . . .

Wm. Caseley:–Was with Crocker at Crammer's Brook; I brought and

Help comes too late for farmer Jonathan May, after Thomas Oliver and John Longley have brutally assaulted and robbed him on the night of 16 July 1835. Left dying, May was found and carried to the "White Hart" inn, Moreton, where he survived until the following morning, though without regaining consciousness.

delivered to my master, Mr. Joses Cleave, some papers I picked up, when Crocker threw the pocket-book to the ground; I believe them to be bills; the papers were rotten and stained.

Gradually, the various objects that the robbers had thrown away were found, gathered up, and passed from hand to hand until they reached Walter May, the deceased's nephew:

WALTER MAY:–Lives in the parish of Dunsford, and is nephew of the deceased. Mr. May produced these papers and the remains of a pocket-book.

CEPHAS COX:–On the 26th February last found the leather part of the pocket-book which Crocker had thrown into the road, and delivered it to Cleopatra Anning.

Who was this woman with the extraordinary name? The report does not explain, but states briefly that:

CLEOPATRA ANNING, delivered this to Mr. Walter May.

It now became clear why the gravely wounded man had been found with "his small clothes open," yet with two five-pound banknotes still within the inner waistcoat pocket: the robbers had searched him for the money-belt that, it may be supposed, the "warm" farmer would have been wearing.

Did the robber–or robbers–find the belt? A friend of the late Jonathan May's, an attorney named Moses Wolland Harvey, determined to answer this question and to find out the identity of May's killers.

In the still very feudal countryside of a century and a half ago, the well-established professional man–attorney, physician, banker–enjoyed not only considerable prestige but a proportionate power as well. Seemingly on no authority but his own, Harvey rounded up all the doubtful characters to be found in the district, notably those known, or thought to have been, at Moretonhampstead Fair at the time when Jonathan May had visited it.

Most of those roped in by Harvey were examined and dismissed from the case; all, that is to say, with the exception of a young man named Avery, who was already in custody on a charge of attempted highway robbery, which, it was alleged by the authorities, had taken place at Alphington, near Exeter, some weeks before the murder of May. Avery's mistress, Elizabeth Harris, declared that she and Avery had spent the night of 16 July –the night of the murder–together, and, in the absence of any positive evidence (though there was strong suspicion in their disfavour), Avery and Harris were dismissed as suspects from the murder case, though Avery still lay under suspicion of implication in the attempted highway robbery, a charge which, if proven, would have ensured for him a sentence of transportation.

Elizabeth Harris, a woman of loose life and recklessly determined character, now planned to do two things: to free her lover, Avery, from the suspicion of May's murder, and to bargain with the Crown for the release both of Avery and herself; his, a release from the charge of highway robbery; hers, from a conviction for stealing at Exeter, a conviction which had got her a sentence of transportation "at the next sailing."

In prison, Harris learned that the attorney Harvey had offered a reward of £100 for any information leading to the detection and conviction of May's murderer or murderers: all the evidence pointed to the fact that at least two robbers had taken part in the deadly assault, but that assumption still remained to be proven.

Elizabeth Harris was now ready, she said, to supply the needed proof: she would name the two men concerned in the robbery—*as she herself had been forced to witness the attack on May.*

She affirmed, under oath, to a Moses Harvey only too eager to "nail" the murderers of his friend, that, though she had, as she had stated, slept with Avery throughout the night of 16 July, they had had a lovers' quarrel and she had risen from their rough bed to "Have a walk" and subdue her anger. That walk had taken her along the road from Moreton to Exeter, and so to Jacob's Well at the very moment when two men had leaped down the high bank and attacked May, pulling him from his horse and beating him with cudgels until he lost consciousness. As Elizabeth Harris remarked, "it was a very good light; I could see the farmer all the way he went before me, quite plain"; and her hearing was as good as her sight, for she heard and remembered all, she affirmed, that had been said on that tragic night: how the two men had accosted May: "You're just going home, Farmer?" "I am." Then, as the men overcame the farmer: "Have you got it?" said one; and the other: "I have"—and very clear in the woman's recollection, the farmer's despairing appeal: "If you rob me, for God's sake don't take my life!"

THE JUDGE:—Were other persons besides you and Avery, taken into custody on this charge?

HARRIS:—Yes, my Lord, several; Black Soph and her man, Carpenter, Pardew.

JUDGE:—Did you never when all of you were subject to a charge of this kind, tell them, or any of them, what you had seen?

HARRIS:—No.

JUDGE:—You were on pretty good terms with them, were you not?

HARRIS:—I never quarrelled with them.

JUDGE:—What caused you at last to tell any one of it?

HARRIS:—I wished to go to another country, and be happy and at peace in my mind. I never wished for pardon: I never asked for it.

RE-EXAMINED BY MR. PRAED:—I did not continue to quarrel with Avery; I went back and slept with him that night, and was taken into custody with him next morning. I first told Tryphena Lampen, the Matron Turnkey.

The learned trial judge, Mr. Justice Williams, did not like this shameless young woman of twenty-two and made no secret of the fact that, though he did not in any way discredit her evidence as regards what she said she saw at Jacob's Well, he was most doubtful that her presence at the scene and at the time of the murder was as innocent as she claimed it was:

> . . . I shall first place before you the woman, Elizabeth Harris, who describes herself as having been an eye witness of this most foul act. Indeed, she describes this occurrence with a particularity, such as shews, that if she at all speaks the truth, then she must have a very accurate knowledge of it.
>
> I have [the learned judge continued] made you acquainted with the character and mode of life of this woman, and now tender her to you as a person whose evidence is liable to remark, and must be received by you with great suspicion and great caution. I freely tell you that it is a species of evidence that you should require to be confirmed, as far as the nature of a case of this description, always dark and secret in its details, will permit of being confirmed . . .

Surely never was the Crown's most important witness in a murder case ever "tendered" to a jury by a judge with less recommendation, yet . . . well, we shall see the value which was placed on Elizabeth Harris's perjured testimony; and see how various quite unimportant elements may result in the gravest miscarriage of justice.

What was it that the woman, Harris, communicated to Mrs. Tryphena Lampen, the matron turnkey of Dorchester Gaol, after Harris's lover, Avery, had been sentenced to transportation and she herself was marked down for that long and usually one-way journey to the Antipodes?

With the shadow of, not merely transportation, but also the possibly life-long separation from her lover, hanging over her; and with the added inducement to "shop" someone–anyone–that Moses Harvey's £100 reward offered, Elizabeth Harris named the two men who, she affirmed, had killed Jonathan May before her eyes. She knew these men only by the nicknames under which they commonly went: "Buckingham Joe" and "Dick Turpin," the latter obviously adopted in posthumous tribute to the noted English highwayman of the previous century.

Now, as Harris claimed that she had seen *and recognized* the two murderers, it was, obviously, necessary that she describe both as minutely as possible. This she did, *and her depositions were carefully recorded*.

This is a fact of vital importance, and was borne in mind by every person associated with the case, save, apparently, the learned judge–as we shall see.

Now, though it be true that Mr. Justice Williams gravely mishandled the case and was guilty of nearly as many misstatements in his summing-up as the judge in the Maybrick case, it has been forgotten by all those who have criticized the judge in the Galley case that, for all that he tried, again and again, to discredit Elizabeth Harris's character, even more than her testimony, she came to the Crown Bar Court in Exeter Castle with a free pardon signed by the Home Secretary, the Right Honourable Lord John Russell–and that she had been given her release from prison and eventual transportation in exchange for her having turned King's Evidence was known to the jury, since the validity of the document bearing Lord John's signature had formally to be certified by a Home Office clerk, Mr. James.

It may well be imagined how impressive the jury found this, and how they must have reasoned from the free pardon how credible the Home Secretary wished *them* to find Elizabeth Harris's evidence. I think here that Mr. Justice Williams felt, and rightly, that he was being overruled from London, and that he went as far as he could–and perhaps a great deal further–in presenting the Crown's "pet witness" in as bad a light as possible.

Harris was not the only one to have perjured herself, and it is beyond rational explanation that her contradictions should not have discredited her at the very beginning of her evidence; even before the trial opened.

Her greatest–and gravest–self-contradiction was in her *correctly* describing both Buckingham Joe and Dick Turpin, for, whether or not she was innocently on the scene of May's murder, Elizabeth Harris had undoubtedly been a keenly observant witness of all which had happened at Jacob's Well on the night of 16 July. Yet, when asked to "recognize" Edmund Galley as the other man that she had seen at Jacob's Well, the man presented to her was in no respect like the man that she had so minutely (and, as we may say with confidence now, correctly) described to Mr. Cole, Governor of Exeter Prison.

We shall see that Galley–the unfortunate Galley–was unlucky

in two most important respects: facetiously, he had been given the nickname of "Turpin" and still bore it as all—led by the very determined Moses Harvey—were looking for a highway robber of that name. And Galley was perhaps even more unlucky in that his alibi failed to stand up to the test:

> The prisoners have always denied ever having been in Devonshire before, and one of them, Galley *or Turpin*, has stated where he was on the 16th of July, last year. He says that he was at the house [*i.e.*, public house, "The Windmill"] of Mr. Rowe, of Dartford, in Kent. Mr. Rowe is here, and you will hear from him that he knows the prisoner and by the name of Turpin, but he will tell you that the prisoner was not at his house in July . . .

Sherlockians ought to note what Galley had to say about his movements on the "fatal day":

> GALLEY . . . was most earnest in his protestations of his innocence. He denied, as he had during the trial, ever having been in Devonshire before last May [*i.e.*, of 1836], when he was brought into it in custody; or that, until then, he had ever seen the other prisoner. He said that on the day this murder was committed, he was at Dartford, where he remained till the 18th. He then went to *Ryegate* races . . . [1]

That the man charged with Edmund Galley—Thomas Oliver, *alias* "Buckingham Joe"—was guilty of having taken part in May's murder, there was no doubt: Elizabeth Harris's naming of "Buckingham Joe" as one of the two murderers had received confirmation from another ex-gaolbird, John Hiscox, who was serving an eleven-month stretch at the same time that Thomas Oliver, "Buckingham Joe," was in Dorchester Gaol with Hiscox, the former having been sentenced to transportation for his having committed no fewer than three highway robberies on one night. A talkative, boastful type, Oliver bragged of his part in the murder of May, whom, with an accomplice named Turpin, he had followed from Moretonhampstead Fair so as to rob the farmer.

(One may credit the veracity of Elizabeth Harris's memory

---

[1] My italics. The name is now spelled "Reigate," as in *The Reigate Squires*.

when she repeated what she had heard Buckingham Joe say to Turpin at Moreton Fair: "It's a fine-looking gaff, and there's some crusty-looking blocks in it, and we must have some gilt in the rot!" The newspaper explains that Harris interpreted thus: ". . . [B]y this was meant, according to the slang phraseology, that it was a full fair; that there were apparently some wealthy-looking farmers in it; that they would rob some of them of their money in the evening. The term *gaff* meant fair; *crusty-looking blocks,* wealthy farmers; *gilt,* money; and '*the rot,*' the evening.")

Oliver's prison confidant, John Hiscox, meditated Oliver's confiding for a couple of months, and, just after Christmas 1836, took his tale to the authorities. So that Buckingham Joe, on a triple highway-robbery rap, was now "up" for murder. Now the problem was to find his *correctly named* accomplice, "Turpin"—real name John Longley, though this fact was not to become known until Oliver, on the eve of his execution, had told it to a young prison chaplain, Francis Vidal.

The hunt for "Turpin" was on . . . and it was Sergeant Thomas McGill, "of the London Police,"[2] who, accompanied by Police Constable Thomas Cannon, found the wrong "Turpin" and brought him, to endure a lifetime of injustice, to Exeter.

The appearance of this Turpin certainly disconcerted Elizabeth Harris when, taken by the revengeful Moses Harvey to meet the newly-arrived prisoner, she found herself not only looking at a man whom she had never before seen but at a suspect whom she had described in quite remarkable detail . . . save that her description in no way matched that of the luckless Galley whom she was now firmly invited by Moses Harvey to "identify."

She had confidently told Harvey that the "Turpin" whom she had seen literally "putting the boot in" on the battered body of May was a good-looking young man (as, indeed, the real "Turpin" was), but, as Lambert says in his excellent account of the Galley fiasco:

> Galley was mean and undersized, was dressed in rags, and looked more like an ill-nourished gipsy than a highwayman. The "Turpin" that she said she had seen had had bushy whiskers when she saw him last, she

---

[2] Established by Sir Robert Peel, as Home Secretary, only seven years earlier.

declared; but the whiskers were now mostly gone or much thinned out – cut off on purpose, no doubt, prompted Lawyer Harvey. There was another discrepancy. Murderer-Turpin was a man with a "cageful" of teeth, which rendered all the more conspicuous the loss of a single tooth in the front of his mouth. Galley-Turpin, however, had few teeth, but one of these seemed to be in the very position where the missing tooth had been before. It was all very perplexing. Still, criminals had been known before now to have had their teeth extracted in order to disguise themselves more thoroughly.

Upon the whole, Elizabeth Harris pronounced Galley strangely altered, but none the less the man she wanted. The longer she looked at him, the surer she became . . .

Of course: since her entire credibility as a witness, and the pardon that, despite her denials ("I never wished for pardon; I never asked for it"), she had not merely "wished" for but had astutely bargained for, depended upon her confident identification of the man whom the authorities had already made up their collective mind to "railroad," she was *forced,* one may say, to stick to her story and identify Galley as the "Turpin" who had been Oliver's even more brutal accomplice.

Her hesitation, though, was so marked that the two examining magistrates responsible for the preliminary hearing of evidence, John Luxmoore and Captain Carslake, showed considerable reluctance to commit Galley for trial and would, in all probability, have dismissed him from the case had not several other witnesses, heartened by Elizabeth Harris's positive identification of Galley as "Turpin," now come forward to add *their* identifications to hers. With considerable misgivings on the magistrates' part, the two men in the dock were committed to stand their trial at the Devon Assizes.

A major mystery in the Galley case, to my way of thinking, is why – and how – the London police, acting on a description of the wanted "Turpin," ever fixed on Galley in the first place. Police Sergeant Thomas McGill never explained, nor at any time was asked to explain, *why* he and Police Constable Thomas Cannon had gone to Coldbath Fields Prison:

The prisoner Galley was there on a charge of vagrancy. I went there a second time; I asked him his name; he said Edmund Galley; I asked him where he was from; he said he was born and bred at Kingston-upon-Thames, in Surrey. *I asked if his name was not Turpin; he said he went by that name . . .* [Emphasis added]

This admission, of course, was the error which effectually damned all Galley's chances of being declared innocent; but he would have answered differently had he known the purport of the question–"Well, that's a sort of joking-like name my mates have given me; my *real* name's Edmund Galley."

In answer to the police officer's questions, Galley denied his ever having been in Devonshire; his ever having known either a "man of the name of Buckingham Joe" or "a man of the name of Oliver." Yet:

I apprehended Galley on the 30th of April when his imprisonment for vagrancy expired. I took him to Bow-street. Before his examination commenced, Galley was standing before the fire in the charge-room; a placard was stuck on the opposite wall containing an account of the murder of Mr. May, and I observed that Turpin was reading it . . .

Obviously, the moral here is plain: Don't read the "dodgers" in a

The revolution that never was! Elegantly-uniformed "New Police"–sergeants and above with side-arms–gather in Bonner's Fields, London, to deal with an expected "popular uprising." The self-important officer in the foreground could well be that Sergeant Thomas McGill who arrested Galley on no evidence at all.

police station. But observe here that Sergeant McGill's "identification" of Galley as the "wanted Turpin" goes completely unchallenged by the Court.

When he had apparently got through [the reading of] it, he turned to me and said, I suppose that is about the thing I am charged with. I asked him how he knew that; and he said, because it is in Devonshire.

A perfectly rational deduction from Sergeant McGill's having asked him "if ever he was in Devonshire." But Sergeant McGill was not in the market for obvious explanations:

He had not been apprised by me of the nature of the charge against him, and I asked him who told him so; he said, Baker, of Mill-lane, had told him so. Baker is the keeper of a lodging-house.

And, the Sergeant, in the interests of justice, ought to have added: "Galley had been gossiping with this Baker in the police station, whilst both were waiting to be examined." The Sergeant —and the Court—preferred to see something self-condemnatory in *all* Galley's answers, as well as in all his failures to support, *at the time,* his account of his aimless wanderings by the production of credible witnesses; though, as he complained bitterly, had he had money he could have collected his witnesses.

It is true: he had no money—as his ragged appearance ought plainly to have demonstrated; but a more convincing proof of his poverty (after having robbed Jonathan May of a considerable sum of money?) lay in his inability to find even a single guinea to brief one of those unemployed barristers who decorate, in graceful idleness, every court in the Realm. Why did the fact that Oliver, supposedly Galley's accomplice in May's murder, could brief the already distinguished barrister (afterward an even more distinguished Judge of the High Court), whilst Galley had to appear on a capital charge without benefit of counsel, pass without comment —especially as Mr. Justice Williams made no secret of the uneasiness that he felt in considering the character (and so, naturally, the credibility) of the various witnesses for the prosecution?

Nor was the learned judge the only one to feel uneasy about the witnesses—especially

Mr. [Montague] Smith objected to the admissibility of the evidence of such a witness [as Elizabeth Harris], she having been convicted of felony. Mr. Praed put in a free pardon under the sign manual [of the King], and countersigned by Lord John Russell, Secretary of State.– Some argument took place on this, this Mr. Praed calling Mr. John Terrell, and that gentleman proving the signature of Lord John Russell, the examination of the witness was directed to proceed.

5

THE KING vs. GALLEY

THE JOINT TRIAL of Edmund Galley, *alias* Turpin (named first in the indictment), and Thomas Oliver, *alias* Buckingham Joe, opened in the Crown Bar Court, in Exeter Castle, on Thursday, 28 July 1836, the last full year of King William IV's brief but revolutionary reign. It was a trial which, in the course of the trial itself, and in the weeks, months, and years following, was to produce many a surprise–most of them of an unprecedented nature.

Elizabeth Harris had no surprises to offer. She had bargained for her escape from the seven-year transportation sentence, and she had been well coached, in particular by the revengeful local attorney, Moses Harvey.[1] She told her story clearly and well, ignoring those slurs on a "character" that, as the learned judge pointed out, she might not justly claim to boast. What the Crown had bought from her was a positive and unwavering identification of the two men charged. This she did–if not with evident pleasure, then at least with more than ordinary self-composure. Any slight embarrassment that she might have felt–or even displayed–when, on her first meeting Galley, he had so obviously not resembled in the slightest degree her description of the murdering "Turpin": this embarrassment had passed, to be

[1]Harvey was also the attorney to the two Crown prosecutors, Messrs. Praed and Kekewich.

replaced by a harlot's impudence nauseating to all but the contriver of Harris's lethal perjury: Moses Harvey.

She faced and outfaced both defendants–but, in particular, Galley. She told how she had overheard the two men plotting their robbery as she passed them at Moreton Fair; and how, having quarrelled with her lover, Avery, she had left in a huff, gone for a walk, and come by accident on the commission of a crime by the two men charged.

"Latimer Country"–and Doyle country, too: old Exeter, as Conan Doyle first knew it when working in unhappy partnership with Dr. Budd in Plymouth, some thirty miles away. This is Frog Street, typical of the picturesque and ancient city now long bombed or "developed" out of existence.

And, following Harris's lead, other witnesses, happy to oblige with a little perjury to get their names mentioned in the Exeter newspapers, identified, in turn, not merely "Buckingham Joe" (who was plainly guilty) but also his supposed accomplice, Edmund Galley:

ANN BENNETT.–Keeps the Lamb Inn, 3½ miles on the Moreton road from Exeter; remembers the day of Moreton Fair, in the summer of last year... These (the prisoners at the bar) are the two men that were at my house...

HARRIET LANGBRIDGE.–I am the wife of John Langbridge; my husband keeps the Golden Lion Inn at Moreton; he did so in July last year. I remember the fair on the 16th of July last year.–In the evening of that day I was tending to my cellar...the prisoner Galley, otherwise Turpin, came into the cellar and asked me to give him a cork... Pointing to the prisoner Galley,–the witness said, that is the man.–I am sure of it; I noticed that he was pitted with the small pox; I found a large vacant space in the side of his mouth, as if he had lost his teeth.

BETTY CROOT:–...I remember the fair; I was there; I know the White Hart Inn; I saw a man at the corner playing the game of the pea and the thimble; it was about 8 o'clock; I stop'd about a quarter of an hour looking at him... Qu[ery]. Look around and tell his Lordship and the jury, if you see that man now. Witness: He with the velveteen jacket (Galley) is the man;–I am quite certain that is the man I saw at the fair...

MARY MARENGO.–...I keep a lodging house in Exeter, and did so in July last year... I know the prisoners at the bar...

ANN CARPENTER.–I stop'd at Mrs. Marengo's; I saw those two men (the prisoners) and a woman that was along with them, there.–The woman with them was called "*Black Ann*"...

JANE CARPENTER.–Am daughter of the last witness, and confirmed the testimony of her mother...

CATHERINE GAFFNEY.–I travel with Mrs. Carpenter and her daughter; I was with them at Exeter in July last year... The prisoners are the same men I saw at Mrs. Marengo's...

And so on; but the really damning witness against Galley was:

WM. ROWE.–I keep the Windmill public house at Dartford, in Kent; I know Turpin, the prisoner; I know him by the name of Turpin; I have known him 4 or 5 years, and by that name. He was at my [public] house in the month of June, last year; he left on the 24th; I have no recollection of his being there in the month of July; I have no recollection of seeing him from June to August. He had then a smock frock on; it

The "Windmill" public house, Dartford, Kent–licensee, William Rowe, who, failing to remember Galley's having been at the tavern in July 1835, failed to support Galley's alibi for the May killing–with tragic results for the accused. Note the "American" spelling on the open door.

appeared an old frock; he remained one night then; I have seen him since at different times.–*By the Judge*–Were you in the habit of seeing him frequently in the year 1835? He was at my house frequently in 1835.

Poor Galley had no better success when he put a direct challenge to the impudent perjurer, Elizabeth Harris:

GALLEY.–Can you look at me with a clear conscience and say you see me do what you say to this man?

HARRIS.–I did, and you know I did, by what I have told you since.

GALLEY *(to the Judge)*.–My Lord, she mistakes me for another man. I never was in Devonshire in my life till I was brought to this prison. I know I am not the man, my Lord–and God Almighty knows I am not the man. She swears to the name they have given me, my Lord, and not my body.

HARRIS.–I'm quite sure you're the man.

GALLEY *(to the Judge)*.–Now, my Lord, that she might get her freedom, she swears my life away. I am not the person who did this, thanks be to God. I never see that woman in all my life, my Lord, till I see her in the gaol.

JUDGE *(to Harris)*.–Witness, attend! Have you any doubt as to these being the men you saw commit the murder?

HARRIS.—None, my Lord. Turpin was the man that came out of the hedge and passed behind the farmer, toward the left side of the horse, and struck the blows with the stick.

The first "sensation"—and what a "sensation" that was!—came from Galley's co-defendant, Thomas Oliver, "Buckingham Joe." It had been noted by the persons in that courtroom, and was duly commented upon by the reporter of each of Exeter's newspapers, that the men at the bar stood, not close together, but as far apart as possible; as though they were not, and never had been, engaged as associates in any felonious enterprise.

The explanation came as soon as the judge, after the jury had returned (after only ten minutes' deliberation) with a verdict of Guilty in both cases, began, as was then customary, to address the two prisoners. Throughout the trial, Galley had never ceased to protest his entire innocence; Oliver, whilst not claiming innocence in so many words, tried to impugn the credibility, not only of the Crown's principal witness, Elizabeth Harris, but also of Charlotte Clarke, who deposed that she was uncertain that Galley was the man that she saw at the Lamb Inn with Buckingham Joe:

. . . I am quite sure that Buckingham Joe is the man I saw at the Lamb, —the other is not the man I saw there.—The Turpin that was with Joe had a nice mouth of teeth; that's not the man *(pointing to Galley)*, it was quite another man—quite a decent, respectable man.—He had no teeth out that I saw: the man at the bar has teeth out.—I am sure it was another man, the man that was at the Lamb had dark whiskers that met at the chin . . .

Which ought to have cast considerable doubt on the identification of Galley as "Murdering-Turpin," the accomplice of Buckingham Joe.

But what of Mrs. Clarke's recollection of having seen and spoken with Buckingham Joe at the inn . . . ?

THE JUDGE:—Witness, have you ever said that prisoner before you *(Oliver)* is not the same man that joined you at the Lamb Inn? My Lord, I never did,—I can swear to him.

OLIVER:—She has five times denied me, my Lord, until that man in the corner there, the magistrates' clerk, tapped her on the shoulder and took her round to the corner of the room. What he said, of course I can't tell, but then she said she would swear to me.

THE JUDGE:—Is that so, woman?

CLARKE:—No, my Lord, I never varied; no man in the corner ever took me on one side:—nothing of the kind ever took place.

The judge appeared to be satisfied with this extraordinarily unsatisfactory evidence.

But it was after all the evidence had been given—mostly perjured (as was revealed later, on the perjurers' own admissions)—and the jury had brought in their hastily-considered verdict, that the sensation came—the first of two. And the explanation for the absence of physical proximity between the two convicted men was now apparent. In a loud, clear voice, Buckingham Joe "electrified" the Court by interrupting the judge, as Mr. Justice Williams was prosily moralizing on the heinousness of the crime:

In your case, however, there is nothing mitigatory—nothing to diminish that violence and brutal outrage by which acts of this kind have but too often been lamentably distinguished. The sentence, therefore, of—

Buckingham Joe cried out:

My Lord, do not,—I hope you will not condemn an innocent man. The man by my side is as innocent as you are. I never saw him in my life till I saw him in the gaol. I was there [at the murder of May], but this man was not. The man who did this is known by the name of the Young Hero, or the Kentish Youth; he is also known by the name of Turpin.

"It is only on proof that we can proceed here," the judge said, "and we must be regulated by the evidence given. On this the jury have found you both guilty—"

More firmly than ever, Buckingham Joe once more interrupted the judge:

My Lord, the man that was at Exeter with me at that time, is a good-looking young man, about an inch taller than I am, and no more like the man standing by my side than that candle *(pointing to the candle in front of the Judge)*, the man at Exeter with me, my Lord, is not at all like this man.

The wretched Galley now burst in with his faltering and self-pitying plea:

My Lord, I am innocent, – but God will forgive me, if you cause me to suffer innocently. If I had had money, I could have proved the truth of what he [Oliver] says; I could have proved that I was not in Devonshire. The witnesses, my Lord, have all sworn falsely against me, but I hope God will forgive them.

The judge resumed his sermon, only to be violently interrupted yet again by the harshly indignant Buckingham Joe:

OLIVER: – I hope, my Lord, you will not hang an *innocent* man; I declare before God this man was never with me in my life!
THE JUDGE: – The evidence —
OLIVER: – The evidence, my Lord, is *false;* they are deceived [meaning the twelve jurymen], – every one of them deceived; – he is not the man, – he is not like the man.
GALLEY: – I never saw this man, my Lord, Gentlemen and Ladies in the Court, – never, till I saw him in prison. – All men for such an offense [as the murder of May] ought to die, – they deserve to die, but I am innocent.

Commented the *Exeter Flying Post:* "The sensation in Court has probably rarely been surpassed." This was not accurate: the Court was to be provided – and that within a few minutes of Galley's whining plea, in such contrast to Oliver's manly bearing – with an even greater sensation.

The newspaper account remarked that the judge "paused for a short space" before resuming his thrice-interrupted harangue, which now was permitted by the self-condemned Oliver and the self-pitying Galley to continue uninterrupted until its traditional end of formal sentence and almost meaningless prayer:

. . . All that remains, therefore, for me is to discharge that duty . . . and that is, to direct that you, Edmund Galley, and you, Thomas Oliver, be taken from hence to the place from whence you came, and thence to the place of execution; there to be hung respectively by the neck until your bodies are dead. – That you be then interred within the precincts of the prison, and may the Lord have mercy upon your souls!

Galley, the account tells us, "continued to declare that he was innocent, which Oliver as constantly affirmed. The sensation in the Court was very great. The judge sat as if pondering on the circumstances of this most extraordinary scene, and several minutes elapsed before the order was given for removing the prisoners from the bar."

Within that space of several minutes, the Court was to witness an outburst quite unprecedented in the long history of the English Bench–unprecedented, that is to say, when we consider the direction from which the emotionally shocking outburst came: from a staid, respectable, and respected officer of the Court–the shorthand writer, George Scherer ("tall, handsome, sensitive and idealistic," R. S. Lambert calls him).[2] He was not the only one in that Court to find his heart swelling in response to the courage of young Buckingham Joe, who had fully admitted his guilt so as to strengthen his pleas for the life of the wretched man at his side–a man so ungrateful (or perhaps merely stupefied with terror) that he could recommend the rope for the man who was trying to save him: "All men for such an offense ought to die!"

Moved by what Holmes might well have called a "wholly irregular impulse," George Scherer could not restrain his feelings. Rising to his feet at the reporting table, placed directly beneath the judge's Bench, Scherer, choking back a sob and with tears in his eyes, yet loudly and clearly shouted this: "Oliver, you are a noble fellow!"

Has any other criminal, self-convicted of a brutal crime for gain, received, in the moment of his self-conviction, such a tribute–and that from an officer of the Court?

For it is true: Buckingham Joe *was* a "noble fellow"–Scherer was not at error in seeing the handsome young murderer's innate nobility; nor did Oliver falter in his continued defense of his involuntary companion in distress. As the hangman, watched by an immense crowd, prepared to end the short life of Buckingham Joe, and as Mr. Vidal, the prison chaplain, read the chilling

[2] Lambert spells his name "Cherer"; I have altered the name, within this quotation, to "Scherer"; it was with that spelling that Serjeant Ballantine refers to George Scherer with affection and admiration.

words of the Anglican burial service, the latter paused, interrupted the reading, and asked Buckingham Joe if he had anything to say before he died?

"I have," said the condemned man; and raising his voice so that he could be heard even at the very confines of the mob at his feet, he added: "All that I have to say is to inform this congregation that I am the guilty man; the other is an innocent man. That is all I have to say."

As he fell at the rope's end into eternity, Buckingham Joe's last thought–and his last words–pleaded for the wretched Galley's life; and I like to think that the long battle for Galley's life, begun even before the two convicts had been taken from the Court, was inspired, not by any sympathy for Galley but by a profound admiration for the "noble fellow" who had cast away all chances of a reprieve, so that the judge should not condemn an innocent man.

Thomas Latimer, the fighter for Galley who was to see the vindication of his and all his co-workers' efforts on Galley's behalf, remembered Oliver–brave Buckingham Joe–with unqualified respect. As the fighting editor of *The Western Times* wrote long after Joe had gone to his end:

> I never saw such an example of quiet courage. He had won the hearts of all his gaolers. Perfectly calm and self-possessed, while all about him were in tears, he said, in a firm voice of deep-toned solemnity: "I have found the truth of that blessed Scripture, As thy day is, so shall thy strength be.[3] I never thought I could go through this." Fascinated by this wonderful example of courage in facing death, I never took my eyes off the culprit till he had ceased to live.

This was what, we may be sure, Latimer had to tell his young friend, that shorthand writer employed by another friend, George Scherer; and that the great novelist that Dickens became did not forget Latimer's moving account of Thomas *Oliver's* noble self-sacrifice and courageous end, is clear, not only from Dickens's having given little Twist (who was snatched by a miracle from a

[3] *Deuteronomy* XXXIII:25. The actual words of the Authorized (King James) Version are: ". . . as thy days, so shall thy strength be."

life of crime) the Christian name of *Oliver*, but even more clearly, in the self-sacrifice of Sydney Carton, who rode in the tumbril to the guillotine with no less dignity than that with which Thomas Oliver, "Buckingham Joe," stood on the scaffold at Exeter, on a brilliant summer's day: 12 August 1836.

6

THE FIGHT TO SAVE GALLEY

To Galley's panicky protestations of his own innocence, Mr. Justice Williams paid a complacent tribute to the many perjurers who had just sworn Galley's life away. "Ah, well!" said the judge; "the evidence of your guilt has been accumulated to such a degree as to leave no doubt on the minds of the jury—or on mine. I never saw a greater quantity of proof adduced."

Three men who had sat in the Crown Bar Court throughout the trial of Galley and Oliver had grown more and more horrified as they listened, first to the evidence of witnesses whose testimony was shaky with contradiction and unacceptable by reason of its obvious untruth; and then the horror mounted as they listened to the judge's grossly prejudiced summing-up, not only grossly prejudiced against the prisoners but also containing a fatal misdirection to the jury on a vital point of evidence.

These three men, who were to spearhead the drive for the saving of Galley, were George Scherer, the shorthand writer; Thomas Latimer, editor of *The Western Times;* and Alexander Cockburn, then "an almost briefless barrister" but who was destined to become one of England's[1] most brilliant and honoured

[1]For the non-British reader, it may be necessary to point out that there is only *English* Law (applying to England, Wales, and Northern Ireland) and *Scottish* Law (applying only within the limits of the Kingdom of Scotland); frequent references, even by British writers—Conan

Lords Chief Justices. He was not engaged in the case either of Galley or of Oliver; but Cockburn had failed to succeed for a client whose defense rested upon an alibi; and now, hearing that Galley was relying on a similar defense-by-alibi, and wondering what *this* judge would make of Galley's defense, Cockburn attended the Galley–Oliver trial.

These three men–all leaders in their respective professions, though each had potential rather than, as yet, solid achievement–were all shrewd judges of human nature, and all had come to the same conclusion in respect of the witnesses called by the prosecution; in their opinion, all–with the possible exception of the Dartford innkeeper, William Rowe, whose memory may have been honestly defective–were perjurers of the most shameless kind, following the lead (though for reasons which are still undiscovered) of the arch-perjurer, Elizabeth Harris; though in Harris's case one might even sympathize with her at her having been forced by the Crown to make the difficult choice between her serving a seven-year transportation sentence and her swearing away the lives of two human beings.

And that perjury had been committed was soon to be not merely a matter of three men's opinion, but of proof, as we shall shortly see.

It was a fortunate thing, too, that of the three, two of the men were professionally equipped to take down a record of the trial in all its details: George Scherer because he had been appointed official shorthand writer to the Court; and Thomas Latimer–already deeply interested in a case which had aroused strong feelings throughout Devon–because, as editor of Exeter's most lively newspaper, he needed a transcript of the trial to hand over, as soon as possible, to his "father of the chapel."[2]

As Lambert relates, no sooner had the two men under sentence of death been taken from the Court than Scherer, the

---

Doyle among them–to "British Law" are wrong. British dependencies, the Isle of Man and the Channel Islands, are governed by their own laws.

[2]The head printer of a newspaper is so called in Great Britain; the reason being that the first English printer, William Caxton, after having learned the new art in Flanders, came to London and set up his press in the abandoned *chapel* of the Almonry at Westminster.

voluminous notes of a nearly fourteen-hour trial in his hand, went quickly over to where Latimer was sitting, tidying up his own notes for the printer. Both men had detected the fatal misdirection in the judge's summing-up, but the correction of judicial error was no easy matter in those days before the establishment of a Court of Appeal, an institution the absolute necessity of which was to be warmly urged by Mr. Serjeant Ballantine in a book that he wrote forty-five years after the conviction of Galley and Oliver.

However, even in those days before establishment of the long-overdue Court of Appeal, there were still legal means by which gross miscarriages of justice might be corrected; the most obvious of these being that free pardon under the Sovereign's sign manual which had freed Elizabeth Harris from the sentence of transportation; though, in her case, it seemed to have been obtained by the authorities merely to promote a perjury to gain a desired conviction. But to effect a righting of judicial wrong was a difficult matter; and the arrogant anonymity of the law was—and still is, of course—most reluctant to admit itself in error by recognizing that a wrong had or has been done.

The attempt to save Galley from a murderer's death depended, as all three of his self-appointed champions realized, on their moving with unprecedented speed to call the judge's attention to a serious doubt of Galley's guilt. In the—to us slow and hesitant, but to the British of post-Napoleonic years speedily revolutionary—changes (and all ameliorating changes) in the law, judges now had the power to order a stay of execution in cases in which even a slight doubt of a convict's culpability might be suspected.

Now, beginning with the three original Galley defenders—George Scherer, Thomas Latimer, and Alexander Cockburn—and the hardly less important persons who were to declare themselves in sympathy with the trio's views (the most important and active of these backers being Montague Smith, Oliver's counsel), the leader, by his vigour, his imagination, and his complete dedication to any cause that he espoused, was, without doubt, George Scherer. In the popular phrase, all the others "did their bit," but the burden of the work involved fell upon those shoulders always prepared to receive the heaviest load in the interests of justice: the shoulders of George Scherer.

For consider the physical effort that George Scherer imposed upon himself as an inescapable duty: the necessity, as he saw it, to collate the views of his fellow protagonists in a long discussion in Scherer's rooms in that old Exeter posting house, "The White Hart," and then to prepare a long memorandum on the case, to be ready for the judge before he left, early on the following morning, for Cornwall. Scherer had already spent nearly fourteen hours in court, *writing all the time;* now, after having heard and assimilated the views of Latimer and Montague Smith (grown most uneasy over Galley's conviction), and having presented his own views, Scherer sat up all night writing the memorandum; the "fair copy" of which was to be given to the judge in the morning; the "working copy" (almost certainly made by Latimer) to be taken away by the editor for publication in the next issue of *The Western Times*.

The memorandum dealt only with essentials, and tactfully left out what men of less diplomatic skill might have felt impelled to include: the judge's inexcusable misdirection of the jury. Mr. Justice Williams was not a kindly man, and he figures now as an unforgettable villain in the mythology of British trade-unionism, in that he sentenced the fourteen "Tolpuddle martyrs" to transportation for having unlawfully "combined"–that is, formed themselves into a primitive trade union.

Now: the memorandum dealt, as Lambert points out, with "the unsatisfactory identification of Galley, the lack of evidence connecting him with any known Devonshire gang, the improbabilities of Elizabeth Harris's story, and the reference by Oliver to the Kentish Youth, the real murderer."

The criticism of Elizabeth Harris's story was, it must be admitted, venturing on very dangerous ground, since that story had been accepted and acted upon by the judge himself; yet his egregious vanity, though deferred to in the omission of the charge that he had misled the jury, could not justify Scherer's omitting the suggestion that Elizabeth Harris's testimony ought not to have been accepted.

Most of the names that we encounter in these accounts of long-past (and mostly forgotten) trials are . . . now just names; though "Johnny" Williams, as this *faux bonhomme* liked to be called when not "my Lord" on the Bench, has acquired, as I have said, a dubious immortality as the trial judge in the Tolpuddle case.

I shall not, I trust, be guilty of an unnecessary digression here when I say a few words about this clever but most disagreeable judge, for it was in the full consciousness of Williams's dangerous idiosyncrasies that Scherer ventured to dispute with him the judgment that he had handed down that same afternoon in the case of Galley. We have seen something of Scherer's energy in the discharge of what he conceived to be his duty; now, with a brief glance at the character of Williams as displayed on the Bench and in civil life, we may form an estimate of the courage that Scherer showed in daring to criticise this tricky, touchy man.

As the reader already knows, the long forty-five-year fight for Galley's vindication and ultimate freedom was successful. More fortunate than Galley in that he had not to wait forty-five years for his free pardon was a man named Barber, who, upon his second trial–this also was before "Johnny" Williams–was sentenced, with his fellow prisoner, Dr. Fletcher, to transportation for life.

What makes this case so notable is that it took place in April 1844, *eight years* after that of Oliver and Galley; yet its resemblance to the earlier case is striking. Charged with Fletcher as being involved in a "very elaborate system of fraud," Barber, an attorney, protested his complete innocence, maintaining he had acted for Fletcher "simply in a legal capacity, without any knowledge of the acts." What is more–and what is so unhappily reminiscent of the Oliver–Galley case–is that Fletcher, from the commencement, entirely exculpated Barber.

But, as Serjeant Ballantine records:

Both prisoners were convicted and sentenced to transportation for life. As regards Barber, the sentence was most unjust, for, without affirming his absolute innocence, it is impossible to say that there was not very grave doubt as to his guilt. After Barber had been sent out of the country in pursuance of his sentence, and had undergone great hardships, he was pardoned and received some compensation. I often saw him during the short period that he survived, his tall form gaunt and haggard, and the sufferings that he had undergone stamped upon his features. He must have been an object of pity to every one possessed of human sympathy.

And off the Bench, in civil life? "Johnny" Williams was no very likeable man, either way . . .

> He was much given to strong expletives [Ballantine continues], which, in the following anecdote I must be excused for omitting.
>
> Upon the trial of a prisoner for a capital charge, he had been induced by an attorney, although against his own opinion, to ask a question, the answer to which convicted his client. Turning to the attorney [Mr. Justice Williams] said, emphasizing, as may be imagined, every word with strong additions: "Go home, cut your throat, and when you meet your client in Hell, ask his pardon."

If one might not approve of the manner of that utterance *from the Bench,* one may hardly disapprove of the content. Less easy to approve of is this:

> Another story told of him is that a clerk, recently married, hanged himself. Another person who afterwards entered his employment expressed a hope that Johnny would not be offended at his entering into the bonds of holy matrimony. "Certainly not," said he. "Marry by all means; but when you hang yourself, do not do so in my chambers," which his former clerk had done.

Ballantine also recalls an anecdote in a lighter vein that I find even more significant than those repeated above:

> [Johnny] was a capital shot, and whilst enjoying the sport upon some gentleman's preserves, and knocking over the birds right and left, the gamekeeper whispered confidentially to his comrade, "They tell me this 'ere gent is a judge. I'll take my Bible oath he's been a poacher!"

The character of "Johnny" Williams was well known to George Scherer, who knew the characters of all the leading men of Bar and Bench. And this was the man who was to be asked to go back on his judgment . . .

If there be a hero in this book, it is not Conan Doyle; it is not Latimer; it is not even Oliver, heroically though he behaved; it is, without a doubt, George Scherer.

No known record is available of the meeting between the judge and the deputation presenting the memorandum, and the verbal arguments with which to back that up. The original three had now found fresh and powerful allies, who shared their doubts of Galley's guilt; now five, and not a mere three, set out on the bright morning of Friday, 29 July 1836, to call at the judge's lodgings:[3] George Scherer, Thomas Latimer, Montague Smith as Alexander Cockburn's "reserve," Ralph Sanders the County Clerk, and John Carew the under-sheriff of Devon: all most influential and highly respected men in their own spheres of activity. I think that we may presume that the arguments—as well as the memorandum—were presented to Mr. Justice Williams by the convener of the delegation: George Scherer.

"Johnny" Williams, petty tyrant on the Bench and affable goodfellow in the society in which he wished to find himself, had no small opinion of both Mr. Justice Williams and of "Johnny" Williams. His self-esteem, never less than remarkable, had suffered no diminution when, with Denman, now Lord Chief Justice, and Henry Brougham, Attorney General for Queen Caroline (and now Lord Brougham and Vaux), he had been one of the counsel briefed to defend the Queen in the scandalous divorce case brought against her by King George IV.

But then, George Scherer—to consider only the leader of the deputation—was no inconsiderable personage himself. Apart from the fact that he was known to, and highly respected by, every mature member of the Bench and Bar, his French connections would have impressed the snobbish "Johnny," who would have known that the English Scherers' first cousin, Charles, was a regular brigadier general in the service of King Louis Philippe and that their other first cousin, Henriette, had married, as her first husband, General Count Jean-Alexandre LeGrand, who died in 1815, and, as her second, Gabriel-Jean-Guillaume, Count Joly de Fleury.

This may well have been the reason for the courteous, if not exactly sympathetic, reception that the delegation received from

---

[3]The modest appellation "lodgings" should not be taken too literally. The English judge, on circuit, travels in sometimes the most elaborate style, always accompanied by his marshal, and is provided, by the city or borough in which the Assizes are held, with apartments and entertainment appropriate to his dignity as the representative of Our Sovereign Lady the Queen.

the judge, who, whilst denying that his belief in the guilt of Galley had in any way been lessened, was still prepared to stay the execution until Friday, 12 August, though, the judge pointed out, he would have returned from Cornwall to Exeter before that "final" date, when he would be willing once again to meet the deputation and hear further arguments in Galley's favour–if any.

Exactly a fortnight now was all that the planners had to reverse the legal decision in Galley's case, and, as practical men, they knew that it was essential that they should have what the wretched Galley had been unable to raise: money to prosecute their search for the witnesses in his favour that he had claimed did exist.

Two subscription lists were at once opened. That headed by Alexander Cockburn was circulated among his fellow barristers of the Western Circuit; that headed by Thomas Latimer, among the editors and senior journalists and general sympathizers with Galley of Exeter, Moreton, Plymouth, and other Devonian towns. Scherer concentrated on one charitable source of cash: the Quaker banker of Exeter, Joseph Sparkes, who immediately advanced a sum sufficient to enable Scherer and his fellow seekers to begin their investigations.

At first, the results of their enquiries seemed to promise an instant and complete success for their cause: in less than a week, the investigators had discovered three persons prepared to affirm that they had been with Galley at Dartford on the day on which Jonathan May had been murdered, two hundred miles away.

But information quite as significant now came from Oliver, awaiting execution and courageously resigned to his fate. The information had been extracted by the prison chaplain, Mr. Vidal, whose sympathy had fully broken through Oliver's–Buckingham Joe's–reserve. To Vidal, the young felon had freely confessed his own intention to rob May, but declared on his honour that neither he nor his accomplice had had any thought save to rob the farmer (admittedly by menaces), and that the resulting death had been an accident, due to the fact that, in the scuffle–after May had been pulled from the saddle–his horse shied, broke free, and kicked both May and the two robbers: Oliver seemed to imply that the bad-tempered "real" Turpin panicked and beat May savagely—and, though we are free to accept or reject Oliver's self-excusing story, it should be borne in mind that, when the judge was making (often interrupted by Oliver) his final remarks to the convicted, Buckingham Joe declared: "I have nothing to say for myself, except that it was not I that killed the man."

Oliver, it will be recalled, had told the Court that Galley was not his companion in the murder of May but that the real fellow-assassin was the man "known by the name of the Young Hero, or the Kentish Youth"—"He is also known by the name of Turpin."

Now, for Vidal, Oliver was to go further and give the real name of this "Kentish Youth": John Longley, "a tall, good-looking man, a native of Kent"—hence one of his two nicknames. Oliver added that, after the murder, he and Longley had parted company, and that the latter had, in all probability, gone to Salisbury. Ralph Sanders, the County Clerk, on receipt of this most important information, sent a constable at once to seek the missing Longley—only to find that the man had left the city "for parts unknown." However, in a negative way, this was further support for Oliver's account, for, though the constable had been unable to apprehend Longley, he had discovered that such a person was known to the criminal element of the cathedral (and horse-racing)[4] city.

But more surprises—and what astonishing surprises! what discoveries!—were to reward the now time-pressed seekers; time-pressed, since the judge was due back now within a day or two, and it was only grudgingly that he had respited Galley for a fortnight, making it clear that for Oliver there could be not even the clemency of transportation. Buckingham Joe must die; whether or not Galley did, too, would depend upon the convincing nature of the arguments (and new evidence) adduced to save him. Mr. Justice Williams made it clear that, in his opinion, such arguments and such evidence would take a deal of finding. . .

---

[4]The significance of Mrs. Ann Carpenter's evidence was quite disregarded: she had testified that she had seen the two prisoners at Mrs. Marengo's, at a time near enough to the murder to have justified suspicion that they had been in Devon *and together* on the critical day. This, though untrue, was accepted by the Court. No one seems to have paid attention to her adding that: "[Afterwards] I saw Oliver at Wilton; it was not at any fair, but after some races, I believe Salisbury races."

There had been nine hostile witnesses and one "neutral" witness introduced by the prosecution; William Rowe, the non-recollecting Dartford innkeeper, being the one "neutral." Now, of the remaining nine, no fewer than three were to suffer, as the phrase has it, all the pangs of a guilty conscience, and to confess to perjury, a crime which, by 1836, though no longer capital, was still visited by the law with exemplary penalties.

The three were Ann Carpenter and her daughter Jane and their companion or partner, Catherine Gaffney: "I travel with Mrs. Carpenter and her daughter."

The excuse that the two Carpenters offered for their having perjured themselves by having stated that they had seen Galley on a significant date at Mrs. Marengo's was that they had wished to exonerate their relative, Elizabeth McKinley, whose attendance at Court, the judge observed, they had been unable to procure, but who, at Wilton, in the company of Ann and Jane Carpenter, had uttered "a remarkable expression" [in regard to the nature of some stains on Oliver's smock-frock]. Catherine Gaffney had backed up the evidence of her two travelling companions by the quite comprehensible necessity of an old friendship. Catherine Gaffney's conscience troubled most of all, though no doubt the penalty for perjury was hardly overlooked in her making her decision to confess. She took extreme measures to purge her guilt: unfortunately for Galley, her confession would have done more good had the authorities to whom she confessed taken her more seriously.

For she *walked* the two hundred miles to London, to surrender herself to the police at Bow Street, on self-confessed perjury—a step so extreme as to be unbelievable, so far as the police were concerned: they sent her about her business, especially after she had offered to conduct them to where the *real* Turpin lay perdu. Then, with the two Carpenters, she wrote, confessing her guilt, to Montague Smith, who thus learned of the real Turpin's whereabouts, but now too late to be able to take the felon.

Three confessions of perjury; three allegations that Galley had been seen in Dartford on the day of Jonathan May's murder; Oliver's revealing the name of "The Kentish Hero"; Mr. Sanders's having established the probable existence of a John Longley, the man named by Oliver: these were decidedly impressive results from a mere week's enquiries. What might be expected from enquiries spread over a far greater length of time, were such grace to be extended to the enquirers?

However, the results were such that even the obstinate "Johnny" Williams could not but take them into account. As we have seen, his decision in regard to Oliver remained unaltered: Oliver was to hang (as hang he did); but the judge now consented to respite Galley "pending further enquiries." For the moment, Edmund Galley had been snatched from the hangman. . . by George Scherer.

Galley was not only an unlucky man; he was an unattractive one–which fact may explain his consistent ill-fortune. And no one found him less attractive than the faceless complacencies of well-dug-in bureaucracy, acting in the name of the Home Secretary for the time being: in Galley's case, Lord John Russell, himself no unrepresentative example of the narrowly prejudiced mind of the aristocrat (he was the third son of the sixth Duke of Bedford) turned revolutionary, always bitterly moralistic and generally disapproving, as he busied himself with his schemes of social reform.

"Johnny" Williams didn't like Galley; Moses Harvey, the murdered farmer's closest friend, displayed a vicious animosity toward Galley in the face of what, to anyone less prejudiced, would have appeared the certain proof of Galley's innocence. In a cockeyed effort to justify this animus against a Galley innocent of the actual murder (or of participation in it), Harvey affected to believe that Oliver, the missing "real" Turpin, *and Galley*, were but three members of a large gang of criminals, of which Harvey's assiduity had contrived–so far–to apprehend and hang only one.

A curious circumstance attending Oliver's execution gave this villainous attorney an opportunity further to cast suspicion on Galley: after having made his noble speech from the scaffold, Oliver went to his hanging still clutching the red handkerchief that he had been holding as he addressed the necrophil rubber-neckers packing the square around him. Harvey–a self-serving opportunist, even for one of his detestable breed–caught eagerly at what *might be* read into the presence of the scarlet kerchief. Harvey, unimpressed by Oliver's courageous bearing and truly noble words (as we hear them echoed by Sidney Carton in

Dickens's fine novel), could only look to his own advantage. He gripped Latimer's arm excitedly. "There!" he cried: "Did you see that he 'died game'? He had the red handkerchief—the 'game flag'—to inform his old pals that he had died without splitting!"

Lambert takes the tale further:

Latimer was profoundly shocked at this suggestion, which seemed so utterly incompatible with what he had just witnessed. But Harvey remained obsessed with the idea that the murder of May had been the work of some organized gang, of which Oliver was a member, and that he had refused to betray his accomplices, including Galley. And unfortunately, the story that Oliver's red handkerchief had been a deliberate signal to his confederates in the crowd, soon gained currency in Exeter [busy Mr. Harvey must have seen to that!] and came to be widely accepted—though Governor Cole wrote a letter to the *Western Times* showing that it was by mere accident that Oliver had come to be in possession of such a handkerchief at all.

With what Galley-exonerating evidence his private Committee of Safety had already presented to the Home Office, and, perhaps even more importantly, the implications in that evidence that evidence more convincing might be confidently expected, neither "Johnny" Williams nor Lord John Russell felt that they could proceed with Galley's execution. Lord John, in an official Home Office communication, instructed Samuel Kingdon, Mayor of Exeter, to "hold an inquiry into the circumstances of Galley's conviction."

Now, authorized to proceed with official backing, and with the Quaker banker's funds to subsidize the most extensive and exhaustive search for evidence completely to exonerate Galley, his friends and the men in their employment spent several weeks, mostly in Kent and Surrey, checking on every statement in his own defense that Galley had made, in or out of court.

As Lambert remarks, "Galley's poor memory greatly hampered the investigators at first":

But at length they came across traces of evidence that Galley had been, as he claimed, at Dartford at the time of May's murder. A carpenter was found who remembered having seen a person like Galley loitering near a building on which he was working, and to have employed him for a few hours as assistant. Then a stall-holder at a local fair told how his stand had been upset, and how Galley had helped him pick up a lot of nuts which had fallen to the ground. And finally, another episode which Galley had quoted found independent corroboration on the spot . . .

This involved Galley's losing half a crown to a man named Phillips, who had fought him, in a "friendly," for that sum, and how Galley, the smaller and now much battered man, had won the half-crown back from Phillips by means of a card trick. In all these enquiries, the most active of all the investigators was George Scherer, who had taken up Galley's case at the very beginning and was to champion him until the end of Scherer's own life—though leaving others to continue the good fight.

Public opinion, though despised by any politician worthy of the name, is a force that the conventions of his disagreeable occupation oblige him always to pretend to respect, and even at times actually to defer to.

So, in this case, Officialdom now found itself under the compulsion of seeming to defer, not so much to public opinion (which, under the malignant influence of the tireless Moses Harvey, was being constantly prejudiced against Galley) as to the important body of fighters on Galley's behalf. Now Galley was granted a stay of execution for the second time; and, more, Lord John instructed the Chief Magistrate of Bow Street, Sir Frederick Roe[5]—"a tall, handsome, gentlemanly man," Ballantine calls him—personally to check every witness and every statement that Scherer had found and taken down in his investigations in Kent and Surrey.

Doubtless realizing that Sir Frederick, on his own, might not check with the zeal that George Scherer and the other original investigators had shown, Montague Smith adroitly offered his help in Sir Frederick's search—and, though it is hard to believe that the Chief Magistrate was unaware of the reasons for Smith's offer of "help," that offer was still warmly accepted, and the two

---

[5]It ought to be noted that, as Chief Magistrate at Bow Street, Sir Frederick Roe succeeded Sir Robert BAKER.

men went off together to examine all the pro-Galley witnesses and their testimony.

In the meantime, those left behind in Exeter were working hard to press Galley's claims to vindication: organized principally by Thomas Latimer, a petition on Galley's behalf was signed by several thousands and forwarded on to Lord John Russell. And, quite unwisely, Latimer authorized (perhaps even wrote) an assured opinion, which appeared in *The Western Times*, that "it is supposed that [Galley] will receive a full pardon."

Never did the foolish practice of jumping the gun receive a quicker or more thorough rebuke. As Lambert explains:

> Unfortunately, Sir Frederick Roe, in compiling his report, conceived that his terms of reference called primarily for a fact-finding report, and not for the expression of his own opinion on Galley's alibi.
>
> Consequently, Lord John Russell, after receiving it, considered it necessary to take the advice, first of Judge Williams, and secondly of the Lord Chief Justice, Lord Denman.
>
> The former, whatever doubts he may have entertained at the time of the trial, had now become fixedly convinced in his own mind that Galley was guilty. Lord Denman, too, was strongly influenced by Judge Williams, whom he had himself promoted to the Bench.

Lambert goes on to explain (in my opinion, inaccurately) what was going through the minds of those Exalted Ones in whose never-compassionate hands lay Galley's earthly fate:

> [Lord Denman] looked at the matter somewhat like this. After all, who *was* Galley? A worthless vagabond, with a bad character. Had there been a miscarriage of justice? Possibily, though by no means certainly–or a level-headed, conscientious official like Sir Frederick Roe would have pointed it out in so many words to the Home Office.
>
> Then again, the convict had had a fair trial, and the verdict of a jury should not be set aside without absolutely convincing reasons.
>
> Finally, no-one doubted that Oliver had been rightly convicted, or that he had had at least one accomplice in his crime. If Galley was innocent, where *was* the guilty man? Let *him* be produced, and then the case for pardoning Galley would be complete.
>
> Such was the reasoning of the Lord Chief Justice and the Home Office . . .

Lambert is wrong here; such was *not* the reasoning of the Lord Chief Justice and the Home Office officials, who certainly did not need Sir Frederick Roe to point out to them that the evidence that he was presenting indicated clearly that there *had* been a miscarriage of justice. Denman, Lord John, and the faceless others were quite capable of making the obvious deduction from

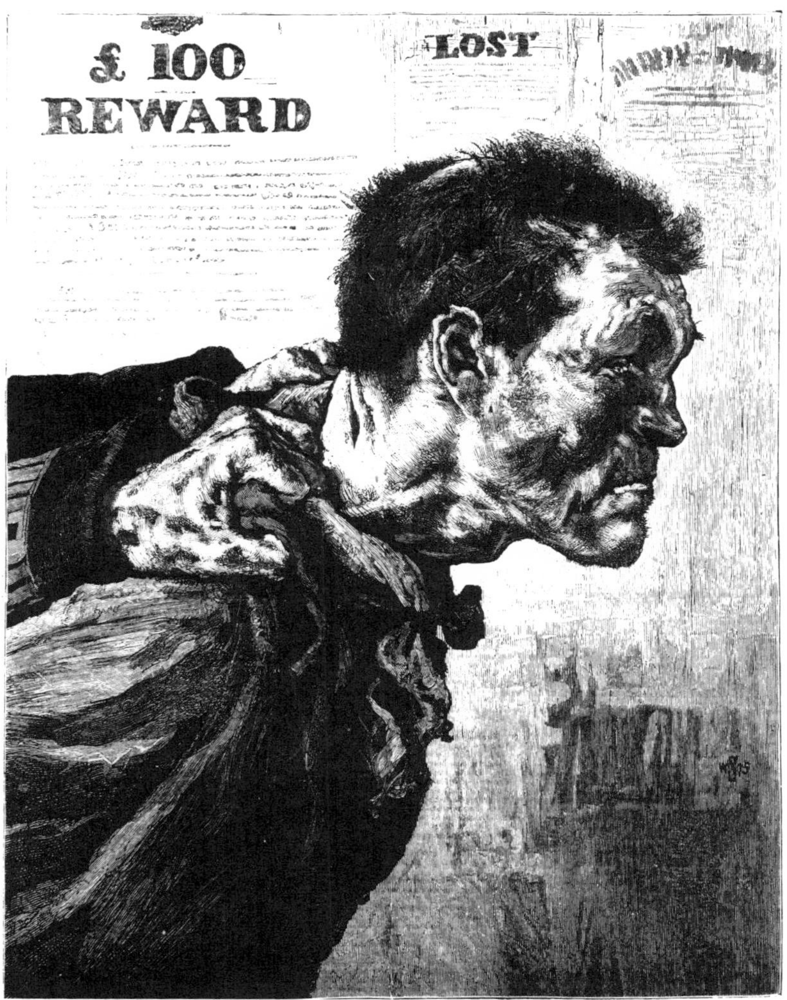

The Galley that Lord Denman might have imagined. "Lord Denman . . . looked at the matter somewhat like this. After all, who *was* Galley? A worthless vagabond, with a bad character . . ." Here is a Victorian artist's idea of the typical "worthless vagabond"–as it was (unfortunately for the unjustly-condemned Galley) Lord Chief Justice Denman's idea, too.

attested facts–the statements of the witnesses that Sir Frederick and Montague Smith had taken down.

In a curiously unemotional fashion, those responsible for Galley's future–I except Mr. Justice Williams, who had developed a personal animus against Galley–were not really against Galley. It was simply that he did not interest them, one way or the other, as the "worthless vagabond" of official opinion. What Lambert had not seen, and what Latimer, for all his sometimes irresponsible outspokenness, had the tact not to mention, is that Officialdom's view of Galley, never very personal, had changed in the weeks since the first stay of execution; he had now acquired a singular value in the eyes of Officialdom: as a weapon by which Officialdom might revenge its outraged vanity on those–led by George Scherer–who had dared to challenge Officialdom's opinion, and had actively "conspired" to refute it.

It was for this crime that Galley was now to be punished, so that, in refusing Galley justice, Officialdom might be even more severely punishing his champions.

And Officialdom was planning a more terrible fate for Galley than a mere hanging. . .

So that, in the autumn of 1836, the Home Secretary informed the Devon County Clerk, Ralph Sanders, that Galley's sentence was to be commuted into one of transportation for life; but that he would not be sent overseas until, with his defenders even harder at work to exculpate him, the possibility of their tracking down the accomplice of Oliver–the "real" Turpin–had been shown to be quite unattainable.

The appalling ill-luck of Galley continued: the real Turpin–John Longley, "The Young Hero," "The Kentish Youth"–*was* found. Governor Cole was told that a man of that significant name had been arrested at Bath and was to stand trial for a felony. But. . .of all the people to whom Governor Cole could have passed that information, he had foolishly to choose Moses Harvey, one of Galley's two implacable enemies; Judge Williams being the other. Harvey declined to take any action, and thus all opportunity of laying "The Young Hero" by the heels was lost. George Scherer was never told; had he known, he would have seen to it that Longley, whether or not the Longley sought in the May murder, would have been questioned.

They had sent Galley, "pending the tracing of the 'real' Turpin," to the hulks of Woolwich, in the Thames, some ten miles south-east of London. The hulks were old derelict warships, verminous and rotten, aptly described as "floating hells." His friends and champions did not desert him; and they all continued the fight on his behalf: George Scherer–enheartened by the compassion that he felt for poor Galley's loyal little sweetheart, Jane Cording (who had been unable to raise more than five shillings–$1.25–for her lover's defense)–never abandoned his fight for Galley; Jane–poor Jane!–"resorted frequently to his chambers in London,[6] humbly but fervently inquiring if there was any hope that her lover might be released. Stimulated by her devotion, Scherer continued to pester the authorities to grant Galley a pardon, and secured reviews of the case by Lord John Russell"–that loudly self-declared champion of Freedom and the Rights of the Common Man–"in 1838 and 1839, unfortunately with negative results."

For his part, Latimer, through the columns of *The Western Times,* sought to keep Galley's case in the public consciousness, and twice in March 1839 reported on Galley's circumstances. They had improved–though, one feels, through official indolence rather than through official compassion–Galley having been put to improving the gardens attached to the Royal Dockyard: "laying out a lawn . . . in parterres for shrubs and flowers."

Latimer was a man of great heart . . . and great energy; and what his heart impelled him to do his energy often snatched away from him–as in the final stages of the first phase of the fight for Galley.

For, though the demands of abstract Justice certainly justified his vehement newspaper attacks on the unjustifiable injustice of the Home Secretary, sound Devonian common sense should have advised him to expose the mean shams of the Autocracy

---

[6] At the chambers in Doctors' Commons where, without doubt, she was seen by, and saw, the tender-hearted young shorthand writer, Charles Dickens, who worked for the Scherer Brothers. There were to be many sentimental remembrances of Jane in the novels that Dickens would come to write.

in terms less wounding to Autocracy's most tender vanity. *Rationally,* there was nothing wrong and everything right in Latimer's crying out, in the pages of his influential newspaper:

A rank and gross injustice has been done in this county. Do not its magistracy possess firmness enough to demand complete justice for the victim of circumstance? Lord John Russell says the real offender must be taken before Galley is released. But though he is to be taken, no real search is made for him. That Galley is innocent and praiseworthy matters not. Fate has woven a net around him. The poor victim may struggle–the web is too firm for him–it breaks not. At length despair takes the place of resistence.

This outcry was honest; it was rational; it was justified by the facts; but Latimer should have known that in their campaign to secure a reversal of the Assizes verdict in Galley's favour, his champions had succeeded merely in altering the direction in which Malice cast its basilisk glance: now it was they and not Galley who were the designated victims of politicians' and civil servants' rancour. Latimer really should have known better . . .

"Officialdom," Lambert had sadly to record, "at Whitehall was growing tired of being pestered by these West Country sentimentalists. Something must be done with Galley; he must be put out of the way."

And so, without a word to Latimer and Scherer, the order suddenly went forth to put the commuted sentence into effect. In the summer of 1839, Jane Cording received from poor Galley a pathetic letter bidding her to hasten down to Woolwich, and take a last farewell of him, as he had been ordered to embark immediately on a transport bound for New South Wales.

And three months later, the little man stepped ashore at Sydney Harbour, branded still as a convicted murderer; a member of a chain-gang; with prospects little better than those of a slave. So for the time being, his champions, Latimer, Sanders and Scherer, were baffled in their fight for justice.

Now a further forty-three years had to pass before that striven-for justice was reluctantly and grudgingly granted.

7

THE VINDICATION OF EDMUND GALLEY

John Longley, "The Kentish Youth," who had, by the criminal connivance of the hate-embittered Moses Harvey, escaped having been charged as Oliver's accomplice in the May murder, was found at last. For the Bath or some later affair, Longley had been transported. The man who found him at last was... Edmund Galley; and in June 1877, Galley, now a more-than-battered sixty-five, wrote a long, semi-literate letter to Exeter, to make his discovery of Longley known (for, if almost all but his champions–George Scherer, who had died on 15 November 1855, no longer one of them–had forgotten that his freedom had been promised by Officialdom contingent on the finding of Longley, the "real" Turpin, be sure that Galley had not forgotten).

It is hard to understand how even so simple-minded a person as was Galley could have addressed his letter to the one man who had hounded him with unremitting malice; and it was the first small sign that Galley's decades-long run of ill fortune was coming to an end that Moses Harvey was dead, and that the letter from Galley arrived on the desk of his son, William Harvey, who had not inherited his father's tenderly nurtured grudge against an innocent man. Harvey Junior sent the letter to the editor of Latimer's rival newspaper, *The Exeter Flying Post,* who printed it in full in a prominent position, retaining all Galley's idiosyncracies of grammar and spelling.

The important fact that Galley had to convey–and in the hope that it would be brought as quickly as possible to the notice of Authority, and as quickly acted upon–was that John Longley, "The Kentish Youth," was living and working, under the assumed name of "John French," in the Young district of New South Wales, not far from Binalong, where Galley was working as a shepherd. The letter made the vital point that, with the arrest of Oliver's true accomplice, the unjustly convicted Galley would be set at liberty.

Well. . .perhaps.

According to his diary, it was on 8 August 1877 that Latimer's attention was drawn to the copy, now more than ten days old, of *The Exeter Flying Post* containing the verbatim reprint of Galley's letter to the deceased Moses Harvey.

The old "Cobbett of the West" was now seventy-five and was enjoying a partial retirement from his duties as editor of *The Western Times;* but Latimer's faculties–at least, his mental ones–were unimpaired by age, and, as he read the repetitious, illiterate, and wholly convincing passages of Galley's pathetic screed, Latimer felt all the old indignation burn up again; heard the old challenge to rouse himself and once again battle for a justice so inexplicably and, in his view, so sinisterly, withheld.

Over forty years had now passed since Oliver, "Buckingham Joe," had gone courageously to the scaffold and Galley's champions had won him a respite from death–though, so far, no more than that. The old excitement returned to quicken Latimer's aged pulses, and, in the first heat of that renewed excitement, he sat down at his desk, took up his pen, and wrote, in perfect detail, the whole history of Galley's indictment; of the courageous efforts of the rightly-convicted felon, Thomas Oliver, to exonerate the unjustly-charged and unjustly-convicted Galley; and of the efforts made by George Scherer, Montague Smith, Latimer, and–less importantly–a handful of others to prove the truth of Galley's alibis; proof that the careful investigations of Sir Frederick Roe had put beyond all doubt.

Latimer dwelt particularly on the injustice of the Home Office's insistence that not until the real "Turpin" was produced, charged, and convicted could Galley be released. The insane irrelevance of this "rule"–thought up, apparently on the spur of the moment, by quill-drivers under orders to save Lord John

Russell's, Lord Denman's, and Mr. Justice Williams's faces—was commented upon bitterly in Latimer's account of Galley's persecution; and he summed up his views in this final paragraph:

> At last the story [of Galley's unjust sentence, and of the many efforts to have it set aside] was forgotten; and now that it is revived in this unexpected way, I feel it to be a sacred duty to Truth and to the memory of that excellent man [George Scherer] who devoted himself so laboriously to clear up the mystery, that I should state these facts, in the hope that Edmund Galley may yet be deemed worthy of the Queen's Royal Pardon.

Two copies of this long and detailed statement of the Galley affair were prepared and sent out, one copy to Galley at Binalong, the other to Latimer's compositors with orders to set the type for the inclusion of the article on the front page of the next issue of *The Western Times:* for Friday, 10 August 1877. It took until 10 November—exactly three months—for Galley to receive Latimer's letter, with the enclosed statement, signed by Latimer himself. And it took until New Year's Day 1878 for Galley's grateful acknowledgment to reach his benefactor in Exeter, who printed the letter exactly as it had been written. The letter is too diffuse and too long to justify reproduction in full; but a few statements of Galley's have not, I think, been given the attention by historians of the case that they deserve.

In the first place, though the son of Moses Harvey had certainly helped Galley by causing to be printed, in *The Exeter Flying Post,* that letter from Galley addressed to Harvey's dead father, the pure essence of generosity had not yet come to distinguish the Harveys. As Galley wrote in his letter to Latimer:

> with this mail i have forwarded letter to Mr W.P.Harvey hoping he will do something for me in this unfortunate affair as i am only a poor man with a heavy family of young children as canot remit the sum he as asked in the leter I have got from him.

Well, as the saying goes, there's no harm in asking...

Then, in the next paragraph but one, there occurs the most astonishing coincidence—if it be a coincidence; and if it be not, then it is even more astonishing that its possible implications have never been examined, even (so far as we know) by Latimer or even mentioned by all the others who have interested themselves in this still-mysterious case. Galley continues:

Know [now] Sir i beg of you as a gentleman if you could not do something for me towards having this man John Longly or alias french taken up for the Murder in question i want to get this mans discripstions sent out to the Athorities out here, that they May see if it corisponds with this french.

Know [now] this french was serving a sentence of 2½ years in Goulbern gail during that time *i went to a place called Marengo* i saw a man there the name of Mr. Mathews and likewise is wife who told me i was on the right scent. Knew him to be the real Kentish hero of former days at home.

ever since I have found any trace of him have been communicating with the home Government and the Government of this Conoly [Colony] and can get No satisfaction.

That Galley had been petitioning both the British Government and that of New South Wales before it occurred to him to try the man–Moses Harvey–who had so relentlessly pursued him in 1836, was a disagreeable eye-opener for Latimer, who now realized that he must deal with a British and Colonial Government already forewarned on Galley's activities–and doubtless already well dug in to meet any revival of interest on the transported "murderer's" behalf.

But what must Latimer have thought of that strange name, "Marengo"; the name of the boarding-house keeper of Exeter, whose testimony, and the testimony of whose most transient lodgers, told so heavily against Oliver and Galley? What must Latimer have thought, not only to find it again as the name of a small settlement in Australia but as a place to which Galley had gone in search of the elusive John Longley, the real "Kentish Hero"? (And what, it must be pointed out, did young Dr. Conan Doyle think as, reading the back numbers of both *The Western Times* and *The Exeter Flying Post*–for he certainly read even the 1836 issues of that journal, as I shall show–that "Napoleonic" name *Marengo* cropped up once more in the tragic history of Edmund Galley?)

So, continued Galley:

as stated in the western times that the Government would not give me up until the right man was found now ie [*sic*] is found will not the

Government have him taken up and punished for the crime that he has Comitted an in justice to a poor man who as been Wronged over 40 years for anothers mans bad deed.

The letter ended on a personal but no less moving note:

As I am far advanced in years with a family to support and can get know [no] satisfaction of this man will not the good gentlemen of exeter do something for me in the way of recompence after so many years of sufring for anothers mans crime that he comited.

Or May i add if her Most Gracious Majesty lady queen victoria was to know my case she might do somethink for a poor sufring man.

It was to be some considerable time before Her Majesty, through her ministers, was to do that hoped-for "somethink" for a poor suffering man, but the good gentlemen of Exeter–and, indeed, of London, too–did not wait, but, under the generalship of Thomas Latimer, almost immediately to be joined by the still vigorous Ralph Sanders, what was left of the original band of champions in the pro-Galley crusade took up the fight once more.

Galley's revenge: frozen carcasses of mutton, product of his sweated labour on an Australian sheep ranch, reach the South-west India Dock, Millwall, London. The plentiful supplies of cheap Australian meat brought ruin, not only to the cattle-farmers of Britain, but to the landowning magnates as well.

Forty years and more had passed since the trial of Oliver and Galley, and it was to be expected that the four decades had not passed without their having effected some profound changes in the fortunes of those who had, in 1836, felt the gravest disquiet at the unsatisfactory conduct of Galley's trial and had "ganged up" to make that sense of disquiet vocal. All the same, it was surprising to find so many of the original "champions" still alive, mentally vigorous, and all now immensely influential.

George Scherer, actively campaigning for Galley to the end, was dead, and so was "Johnny" Williams–obstinately anti-Galley to the last.

But most of the others who had saved Galley from the hangman, but had failed to secure his acquittal, were, as they say, "around"–and, as was to be expected, all had risen in the world–some very high, indeed.

Thomas Latimer was now Exeter's Chief (or Senior) Magistrate; Montague Smith was a High Court judge; Cockburn was not only Sir Alexander now, but Lord Chief Justice of England. Lord John Russell had been created Viscount Amberley and Earl Russell in 1861 and retired into unimportant authorship after having been twice Prime Minister. Unfortunately, in 1877, he was still alive, and would not die until the following year, by which time the Latimer-directed pro-Galley agitation had got well into its stride. It is true that the former Lord John was no longer Home Secretary, but, after Scherer's death, Galley–unwisely, but most understandably–had endeavoured to achieve, by his own efforts, what George Scherer had failed to do: he continued to address petition after petition to the Home Government, irritating, by his importunity, every successive Home Secretary, no matter to which of the two political parties the Minister belonged.

What Galley did not realize–though, of course, Scherer, Latimer, and all Galley's other friends too painfully did–is that a Minister, any Minister, in any country, and at any period of history, when asked to hear a plea or investigate a complaint, inevitably and naturally "calls for the file," and there in the file is what may be called the general opinion of the Ministry in the past. It is usual, of course, to save the Great Man the tedium of reading his way through the file, that the Permanent Under-Secretary instructs a clerk to prepare a Minute: a résumé of the case. In this traditional manner, the present incumbent of the Minister's chair could see at once that all of his highly respected predecessors – their political allegiance being of no consequence – had dismissed all Galley's pleas, whether made through George Scherer or on Galley's own initiative.

The present (1877) Home Secretary, Sir Richard Assheton Cross, was a narrow-minded jack-in-office – bigoted, self-assured, and, as with so many persons of his type, a great collector of "honours,"[1] all gained, as a cynical contemporary observed, in having studied the art of never rocking the boat.

As Sir Richard read through the Minute relating to Galley, no thought of boat-rocking entered his complacent mind. He saw that Lord John Russell, his predecessor, had, on the urgent representations of George Scherer (who the devil was *he?*), graciously consented to review the case of Galley in both 1838 and 1839, and Cross noted with approval that Sir John had seen no grounds for going beyond his already perhaps far-too-merciful action of commuting Galley's death sentence to a mere transportation for life. The persistence of these pestering busybodies! Scherer . . . Scherer . . . Scherer again . . . and yet again. Would the man never take no for an answer? (Ah, he was dead now, after having had, as his last refusal, Lord Palmerston's curt negative during the Crimean War of a quarter-century before.)

And now here was this Galley, on his own, apparently, pestering both Lord Aberdare and Mr. Robert Lowe, successively Home Secretaries in Gladstone's first Ministry of 1868–74; worthy gentlemen both, for all that they belonged to the Liberal Party. Still . . . they had each given a decided no to a request that they reopen the case.

And why was Sir Richard Assheton Cross reading the résumé of the Galley file? We shall now see.

In the reign of Queen Victoria, there were only two "main" political parties – and party divisions were taken seriously indeed,

[1] The Right Honourable Sir Richard Assheton Cross, G.C.B., G.C.S.I., P.C., D.C.L., LL.D., F.R.S.; created Viscount Cross, of Boughton-in-Furness (Peerage of the United Kingdom), 1886; Secretary of State for the Home Department, 1874–80 and 1885–86.

though, since almost all of the Members of Parliament shared the advantages of family, landed possessions, conventional education, and wealth, they could meet their political opponents on easy terms. Only in the fact that each party had its own clubs–the Reform, Liberals' principal; the Carlton, the Conservatives'–and attended, generally, the luncheons, dinners, balls, and soirées of those grand hostesses clearly identified with either party, was it possible to make any clear distinction between the two.

However, it was sometimes necessary to move cautiously in any matter in which a Minister of the Crown might need to become involved; for the Minister was not only most clearly to be identified with his party; he *was* the party–especially and unmistakably so when it was his duty to rise in the House of Commons or the House of Lords to pronounce on Government policy.

The position of Galley is not at all difficult to understand, when his abysmal poverty, lack of education, "simplicity" bordering upon feeble-mindedness, lack of influence, and irregular social standing are borne in mind. He was in possession of information which, in competent hands, might have helped him considerably, but, after the death of his prime champion, George Scherer, in 1855, Galley had made the mistake of deciding to "go it alone" –and if the mandarins of the Home Office could deal contemptuously with a George Scherer or a Thomas Latimer, one may well imagine how far Galley got with them.

The identity of the "real" Turpin had been known to Galley, apparently, soon after his arrival in Australia in 1839; and, from that time on, Galley had obsessively (but understandably) tried to find John Longley, "*alias* French." That it took Galley so long even to get news of Longley is easily explained by the fact that Galley was not, in any sense of the word, his own master, but a "ticket-of-leave" convict, licensed to work for a private employer but strictly bound, like any mediaeval serf, to remain where he had been put to work. The principal source of news to those dwellers in the Outback (as was Galley) were the wandering men; and it was not until 1859, twenty years after he had arrived in Australia, that Galley learned that Longley had settled not far from him in New South Wales.

Naturally [Lambert writes], Galley took every opportunity to seek him out; but his occupation hampered him, and he rarely found himself free to journey in pursuit of Longley. Nevertheless, once he had discovered his whereabouts, Galley renewed his pleas to Authority at home; with the result that both Lord Aberdare and Robert Lowe—successive Home Secretaries in Gladstone's ministry—reviewed the case once more, but only to record the discouraging opinion: "No action necessary." Meanwhile, Galley's appeals became known to his employers and fellow-workers, who came to regard him as a "character" who was at least sincere in believing in his own innocence.

That Galley should have waited nearly twenty years after having run Longley to earth before switching his pleas from the Home Office to a possible unofficial helper seems inexplicable, even taking Galley's lack of *savoir faire* into account—but so it was: not until 1877 did the son of Galley's implacable enemy, Moses Harvey, receive the appeal from Galley.

Latimer saw that Galley's case needed to be strengthened considerably if the permanent officials of the Home Office were to be made to approve of some mercy for Galley—and so advise their Minister-for-the-time-being.

The experienced old editor saw that this *might* be accomplished in three principal ways:

a. By mounting a *sustained* propaganda campaign in Galley's favour, by press articles appearing every few weeks, to inform the public of the miscarriage of justice forty years before and to arouse the public's interest in a case either forgotten or never known.
b. To gather around him all those earlier champions who were still alive and who had not altered their opinion that Galley was innocent.
c. To collect and "codify" all the evidence in Galley's favour; that evidence being reinforced by the opinions of the (mostly legal) friends of Galley.

Two of those friends, as I have already said, had acquired great eminence in their profession: Montague Smith was now a High Court Judge; Sir Alexander Cockburn had risen to even greater eminence to become Lord Chief Justice; and Latimer decided to invoke the authority and prestige of these two distinguished men. There was, however, a difficulty in approaching them officially:

Montague Smith was a Conservative–a Tory–whilst Sir Alexander Cockburn was a Liberal. . .as was the unyieldingly Radical Latimer.

Accordingly, Latimer asked his friend Ralph Sanders, who had never wavered in his belief in Galley's innocence, and who was a Tory, to approach Mr. Justice Montague Smith, to seek his support in asking that the Galley case be reopened. Latimer approached, with the same object, his fellow Liberal, the Lord Chief Justice. Latimer's first letter to the Lord Chief Justice was written in January 1878. The answer came immediately: the L.C.J. had read all the documents enclosed in Latimer's letter; remembered the Galley case perfectly, and his own deep misgivings on the justice of the verdict and sentence even at the time; advised Latimer to see to it that a much more detailed and accurately drawn up petition were presented by Galley to the Home Secretary; and that the Lord Chief Justice himself (though a Liberal) would approach Assheton Cross, the Tory Home Secretary, in person. Latimer written to, the Lord Chief Justice then took pen and paper and wrote a detailed summing-up of the entire Galley case, paying particular attention to the admitted perjury of witnesses for the prosecution; to the obvious perjury–though unadmitted–of the Crown's principal witness, Elizabeth Harris; to the faulty and misleading summing-up of the trial judge; and, most importantly, to his own inability to understand how the Home Office could decide to accept evidence so as to reprieve Galley but decline to permit that evidence to set him free.

> I know not [the Lord Chief Justice wrote] on what ground this strange proceeding was based; but I can say with truth that I have never thought of it without a deep sense of the flagrant injustice of such a decision. No question of the degree of guilt could arise in this case; the man must have been wholly guilty or wholly innocent. Had the evidence of the *alibi* been brought forward on the trial, and had it only sufficed to create a reasonable doubt of the prisoner's guilt, it would, according to the humane principle of our law, have been sufficient to warrant an acquittal. But the evidence was far more than sufficient to create a reasonable doubt of guilt. *It excluded all reasonable doubt of guilt.* [Emphasis added]

The writer touched on the evidence for Galley's innocence; told how it had been collected, and by what disinterested men; and ended this official memorial with these emotionally charged words:

[Galley] has passed forty years and upwards in the Colony without reproach. For many long years he must have worked as a slave on the public roads[2] or works, leading a life of misery and hardship . . .

Now the writer turns to the evidence of Galley's Australian life that Latimer and others, working in the same interest, had collected:

He has now been twelve years in the service of the same master. He is married and has a family.[3] He desires, before he passes away, to have the stigma of murder and felony wiped out by Her Majesty's pardon. I cannot refrain, under a strong and imperious sense of duty, from earnestly and anxiously pressing this case upon your consideration, that justice and right may at length, however tardily, be done to an injured man.

The Lord Chief Justice's memorial was sent to Assheton Cross, under cover addressed to the Minister *personally,* was dated 16 March 1878, and the feelings of outrage with which it was received by Cross and his permanent officials may well be imagined. Lambert remarks caustically that:

Such intervention as this, by the Lord Chief Justice himself, was almost unprecedented, and made a deep impression at the Home Office–so deep, indeed, that it took the officials there a year to make out a reply . . . At first the hopes of Galley's champions ran high; but as time passed by, and delay lengthened, they faded into doubt and disappointment. At length, on March 27th, 1879, a brief and unconciliatory reply was sent to Cockburn by the permanent secretary at the Home Office, Mr. Godfrey Lushington.

The letter, for official arrogance, insolence, and the deeply-ingrained sense of invulnerability that a non-terminable (save by retirement or death) employment gives most "established" civil servants, may stand as a model of all such communications:

---

[2]Galley served his first six months in New South Wales in a chain gang.

[3]Here is an example of Cockburn's delicacy: the marriage was a common-law union, though of the most respectable kind. Galley's "wife" had been deserted by her husband, leaving her with seven children.

My Lord,

Adverting to your letter with regard to the case of Edmund Galley, I am directed by Mr. Secretary Cross to acquaint you that he has long and earnestly considered this case, which, from the peculiar circumstances which surround it, and from the weight which attaches to the recommendation of your Lordship, has required at his hands more than usual anxiety and deliberation. The peculiar difficulty which more especially presents itself in the case appears to Mr. Cross to be that all the facts which are now laid before him and upon which the recommendation of your Lordship is based, were, while they were fresh, and while Galley was under sentence of death, brought under the consideration of Lord John Russell and Lord Denman, the Secretary of State and the Lord Chief Justice of the day: and moreover, in Mr. Cross's judgment, the question for him to decide is not so much whether, had he been in Lord John Russell's place, he would have arrived at the same conclusions as his Lordship, as whether at this period of time, so long after the event, and upon the same facts, he would be justified in overruling the solemn decision of the then Secretary of State, acting under the direct advice of the then Lord Chief Justice. There is an additional element in the case which weighs upon Mr. Cross's mind, which is that he finds that the matter has been more than once brought before his predecessors, and that both Lord Aberdare and Mr. Lowe felt compelled to decline to reopen it. Under these circumstances, I am directed to inform your Lordship that Mr. Cross feels himself constrained to abide by the previous decisions in the case, and cannot take upon himself the responsibility of overruling them.

And that, the malignant Mr. Godfrey Lushington must have told himself, as he rubbed his hands in self-satisfaction, is *that!* . . . How *dare* that Scotch interferer apply the word "strange" to any Home Office decision . . . ?

However, though Lambert calls this offensive missive "a severe setback to Latimer and Sanders," it proved itself to be no irremediable disaster but merely a setback with the power to encourage the champions to renew their assault on complacent Privilege in even greater force. Latimer, as all in his day, knew his Bible well, and Christ's words, as recorded in *Luke* XII:2–3, must have come most appositely to the old editor's mind:

For there is nothing covered, that shall not be revealed; neither hid, that shall not be known.

Therefore whatsoever ye have spoken in darkness shall be heard in the light; and that which ye have spoken in the ear in closets shall be proclaimed upon the housetops.

Anyone foolish enough to write such a letter to a Lord Chief Justice may well have been foolish enough to believe that Sir Alexander would, out of very shame to have merited such a rebuke, keep the communication to himself. Of course, the Scotsman did no such thing: he sent a copy to Latimer, and Latimer promptly printed it in *The Western Times* and saw to it that all the national newspapers had a copy of Latimer's, containing the Home Office rejection of the Lord Chief Justice's emotional though soundly reasoned plea on Galley's behalf. It was an adroit move on Latimer's part, and the results were soon to appear.

In its issue of 2 April 1879, *The Times* headed and began a long article thus:

A PLEA FOR MERCY.–The *Western Times* of yesterday publishes a correspondence between the Lord Chief Justice of England and the Home Secretary in reference to the case of Edmund Galley, who was tried in 1836, and sentenced to death for the murder of a farmer named May, in the county of Devon . . .

There was a further brief reference, in *The Times* of 28 May, to a petition which was being prepared in Galley's favour; this brief article was headed: THE CASE OF EDMUND GALLEY.

And, in its issue of 11 June 1879, *The Times* had reason to print a very long article under the heading THE CONVICT GALLEY, as the outcome of the most energetic campaigning that even Latimer had ever done in his vigorously combative life.

For that element of luck which is an essential ingredient of a long striven-for success was, at this critical moment, to give the champions an unexpected argument in their favour. If the obstinate Assheton Cross entrenched himself behind precedent, fate was now to provide his opponents with a precedent more to their advantage. In the very month–March 1879–in which, at the direction of Cross, Lushington sent the offensive letter to the Lord Chief Justice, Cross himself arranged a free pardon (with monetary compensation of £1,000) for a young man condemned to death for having murdered by shooting Police Constable Cock; the death-sentence being commuted to that of penal servitude for life. The convicted prisoner, William Habron,[4] who actually admitted having threatened that he and his brother would "get" P.C. Cock, was released and compensated when the notorious burglar-violinist, Sherlock Holmes's "friend," Charlie Peace, confessed to the crime for which Habron had so nearly gone to the gallows. The analogy with the Galley case was so striking (save that Galley, unlike Habron, had never uttered threats) that everyone was asking why, if Cross could extend justice to Habron, the Home Secretary should be so intransigent in the case of Galley?

The "reasons" given in the Home Office letter for Cross's rejection of the Lord Chief Justice's plea on Galley's behalf were seen, accepted, and worked on by the champions as a challenge; and the references, in Lushington's letter, expressed or implied, as to the non-availability of evidence or witnesses after a lapse of forty years spurred the champions on to finding the "missing" witnesses. One of the most unlikely was the last surviving member of the jury which had brought in a verdict of Guilty in the Oliver–Galley trial, and he was discovered through a letter that he wrote to *Lloyd's Sunday Newspaper;* an "open letter" to Assheton Cross:

> I implore and beseech you in the name of humanity, to release this poor man. It will relieve a burden from my mind in the agony of death, which at my time of life cannot be far distant.

Now the entire British press, alive to the importance of what once had been a news story of purely Devonian interest, were printing "the continuing saga" of the wretched Galley, as the indefatigable Latimer kept the papers of all his rivals supplied with material. *Lloyd's Sunday Newspaper* had found the last juryman; now Latimer was to find the prison chaplain who had attended Oliver

---

[4]That this name, too, stuck well in Conan Doyle's memory is evident from his use of the name, only slightly altered ("Habron" to "Hebron") in *The Yellow Face* (1893), written fifteen years after Habron had been free-pardoned and compensated for false imprisonment.

during that man's last days: the Reverend Francis Vidal. He was to add to the now impressive mass of testimony his firm belief that Oliver's exoneration of Galley ought to be accepted without reservation.

The self-assured quill-drivers of the Home Office went calmly about their business, sending Galley, in Australia, formal notice that the petition that he had addressed to the Home Office at Latimer's suggestion had been rejected (once again!). But if the Home Office went about its customary duties in its customary way, Latimer and his friends went about their extraordinary and self-assumed duties at ten times the rate and with far more energy and zeal. For now the ranks of the champions were swelling; and Latimer, through the pages of *The Western Times*, never let the public forget the Galley campaign. In answer to Cross's insolent rejection of the Lord Chief Justice's plea, Latimer got up a petition in Exeter to which over two thousand Devonians were happy to affix their signatures; the petitioners including both the Bishop and the Dean of Exeter. The strategy and tactics of the Latimerians were now planned to overcome Cross's obstinacy by what is called colloquially "going over his head"–and to the only body with powers superior to his: the High Court of Parliament. For Galley had not only found a new and powerful friend, this friend was one who had a declared interest in the establishment of a Court of Appeal. Had such a Court existed in 1836, Galley would never have been shipped to Australia.

This new and powerful friend was Sir John Eardley Wilmot; a wealthy, politically independent baronet, nominally attached to the Conservative (that is, Cross's) party, who represented the "free and independent" electors of South Warwickshire in Parliament. Sir John, approached by Latimer and, almost certainly, by the Lord Chief Justice, agreed to ballot for a place to bring forward, in Parliament, a motion which should declare Galley innocent and pray Her Majesty to grant the convict a free pardon. On 25 July, Sir John rose to address the House, which had had the petition from Exeter presented to it on 10 June. Its members had already had an opportunity to acquaint themselves with the facts and arguments that Sir John would produce, for, on the morning of the debate, a pamphlet, containing all relevant material, had been laid on the desk of every Member of Parliament: a pamphlet written, produced, and paid for by Thomas Latimer.

In those days, Members of Parliament were not paid, and their last privilege—that of franking their (and their friends') mail by a mere signature, with "M.P." after the name—had been withdrawn on the introduction of national penny postage in 1840. There were, even in those independent times, fairly strictly-drawn party lines; but party discipline, for all practical purposes, controlled only those greedy for the rich rewards that unswerving loyalty promised. For those whose ambitions lay elsewhere, the absence of a Parliamentary salary gave them a freedom of opinion and the expression of that opinion not, alas, ever again to be enjoyed by our over-salaried "representatives"—a term which has now become, for all practical uses, meaningless, but which, in the last century, had a real significance. In those days, Members of Parliament were always fully conscious, not only of the national interest, but of the interests of the electors who had sent them to Westminster. The cherished independence of members of both parties was now to be demonstrated, in no uncertain fashion, throughout the House—to the great discomfiture of Disraeli's government in general, and of Assheton Cross in particular.

For now, as I have said, Galley's cause had gathered about it some most important additional recruits: leading them, the passionately humanitarian Tory, Sir John Eardley Wilmot; but, backing him, the even more respected figure of old John Bright, the Quaker Apostle of Reform, who had fought for that Free Trade which, in the second half of Victoria's reign, was to make Great Britain the richest nation in the world. Bright spoke from the Liberal benches, but his plea for justice for Galley was no less emotional, no less forceful, than was Sir John's.

So then, on the hot evening of Friday, 25 July 1879, in a crowded House, Sir John Eardley Wilmot rose to present the case for "the convict Galley." Sir John spoke well, and, from both sides of the House, private Members rose in his support—and perhaps it was as well that the Government had chosen its own spokesman so clumsily: the coldly arrogant and irritatingly sarcastic Robert Lowe, one of the five Home Secretaries between Lord John Russell and Assheton Cross who had turned down pleas for Galley's release and rehabilitation.

Lowe began badly and ended up worse; with an argument which not only did not impress the hundreds of assembled

Members of Parliament but only infuriated all save the Government ministers. The House of Commons was not, Lowe explained, a judicial body, with powers to try a case which had already been tried forty years before, ending with a decision given, with due respect of legal forms, in a Court of Law. Now this angered his listeners, for two excellent reasons: the first, that Parliament *had* (and has still) the power to overturn a jury's verdict, and, second, that Galley was not in Australia, forbidden, under pain of death, to return without official sanction, because of a decision "long ago in the Law Courts," but merely because of a decision by the then Home Secretary, who had ordered Galley out of England because his continued presence there was embarrassing Lord John Russell, Lord Denman, and "Johnny" Williams–and, of course, to muzzle Galley's defenders, led by George Scherer.

It must have been considered a splendid strategic move by some fat-headed adviser of the Government to have let–or asked –Robert Lowe, a Liberal, to rise to defend Assheton Cross, the Tory Home Secretary. It was a strategic blunder; for now Lowe was succeeding in irritating members of both parties–in particular those of his own. Not one of Lowe's arguments elicited any sympathy in the House; and, as each harsh opinion followed the next, the House, as the Parliamentary reporter of *The Times* recorded, "shewed unmistakable signs of deep uneasiness and a growing agitation." As well they might have done . . .

For what was Galley suffering now? Lowe asked the House. The man's sentence had expired (which was untrue: Galley had been transported *for life*), and "he no longer lay under any practical disability." And then, the chillingly unsympathetic Lowe continued, Galley was a member of the criminal class–an assumption quite unsupported by proof–"If Galley was wrongly convicted, he certainly assisted very much in his own conviction by the irregular and improper life he led"–a statement so contemptuous of fact, of law, of common justice and common humanity that the House gasped as one man. But, if Lowe heard the gasps and saw the looks of astonishment and condemnation, nothing now was to halt him in his arguments. Of course, Cross should adhere firmly to his decision not to reopen the Galley case; and there was no reason to do so "simply because it was now forty-three years old."

The public welfare [Lowe blithely continued] requires that there should be a term put to all proceedings . . . If the House thinks that it is the right and duty of a Secretary of State, who had only held office for a short period, to overthrow a decision of the most respected and most honoured men who have lived in this country [a group, no doubt, in which Lowe wished to be included], we shall be adopting a principle which will render the continuity of the administration of justice in this country impossible.

The impudence, as well as the immorality, of his preaching a doctrine that, once a decision had been given "in the Law Courts," that decision, even if manifestly wrong, could never be set aside, infuriated the House–and brought the Grand Old Man of Liberalism, John Bright, the Quaker humanitarian, to his trembling feet. Lowe tried to interrupt him, but Bright contemptuously brushed the interruption aside.

If [said Bright] I wanted anything to convince me of the force of the case brought before us, it would be the speech which [Mr. Lowe] has delivered. My Right Honourable friend [Lowe] has said that the man is now suffering no punishment, except that he cannot return to England. But surely, if he cannot return to England because he has the mark of Cain on him and the brand of the murderer, it is a punishment of which, if we can relieve him, we ought to do so.

The lapse of time makes the weight of Galley's unjust punishment all the more excessive, and the House ought to recommend the Crown not to bring this man back to England, not to take him out of slavery, but to say that there had been a miscarriage of justice, and that for the rest of his life there will be taken from him the dark spot which has so long rested upon him.

In that way, proof will be given to the world that, whatever may be the failings of our Judicature–and it has many failings, as Courts of Justice in all countries have–whenever its errors are discovered, the Parliament of England, even at the last hour, will do its best to remedy the damage which has been occasioned, and to do justice to an unfortunate, poor and long-absent man.

The prestige, no less than the impassioned eloquence, of the House's most respected senior statesman moved most of the Members to sympathy; but Assheton Cross, though obviously (from a characteristic jerking of the left leg) greatly uneasy, had his orders, and, though with a patent reluctance, he trotted out the old arguments in support of earlier decisions in the Galley case, and concluded: "I have no new facts before me. I have no better opportunity of forming an opinion than those who have preceded me in office. I have come to the same conclusion as Lord John Russell–and I cannot advise the House to accept the motion."

The Times's reporter noted the House's response with the simple journalistic cliché of "Uproar"–but it was more than that. If Assheton Cross had thought that his denial of justice for Galley, on the weak grounds that "Galley's *alibi* had never been investigated at all, or submitted to the only valid test, that of examination in a Court of Law," would be accepted by the majority of the House, he was in for what must have been the greatest surprise of his life.

Eardley Wilmot bounced to his feet, waving his Order Paper and now shouting to be heard. Above the roar of the other outraged Members, he could be heard telling Cross that he intended to "divide" the House–that is, ask the House to vote on his motion, whether or not Cross would wish or Mr. Speaker permit it. And the temper of the House was such that Cross gave way, Mr. Speaker did not intervene, and the debate continued.

It became clear that not all the Members were of one mind, even those sympathetic to Galley, and there was a strong sentiment in favour of a compromise which would, whilst allowing justice to Galley, save the face of those who had declined to allow such justice to "an unfortunate, poor and long-absent man," in Bright's words. The Member who came forward with a suggestion to pour oil on these now very troubled waters was Sir Henry James, and he made a proposition which was taken up (not improbably with a sigh of relief) by several other Members, including one from Latimer's county of Devon: that the House should not insist on declaring Galley's complete innocence, but only the serious doubt of his guilt, and that, so long as this hair-splitting difference were adopted, the motion to grant–or pray Her Majesty to grant–a free pardon to Galley should be pressed.

Cross, seeing that his face might now be saved, jumped in now to assert his authority, by insisting that Sir John Eardley Wilmot's assertion of Galley's innocence be unreservedly withdrawn, and so Sir John, on the excellent principle that half a loaf is better than no bread, salvaged what he could from the almost wrecked motion and asked leave to amend it so as now to read: "That an Humble Address be presented to Her Majesty, praying

Her Majesty that she will be graciously pleased to grant a Free Pardon to Edmund Galley." The House murmured its approval; but even now, with the sentiment of almost the whole House of Commons plainly against him, the obstinate Assheton Cross did not yield, and only a further passionate speech by the old Quaker, Bright, convincing him that a forced "division" would defeat the Government on this issue, decided the Minister to submit. Even so, the disagreeable task of assenting to the obvious feeling of the House was given by Cross to the Right Honourable Sir Stafford Northcote, Chancellor of the Exchequer, who, in a surly manner, announced that the Government would accept the amended motion without further conditions.

The triumph of the champions was incomplete, and, in paying a generous tribute to the more successful Thomas Latimer, the editor of *The Exeter Flying Post* somewhat exceeded his brief when he commented upon the outcome of the Parliamentary debate:

> Through the lengthened period of forty-three years, we in the West of England know that there was one master mind present at the trial, that, as the chief engineer, in season and out of season, set in motion the whole of the machinery that was ever and anon at work to obtain an acknowledgment of Galley's innocence from the authorities, and to bring him before the world a free man. Many times and oft has the veteran penman of the *Western Times* issued his broadsheet advocating the claims of the wronged and oppressed, pleading in the cause of justice. Making known Galley's injustice and long-suffering is no isolated case in his labours. But the Free Pardon graciously granted by Her Majesty to Galley will afford Mr. Latimer an enduring satisfaction to the end of his long, upright, laborious, useful and valuable life.

A generous tribute indeed, even if richly deserved, from the editor of a rival newspaper which was being slowly put out of business by the greater skill of Latimer as a journalist. But the tribute erred in that it had congratulated Latimer on having obtained "an acknowledgment of Galley's innocence from the authorities"–for this was what neither Latimer nor his principal Parliamentary colleague, Sir John Eardley Wilmot, had managed to do. To obtain a free pardon from the very reluctant Cross, Sir John and his supporters on both sides of the House had had to accept "suspicion of his guilt" rather than the plenary "perfect assurance of his innocence" as the terms on which the free pardon could be granted to Galley–and this half-triumph left both Latimer and Eardley Wilmot with yet more fighting to be done.

Lambert says that

> the intention behind the terms of the first resolution moved by Sir [John] Eardley Wilmot in the House of Commons had been to secure for Galley, not only a Pardon, but also compensation for his wrongful conviction. Probably this accounted for the stubborn resistance of the Home Office, and of Authority generally, to the declaration of Galley's innocence.

Well, the intention to ask compensation for Galley was doubtless in the minds of both Sir John and of Latimer, as well, we may certainly believe, as in that of the Lord Chief Justice, who had added to the literature of the Galley case by publishing his own "intervening" pamphlet and who would hardly have been human had he not smarted under Cross's insolent rejection of his plea for Galley. But it must be recorded that no specific demand that Galley be compensated was written into the original petition presented to the Commons by Sir John Eardley Wilmot, nor, obviously, into the amended petition, which merely dropped the demand that Galley's "innocence" be recognized. Lambert, then, is wrong in assuming that a demand for compensation for Galley "accounted for the stubborn resistance of the Home Office, and of Authority generally, to the declaration of Galley's innocence." As no compensation had been demanded–even though dearly hoped for–the Home Office, in this respect, had nothing to resist.

It was something a good deal more sinister which motivated and strengthened that opposition to justice for Galley which had been the *consistent* policy of the Home Office for over forty years, and which, as Eardley Wilmot and Latimer were soon to discover, would not alter with the change from Conservative to Liberal government which took place in the year following the Queen's granting Galley a free pardon. Nine years earlier, the Pope had startled the world by promulgating the dogma of the Papal Infallibility. With far less publicity, the Authorities of England had been upholding and imposing the doctrine of the Infallibility of the English Judicature: not only were English judges (and their lackeys at the Home Office) never at fault; they never *could* be at fault. As Pilate said, many centuries before: "*He gegrapha, gegrapha!*"–"What is written is written."

In the matter of compensation for Galley, it is obvious that Sir

John and Latimer had relied too much on the fact that, after only two years of wrongful imprisonment, Habron had been awarded £1,000 by Cross as Home Secretary. The motion in the House of Commons as carried, by denying the innocence of Galley (and thus that his sentence had been wrongful), put the wretched Galley out of all claim for compensation.

The free pardon carried no *solatium* of monetary compensation for years of obloquy and physical and mental suffering. Any other man than Latimer would have "called it a day," in the reflection that he had done all that he could and that what he had done had been more than any normal man could have hoped to effect. But Latimer being who he was, he decided, with Sir John's help, to return to the attack.

The new Government was nominally, not only Liberal, but "liberal" also, and from Sir William Harcourt, the new Home Secretary, a response much more sympathetic than that received from the stubborn Cross was confidently expected by both Sir John, within the House, and by Latimer, campaigning outside. Alas! the doctrine of Judicial Infallibility still governed; and, as Lambert says: "When Sir [John] Eardley Wilmot asked a question in the House on the subject [of Galley's compensation], he received a reply from Harcourt not very different from that which he would have expected from the obstinate Cross."

But victory was in sight for the dedicated campaigners. Latimer, at his own expense, had published a second edition of the Lord Chief Justice's *A Plea for Pardon*, and though, on Friday, 5 August 1881, Sir John rose to address a poorly-attended House (it was Friday: a hot day, with a hotter week-end to tempt most Members away from London), the House's common response to his second plea for Galley made up for the relatively few who heard him with full attention and cheered him warmly. The support was needed, for Harcourt, true to the principles which seemed to have actuated every Home Secretary since at least 1836, put forward the curious "defense" that the Government ought not to be expected to compensate every prisoner wrongly convicted. He suggested that, if Galley wished to return to England, there was now no legal objection to his doing so, and that the cost of bringing the poor shepherd, his "wife," and seven children back to the Mother Country might be (Harcourt really meant "ought to be") defrayed by public subscription. The indignation that this reply inspired angered men of all shades of political opinion: Tory, Liberal, Radical.

One after the other rose to urge the Government to compensate Galley; and at last, sensing the unity of the House's opinion and fearing for the Government's popularity in the House's growing enmity, the Government caved in, and Sir Henry James, Q.C., now Attorney-General—the very man who had suggested the compromise on the original motion—rose, and with no marked enthusiasm declared that, as Galley's case was exceptional, and must in no wise be construed as a precedent, and agreed to arrange what the House so obviously wished: "adequate" compensation for Galley.

From the small post office within the Palace of Westminster, Sir John Eardley Wilmot telegraphed to Latimer, giving him the news that the compensation for Galley had been, at last, allowed: one thousand pounds—and, as soon as possible, Latimer, authorized to do so by the organizing committee, cabled the following message:

> From Latimer, Exeter
> To *Sydney Herald,* Sydney
> Government Galley Thousand. Inform him.

The rate to Sydney, New South Wales, in 1881 was ten shillings and ninepence a word: a twelve-word cable, then, cost £4 16*s*. Sherlock Holmes, whose telegrams cost him only one shilling (24¢) for *twenty* words, with 3*d*. (6¢) an additional word, was yet rarely more laconic.

Of course, none but the most *naïf* believed that, with Sir Henry James's admission of defeat in the House of Commons, that the matter of Edmund Galley had been closed with Latimer's cable to the *Sydney Herald*. It was one thing for a Government department to defy pleas for mercy over a period of more than forty years, and it was quite another to pay what the faceless and not-so-faceless men of that Department thought of as the penalty for defeat.

It was by no means a simple miserly desire to defer that payment as long as possible which caused the Home Office to

GALLEY'S COMPENSATION

WESTERN TIMES OFFICE,
Aug. 26, 2 p.m.

Mr. EDWARD JOHNSON Telegraphed us that EDMUND GALLEY is to have

£1,000

Compensation for Galley—at last! How Exeter heard the news: the poster which appeared in the window of the *Western Times* office on the early afternoon of Friday, 26 August 1881. The long fight for Galley was won . . .

suggest that, rather than remit the £1,000 to Galley, as that Department had (through the Attorney General, in the House of Commons) promised to do, the Home Office should invest the capital sum "on Galley's behalf," sending him merely the interest, which would have been paid quarterly. The suggestion came from the sort of low cunning characterizing far too much Officialdom; and the advantage to the Department in its being able to retain possession of Galley's miserable thousand pounds was that, *on the interest,* he would be able, by the exercise of rigid economy, to buy himself a *steerage* passage on, say, the S.S. *Lusitania*[5] (J. J. de Gardoqui, Master) after the receipt of a whole year's interest—provided always that the Home Office remitted the interest punctually. The intention behind the suggestion was, obviously, to try, as far as possible, to keep Galley where he had been brushed in the first place—under the carpet. Politicians are very

[5] This, of course, was not the *Lusitania* which was torpedoed off the coast of Ireland by a German submarine in 1915, with great loss of life. The Cunard Line's *Lusitania* was only eight years old at the time of her destruction.

sensitive people, and Galley, returning to a hero's welcome at Exeter, could well have embarrassed the ardent seekers after a bogus popularity.

No one, so far as I know, has examined this aspect of the Home Office's intransigence, against which Ralph Sanders took it upon himself to fight with all the energy worthy of one of the principal champions.

As Galley's grudged thousand pounds would be granted from Treasury funds, it would be invested, as a matter of course, in British Government Three Per Cent. Consols, which, in 1881, stood at par. So that £1,000 worth of Three Per Cents. would yield an annual thirty pounds. There would have been no income tax chargeable on so trivial a sum.

To get back, *only by himself,* at the very cheapest rate, Galley would have had to buy bunk-space in the steerage for sixteen guineas ($73.53 at the then current rate of exchange). The voyage lasted forty days, and Galley could not have expected to go ashore, save for a walk, as the ship touched in at some of the hottest places in the world. Food–of a sort–was provided; but he would have been unable to supplement the ship's menu, save in the most meagre degree, had he hoped to arrive in England other than penniless. And what of the wife and children that he would have had to leave behind . . . ?

Sanders did get Galley his intact thousand pounds, after all, but he used none of it to return to England. For, dying two years later, Galley had passed out of the animosity, as doubtless he was to pass out of the very fugitive memories, of those who had fought so valiantly and so long to uphold the tradition and prestige of the Home Office.

Lord John Russell had died three years before: those who held his lordship's memory in affectionate respect must have been gratified to realize that, even though they had failed to prevent Galley's getting the free pardon that Lord John would never have authorized, they had at least achieved what his lordship had always desired: they had kept Galley out of England for good.[6]

---

[6]It is one of the most curious twists in this most twisted story that, though Lord John Russell, first Earl Russell, had set his face against

If, as I have said, the year 1881 was so "pivotal" for Conan Doyle, it was a year which, perhaps more than any other in his life, emphasized the truth of that piece of ancient folk-wisdom which points out that "when one door closes, another opens." For Conan Doyle, the St. Luke's Mystery began in 1881, and, though he was not to become aware of it until he read the newspaper accounts of the trial of Frau Stanger and Fritz Stumm late in the following year, that door to success, which was never to close for him, had opened in 1881. It was, too, the year in which the long fight to vindicate Galley came to its partial—only partial, remember!—end; though, to be realistic, it was still dead-and-gone George Scherer and Lord Chief Justice Cockburn, and still-living Thomas Latimer and Sir John Eardley Wilmot, who were vindicated, rather than was far-away Edmund Galley. But for them all, 1881 was a year of endings, of closure. . . . Only for one young doctor, caught in the petty machinations of a small-time con man—a half-despairing young doctor who was still unaware of what Fate had in store for him—did the door open . . . and open wide.

The accounts of the Galley affair make, even now, for sad reading, and I often felt myself growing warm with indignation as I visualized the smooth rotters inside and outside the House of Commons, with their shameless evasions and out-and-out lies,

---

asking either King William IV or Queen Victoria to grant Galley a free pardon, the passing of thirty-three years after Russell's death witnessed the second Earl, John Francis Stanley Russell, petitioning King George V to grant *him* a free pardon. (He got it, of course: he was no Galley.) What had happened was this: the second Earl, "Lord John's" grandson, had married, in 1890, Mabel, daughter of Sir Claude Scott, Baronet, and endured the lady's unattractive ways until, in despair, the second Earl went to Nevada, where he got a divorce from his wife and re-married: this time to Miss Mollie Cooke (who divorced him in 1915). A Nevada divorce not being recognized by the British authorities, it was plain that Lord Russell had, in marrying Miss Cooke, committed bigamy. On his return to England, he was arrested, tried by his peers, and sentenced to imprisonment.

denying justice, not out of any particular spite against Galley, but because criticism of themselves, even by one of their own caste, deserved to be punished.

I mention my own feelings of resentment against these malignant jacks-in-office because I would wish the reader to bear in mind the fierce passion of indignation that such flaunting of justice must have aroused in the breast of young Dr. Conan Doyle—for it is of him and his greatest creation that this book set out to tell; the story of Galley—though vitally important as a source of inspiration to Conan Doyle—is really only incidental to the main theme of my book, which is to show the different elements which went into the making of Sherlock Holmes; elements which, all the same, may not be treated save as elements which went into the making of Conan Doyle.

If I were asked to name the most outstanding characteristic of Conan Doyle, I would name that sudden, indignant response to the knowledge of injustice which never permitted him to leave injustice undenounced and, where possible, uncorrected. If I may now feel my blood rise at the long agony through which poor Galley was so unjustly put by the fat cats of a worthless Ministry, think how much more fiercely Conan Doyle's heart must have beaten with indignation at an age younger than my present age by forty years—the time that it took Galley to obtain a grudged and insufficient justice.

The life of Conan Doyle is one long outcry against men's wrongdoing; one long outcry on behalf of those to whom the wrong has been done. One of Conan Doyle's heroes, Oliver Wendell Holmes, had burst into indignant poetry when it was proposed to scrap the famous and historic frigate, U.S.S. *Constitution:* "Ay, tear her tattered ensign down . . . !" And with a similar patriotic sentimentality did Conan Doyle read that Nelson's old flagship, *Foudroyant,* had been sold to the Germans to be broken up. And, like Holmes, he put his indignation into verse as bitter as it was sincere:

Who says the Nation's purse is lean,
    Who fears for claim or bond or debt,
When all the glories that have been
    Are scheduled as a cash asset?

If times are black and trade is slack,
 If coal and cotton fail at last,
We've something left to barter yet—
 Our glorious past . . .

He took up the cudgels on behalf of the maltreated slaves of the Belgian Congo; he went to the aid of the wretched Parsee solicitor, George Edalji; he fought for the ungrateful Oscar Slater; and, if he got, in all these struggles for the underdog–struggles into which he flung himself with all that passion for Lost Causes which is at once the strength and the weakness of the Irish temperament–more kicks than ha'pence, as the saying goes, he emerged from each battle, victorious or not, in the warm assurance that he had fought valiantly in a good cause. It is in no spirit of denigration that I say that, for Conan Doyle, indignation was a passion, and that those who have written of him (sympathetically or critically) have failed to realize–as, perhaps, he himself never fully realized–this indignation was the one passion on which he never put restraint. His biographers may never claim to have understood him completely so long as they fail to be aware that it was not so much that injustice aroused his indignation, as that he had a continual need to maintain his indignation at fever-point through a constant hunt for injustices which might be corrected or, at least, constructively criticized.

To this must be added another need–again so typically Irish (or, more precisely, Celtic): the need to find and worship the Heroic. There is probably, in all Conan Doyle's writings, no story so truly autobiographical, so truly, in its symbolism, self-revelatory, as that in which Brigadier Gérard devises a plan to rescue his adored hero, Napoleon, from St. Helena, and arrives only to find that the Emperor has just died. There is more of Conan Doyle, there is more of the quintessence of Conan Doyle, in this fiction of an impossible adventure which failed of its glorious object, than in all the autobiographical sketches of *The Stark Munro Letters,* which do no more to "reveal" Conan Doyle than in "revealing" what he thought of a conman who had taken advantage of a young man's credulity and need.

In George Scherer and, though to a lesser degree, in Thomas Latimer, Conan Doyle found two Heroes—and heroes on which to model himself. Heroes to inspire him and arm his indignant right-thinking he had always needed, and would need to the end of his days. The two Scherers—George, of the long fight for Galley, and Wendel, of the fight for a private detective's right to command the respect of entrenched Privilege—added "body" to the developing concept of the Superhuman Detective; not least in name, as I have pointed out.

Sherlock Holmes, indeed, has a long pedigree and, to use a homely analogy, is "the son of many fathers." It suited Conan Doyle, in later years, to claim that the original of Sherlock Holmes was one of the lecturers at the Medical School of Edinburgh University, Dr. Joseph Bell; but, apart from Bell's impressive deductions from an examination of a patient's appearance—that characteristic which, in all the Sherlock Holmes stories, is made to impress Watson (who could never become used to it and was as impressed by the hundredth demonstration as he had been by the first)—there is nothing in *all the rest of Sherlock Holmes* of what has been recorded of Dr. Bell, and it is significant, as a pointer to what Conan Doyle *really* thought of Dr. Joseph Bell, that, of the three characters in the Canon to whom Doyle has given the forename of "Joseph," not one is a hero, and two—Joseph Stangerson and Joseph Harrison—are thorough-paced criminals. Is this naming consistent with that warm declaration of respect for Dr. Joseph Bell with which Conan Doyle prefaced later editions of *A Study in Scarlet?*

I have stated already that the character of Sherlock Holmes is a synthesis of many elements, gathered, consciously and subconsciously, by that character's maker, over many years; and every element, however seemingly trivial, inspired by, and recording, for the patient analyst of the Canon's names, an experience of Conan Doyle's.

Briefly to recapitulate the accident by which the personalities—and thus, the names—of the two Scherers came to be dominant in the making of Sherlock Holmes, it must first of all be emphasized that the two Scherers were encountered not only in the same year, 1882, but at a time of great emotional tension for Conan Doyle. In the early part of that year, following his return, in not altogether excellent health, from West Africa, he had had to decline the powerful backing of his influential London relatives in launching him as a *Roman Catholic* doctor, with a promised ready-made practice among his co-religionists in the English capital. Conan Doyle was of too independent a mind to accept the conditions under which the help was proffered, and, already unsure of his own status as a practising Catholic, refused to take up the offer, sadly disappointing his mother (the "Ma'am"), and broke for ever with these would-be helpers, to whom their religion represented a Truth not to be doubted or even, in the mildest degree, to be criticized. Now, with that final break, Conan Doyle was very much on his own: with a profession, to be sure, but with no practice.

By his own courageous show of independence, he had made his own future most bleak, indeed. At twenty-two years of age, a bleak future may look—and it must have so looked to young Dr. Conan Doyle—even bleaker.

Needs must when the Devil drives, and, though against the Ma'am's warnings and against his own judgment and, indeed, his own inclination, he felt compelled to accept get-rich-quick Dr. Budd's illusory offer of a "partnership" at Plymouth; a move made with misgivings which were to be far too quickly justified. Yet what is essential here to note is that Conan Doyle's joining Budd was not at all what it seemed then and for several years after —a mistake.

It was anything but a mistake, for, at Plymouth, when Doyle arrived there in the early part of 1882, the principal subject of conversation was still the triumph of Thomas Latimer, Devon's "Grand Old Man," in the preceding year. I shall demonstrate in the next chapter the proofs that Conan Doyle absorbed every item of information relative to the Galley case that he could lay hands on—a case in which the name of George Scherer was far and away the most prominent.

Names meant a great deal to Conan Doyle. He might have noticed them, on occasion, rather subconsciously than consciously: but once seen, they entered his mind permanently; and rarely did he fail to make use of them. (An example: the whaler *Hope* that Conan Doyle joined as ship's surgeon in February 1880 left *Peter*head for the Greenland waters. Of the two names—*Hope* and *Peter*—dormant in Conan Doyle's "name store," the first was used six years later [as that of the vengeful Jefferson Hope of *A Study in Scarlet*] and again in 1904 [as that of the Rt. Hon. Trelawney Hope in *The Second Stain*], whilst, though "Indian Pete" occurs early [in *A Study in Scarlet*], the full form "Peter" occurs first only as late as 1893 [as the name of *Peter* Steiler of *The Final Problem*], "Peter" being used again in 1903 [*The Solitary Cyclist*] and 1904 [*Black Peter*]. With "Peter" slightly altered to "Peters" and used as a surname–"Holy" Peters–the name is used in *The Disappearance of Lady Frances Carfax* [1911], thirty-one years after young Dr. Conan Doyle had shivered near "Greenland's icy mountains.")

Then, after having read all that he could find of the Galley case, including the name-suppressed reference in Serjeant Ballantine's memoirs, which appeared in that same year of 1882, Conan Doyle, having left Budd and set up in practice on his own at Southsea,[7] once more encountered the already impressive name "Scherer"–this time as the "hero" of the St. Luke's Mystery.

Thus the shared name and the two different characters of the two Scherers–different, yet with a master quality in common–went, with all their potentialities, into the fashioning of Sherlock Holmes. As Conan Doyle went slowly but surely about the perfecting of his super-sleuth, the name "Scherer" was not only engraved on his consciousness but, one may well say, deep-etched.

In one of his writings, Aldous Huxley refers to what he felicitously calls "Adrenalin Addicts"–persons who know a subconscious need to keep that powerful gland-produced drug "hopping them up" and who meet that need by a continuous resort to emotional tension. They need to, and they can always, find the effective stimuli–sometimes in domestic "scenes" but as often outside the house–in finding objects to arouse their indignation. In the sense that he was always on the lookout for social irregularities to be

[7]A suburb of the naval base of Portsmouth, Southsea, separated from Portsmouth by a narrow stretch of water, stands on *Hayling* Island –hence the name that Conan Doyle gave to Jeremiah *Hayling* in the adventure of *The Engineer's Thumb*.

corrected through some more-or-less violent action on his part, we may certainly (and in no denigrating fashion) include Arthur Conan Doyle amongst the Adrenalin Addicts.

All his life, he was to survey the social economy and let his easily-moved indignation be aroused–and the objects of his many crusades are so varied that we may be sure that it was in response to a single emotional stimulus that he reacted, in an unvarying manner, to so many different injustices. I have read, far too often, the facile and unthinking description of Sir Arthur as a "many-faceted man," or terms of similar meaning, simply because the biographer was deceived into thinking that, because the objects of Sir Arthur's compassion have been of so striking a diversity, his emotional impulse was not the single thing that it was, but was as multiplex as the causes that he took up, the persons whose causes he made his own.

This is fallacious reasoning; one might as well deny a single all-dominant craving to the bibliophile because the books that he desires and secures for his own pleasure are so diverse in subject; to the numismatist or philatelist, because each collects his stamps or coins from all countries and from all periods; to the sensualist, because the women whom he (successfully or not) pursues display every conceivable variation of face, form, colouring, character, and personality: to him they are all equally desirable. With a passion not dissimilar in its single-mindedness, only in its object–the correcting of error, with the concomitant gaining of justice–Conan Doyle threw himself into every cause that he thought worthy; all, of course, having the aim in common of helping the helpless.

The results of this single-minded ambition were various, indeed: it would be impossible for me to list, even with no more than a line of description, all the causes that Conan Doyle made his own.

Here, though, is a handful of the more representative cases of Doyle's high-minded self-involvement in other people's affairs: involvements, most of which, in the remembered and always admired tradition of Sir Alexander Cockburn's and Thomas Latimer's strategy of arousing public opinion by inflammatory pamphlets, were always accompanied by Conan Doyle's printed arguments–paperbound books or book-length articles in the national press.

He set out to clear the name of an unjustly-convicted Parsee solicitor, George Edalji, accused of cattle-maiming (shades of *Silver Blaze!*); in typical Cockburn–Latimer fashion, Doyle gave his arguments in Edalji's defense the widest possible publicity in an eighteen-thousand-word statement in the (London) *Daily Telegraph*–just as he set out to reverse the conviction of murder of Oscar Slater with arguments put forth in the 1912 pamphlet *The Case of Oscar Slater*. To safeguard the disgracefully neglected health of the British soldiers in South Africa, dying in the tens of thousands of the enteric and typhoid fevers originating in horribly insanitary conditions, he accepted the direction and control of the big military hospital organized and paid for by his friend John Langman and went *to the front* with it. He defended, in print, the attack, by the anti-Boer War Liberals on the misconduct of the campaign by military inefficiency, but hotly rejected the charge that the "forgotten" orderlies were in any way responsible for the appalling conditions in the British military hospitals, as he no less indignantly rejected the "lies" about the alleged barbarities inflicted by the British on Boer soldiers, their women, and–particularly–their little children. His explanatory account of the ill-judged and ill-handled war, *The War in South Africa: Its Cause and Conduct,* sold three hundred thousand copies at sixpence (12¢) in six weeks; an additional fifty thousand going to the United States and Canada.

No injustice–no mere irregularity–escaped his interest; nor was any worthy case judged by him unimportant. A young nurse on the staff of the North-Western Hospital, in Hampstead, London, wrote to Conan Doyle in her distress. "I am writing to you," Miss Joan Paynter beseeched, "as I can think of no-one else who could help me. I cannot afford to employ a detective myself, as I have not the money, neither can my people, for the same reason. About 5 weeks ago, I met a man, a Dane. We became engaged..."

The Dane had given Miss Paynter many presents; had persuaded her to resign from her job at the hospital; and then... vanished. The Dane had not seduced Miss Paynter, nor even attempted to do so; he had simply disappeared, and neither Scotland Yard nor the Danish police had been able to trace him.

But Conan Doyle traced him...and explained to the jilted girl that she should forget the Dane and return to her admirable vocation of nursing the sick. (I think that Conan Doyle must have had Florence Nightingale–then still living–in mind when he set out for South Africa to do for the British soldiers there what Miss Nightingale had set out to do for the British soldiers in hospital in Turkey, fifty years earlier; and I am sure that he had the revered Miss Nightingale in mind when he counselled Miss Paynter to resume her noble occupation . . .)

I once heard an admirer of Conan Doyle refer to this aiding of the impecunious young hospital nurse in these terms: "He'd help anyone who needed helping, even a nobody . . ." But here was mistaken fact: Miss Paynter (for it was she whom we were discussing) was not a "nobody"; her appeal provided Conan Doyle with yet more of that essential pabulum on which his emotional life depended for sustenance. To quote what Bardolph said in quite another connection, hers, and all the other cases calling for Conan Doyle's helpful attention, were "the fuel that fed those flames" of his necessary emotional warmth.

All this has been told before–how, when the organizers of the fight between Jim Jeffries and the Negro challenger, Jack Johnson, for the heavyweight championship of the world were seeking for a referee whose impartiality could be trusted to pour oil on the possible tempest of aroused racial prejudice, their choice fell at once on Conan Doyle, as an obviously impartial foreigner whose fame and popularity had earned him the confidence of all. He did not go, but that he had been the unanimous choice of all concerned shows well the world standing he had achieved at the time of the fight.

And told, too, how Conan Doyle, again with a many-paged pamphlet, *The Crime of the Congo,* set out to champion the maltreated slaves of King Leopold's vast African estate, and succeeded in his purpose. How Conan Doyle, himself a happily-married man, had joined and led the Divorce Law Reform Society to help the unhappily-married. How he had invented body armour for the fighting British infantryman and had pestered the War Office to adopt it . . .

Of course, this has all been told before, but it has not always, if at all, been correctly interpreted. And this brings us back to the subject of this book: Sherlock Holmes.

Over a period of many years, in lecture-halls, at anniversary dinners, in smaller but more intimate Sherlockian gatherings, at private luncheons and dinners in the company of my fellow-Conanicals, I have been asked the important question: "Mr. Harrison, how do you account for the world-wide and continuing success of the Sherlock Holmes stories? How do you account for the tremendous appeal of Sherlock Holmes as a character . . . ?"

I have given that question a great deal of thought; and though, even now, I may at best hazard an answer, I do think that I know why it took me so long to come up with an answer as satisfactory to myself as to any of my many questioners. The answer, in my opinion, is that the appeal–the appeal which accounts for that "world-wide and continuing success"–comes, not, as we have all assumed, from the stories; not even from any admiration that we may feel for Holmes's detectival powers (for, to be completely honest, Conan Doyle, especially in his later years, was a far better detective than Holmes ever was); but, and I maintain solely, from the admiration that we feel *for Holmes himself.* As what, then, if not for Holmes the detective, as Holmes the super-sleuth?

What appeals irresistibly to all of us who have fallen under the spell of *Sherlockismus* is that synthesis of qualities which represent, not at all any Walter Mitty-like daydreams, but the firmly envisaged ambitions, the hoped-for self-realizations, of Conan Doyle. I have known many a successful author of tales in which the hero is an incredible Superman; Holmes may be a Superman, but he is not incredible, and Conan Doyle is, without doubt, unique among all the authors of the world in that he drew up, in the fullest detail, the pattern of the man that he actually succeeded in making himself. Holmes is not, as has been unrealistically said, "a glorified Conan Doyle": rather, Holmes is what Conan Doyle set out to become, and succeeded.

The indignation with which Conan Doyle read what Officialdom had done to Galley, to save its contemptible Civil Service "face"; the admiration with which he read how Scherer, Latimer, and their associates had refused to take Officialdom's *No!* for an answer: these, principally, are what have generated the most distinguishing characteristics of the Holmesian *persona*. Holmes, then, is–*and was intended to be, from his creation*–the perfected Conan Doyle, and, since "perfection" is all the better, all the more acceptable, if it have a little element of human imperfection in it, so Conan Doyle has given Holmes, not only all the to-be-striven-for virtues, but also some faults, though the principal of these is presented to the reader symbolically.

Conan Doyle, as a fully-qualified medical practitioner even before he began work on the final draft of *A Study in Scarlet,* knew well the compulsions imposed on him by his "adrenalin addiction"; admitted honestly the chronic compulsion to act; recognized as honestly its cause. For Holmes's seven per cent. solution of cocaine, read Conan Doyle's adrenalin.

Otherwise, there is no symbolism: Holmes's dislike of, contempt for, Officialdom and its "running dogs" the Police; Holmes's nervous energy, always finding–or, at least, always on the look-out to find–work to effect the discharge of that energy: these are what Conan Doyle recognized in himself–these and many other qualities. And perhaps there *is* one more piece of not-altogether-charitable symbolism: in Conan Doyle's making of Dr. Watson an amiable simpleton. Here, I think, Conan Doyle, with a consciousness of guilt in that he had failed Medicine (and not the other way about), and had flown for rescue to Literature, was indicating, in a sour-grapes type of self-justification, that he had made the better choice–as Holmes was superior to his companion and butt, Dr. Watson.

So, if Holmes is merely the foreshadowing of what Conan Doyle wished–intended, nay, more, *determined*–to be: what is it in that composite Doyle–Holmes character which has attracted readers for almost a century? Or, to be more precise, who and what is this Holmes which attracts us?

It is not Holmes the Super-Sleuth–I don't think that anyone cares a damn for Holmes the Detective's "detection." What attracts is what Doyle planned him to be, and what Doyle planned himself to be: Holmes the Help of the Helpless, Holmes the Redresser of Wrongs, Holmes the Adjuster of Balances, Holmes–always and forever–the perfect Guardian of the Eternal Equipoise . . .

8

GALLEY: THE PROOF FROM NAME-USE

The little sister is one of the best of Raymond Chandler's detective novels. Its main character is the private eye Philip Marlowe, and its action revolves about, as it springs from, the murderous activities of the gangster Weepy Moyer. On one occasion, a female associate of Moyer telephones Marlowe, to hear the facetious acknowledgment of her call: "Utter McKinley Funeral Parlors."

Now, both "Moyer" and "Utter" are distinctly unusual names, and, if each occurs elsewhere, they are found together, as far as I know, only in an account of Wild Bill Hickok's last days at Deadwood City: one of Hickok's closest friends being the gambler Colorado Charlie *Utter*, and S. L. *Moyer* having been the one who introduced Hickok to his relative, Mrs. Agnes Lake, the circus equestrienne whom Hickok married.

We may therefore confidently conclude that Chandler found these names in the closest association in a detailed account of Hickok's death, and of the events leading up to his murder. And though William McKinley did not become President of the United States until twenty-four years after Hickok's death, Chandler must have noticed the association between the two men's mode of dying: both were assassinated.

The names that authors give to their characters—their fictional characters, to be precise—seldom come "out of the blue," though they may well have come out of the authors' collective subconscious. "Once seen, always remembered" would appear to be the general rule by which authors name their characters, but in this naming, personal impulses, personal tastes, personal naming-patterns, are always evident. All authors, in common with all other people who read, encounter hundreds, even thousands, of names as they go through life, and these names, consciously or subconsciously remembered, are gathered up and scattered by them throughout their writings.

Few authors employ names in contemporary use, such as are to be found in any telephone directory: this is too hazardous a practice, where "any living person" may well (and profitably to himself) identify himself with a person named in a book: the greatest hazard in authorship, the greatest hazard in publishing, as the many and expensive libel actions which have been heard in court or settled out of court confirm.

"Making up" names is an unsatisfactory solution to name-finding; for the name made up, however unusual, even improbably grotesque, *may* exist: Matthew Arnold cited, as an example of a decidedly coarse streak in the British character, its tolerance of ugly, even obscene, surnames. Most authors, "playing it safe," use the fairly safe method of using the common names–the Harry Browns, the Matthew Robinsons, the Mary Smiths–of the telephone directory's *multiple* columns. Conan Doyle, of all the authors whose naming-patterns I have studied, used remembered names *en bloc*. Not by any means used all at once, in the same novel or short story; but gathered up in one reading, as it were, and used throughout the remainder of his writing career. It is this habit of using–or, one may say, "using up"–a stock of names gathered from one source which enables us to say with confidence that Conan Doyle read, and was mightily impressed by, a certain newspaper report, just as the use of the names "Moyer" and "Utter" make it clear that Chandler had read, and been impressed by, the tale of Wild Bill Hickok. I shall now demonstrate that, in the short time that Conan Doyle was at Plymouth, getting his speedy disillusionment with Dr. Budd and all that Budd stood for, he heard, and read, all the facts of the Galley case of which he could find the record. And that Conan Doyle was fascinated by the tragedy of Galley, and even more so by the efforts of Scherer, Latimer, and others to secure the man's deserved acquittal, is apparent from a curious piece of evidence–evidence, I mean, that he had read the full account of the trial of Buckingham Joe and Galley in *The Exeter Flying Post* of Thursday, 4 August 1836. The evidence is this: above the crosshead in bold capitals–TRIAL OF THE MURDERERS OF MR. JONATHAN MAY–is the report of another case, in no way connected with that of Oliver and Galley. This was the trial, for attempted murder of her husband, of Elizabeth Bird, 30, arraigned on a charge of having administered to, or caused to be taken by, Daniel Bird, "a quantity of a certain deadly poison, called Sulphate of Copper, or Blue-stone."

I had never heard the term "blue-stone" before, nor, I feel, had the quite undomesticated Dr. Conan Doyle; nor again did his reading, in the account of Mrs. Bird's trial, that she had not bought the blue-stone in order to poison her husband (though the evidence called in her defense by Mr. Cockburn, the future Lord Chief Justice, made it clear that Bird had richly deserved an unpleasant death), but, as she explained, "had bought a penny-worth in Honiton, in order to use it in dyeing," make Dr. Doyle any the wiser. But the hitherto unencountered term "blue-stone" stuck in his mind, to emerge, ten years later, in 1892, as a *Strand* magazine short story concerning a blue stone: the Countess of Morcar's *The Blue Carbuncle.*

Sometimes, like the legendary toad in the rock, a name, even though first encountered in a most important context, would remain dormant–unused–for many years. Despite the unique importance of the Galley case in Conan Doyle's experience–it brought him the knowledge of George Scherer, a master element in the making of Sherlock Holmes–Conan Doyle did not use the name until 1910, twenty-eight years after he had first encountered it.[1]

---

[1] But, as an assiduous reader of the daily prints, and as a dedicated student of crime in all its forms, Conan Doyle cannot have missed encountering the name in 1896, when, on 4 July (Independence Day!), Elijah Galley was sentenced to twenty years' penal servitude for having killed Mr. and Mrs. Riley, "in a fit of passion," in North Street, Pentonville (where a great London prison is still situated). Note that the name, with the more usual spelling, of the *victims,* is used twice in the Canon, though both in *The Valley of Fear:* Reilly, a lawyer, and Reilly, a *killer.* It is typical of Conan Doyle's unusual mentality that he should bestow the

For this first and last time of the name's use, Conan Doyle gave it its literal significance in the title of one of his excellent stories about the passing of the Roman rule in Britain: "The Last Galley."

As was the case in Chandler's use of the names "Moyer" and "Utter," Conan Doyle's use of encountered and remembered names is, as the servants say, "promiscuous"–there seems to be no discernible relation between the character of the original owner of the name and the character of the fictional person to whom Conan Doyle gave that name. It is observable, however, that the reappearance of an encountered name tended to fix the name more firmly in Conan Doyle's memory (a phenomenon which, I imagine, applies to all of us?), and this use of a name doubly-impressed by a second encounter brings together the case of Galley (in 1882, so far as Conan Doyle was concerned) and the case of Mrs. Walter Carew, originally of the little seaside town of Bridport, in the county of Dorset, and on the border between that county and the county of Devon. (For the benefit of non-British readers, the well-known Devon name "Carew" is pronounced "Carey," as Conan Doyle spells it in *Black Peter:* this fact should be borne in mind.)

Now: first, the Galley case, in which Conan Doyle encountered the *very well-known* Devon name (no one living in Devon could have failed to know that the Carews were an ancient "county" family) in the person of John Carew, Acting Under-Sheriff of Devon.

Returning to Mrs. Walter Carew: she was twenty-one when she married thirty-five-year-old Walter in 1889. In 1896, after the Carews had lived for several years in Yokohama, to which city Carew's business interests had taken him, he fell ill of what the doctor diagnosed as disease of the liver–no uncommon complaint

---

name of the murdered on a murderer–not the only instance of this curious inversion, as I have pointed out.

He must have encountered the name again in 1903, with the case of the two "baby-farmers," Mrs. Amelia Sach, 29, and her dimwitted assistant, Mrs. Annie Walters (name used in *Wisteria Lodge,* 1908). Both women were charged with having murdered babies entrusted to their so-called "nursing-home," the *corpus delicti* being the alleged murder of the illegitimate newborn baby of a Miss *Galley*.

among the English expatriates of that day. Mrs. Carew not only made the mistake of buying arsenic and sugar of lead but made the even graver mistake of sending her children's governess, Miss *Jacobs,* to buy the arsenic and sugar of lead. It was, as the late Miss F. Tennyson Jesse observed,[2] the Maybrick case all over again: "Like Mr. Maybrick [whom Mrs. Maybrick was accused of poisoning], Mr. Carew apparently had been an arsenic-eater"—to which I may add that the case of the jilted Miss Joan Paynter bore some resemblance to the Sherlock Holmes story *A Case of Identity,* written by Conan Doyle five years before Mrs. Carew, of Bridport and Yokohama, was tried by the British Consular Court and sentenced to death.

Though (as we recognize now) patently innocent of her husband's murder, Mrs. Carew was, like Mrs. Maybrick, guilty of a grievous social crime, in that she had been conducting a sentimental love affair with a young Englishman, Dickinson, employed in a Yokohama bank. Mrs. Carew's defense involved a curious and—for almost everybody—unbelievable "story of a mysterious veiled woman, calling herself Annie *Luke,* a former mistress of her husband's, who had called at the house, and had sent letters declaring that she had revenged herself upon him."

This is no digression: I have told briefly the facts behind the Carew death (it obviously was not murder, save that it might have been self-murder) to call the reader's attention to a typical example of Conan Doyle's reaction to already-encountered names.

1. He remembered CAREW (Carey) from the Galley case.
2. He remembered LUKE from the St. Luke's Mystery

—and used the first in *Black Peter* (1905); the second in *The Three Students,* published in the same year, in which St. Luke's College is mentioned. As for Mrs. Carew's children's governess, Miss JACOBS, Conan Doyle had certainly encountered this name before, from the Galley case, in which the murder took place at JACOB'S WELL (all the witnesses to the finding of the murdered man's body mentioned Jacob's Well).

A problem now makes itself apparent: it is clear that a double encounter with any name fixed that name more firmly in Conan

---

[2]Miss F. Tennyson Jesse, *Murder and Its Motives* (London: George G. Harrap & Co., Ltd.), 1924.

Doyle's memory; but *why* did he often feel compelled to use any name more than once? (He uses the name of Ralph SANDERS, County Clerk at Galley's trial, no fewer than four times, all–fictionally–borne by persons of greatly varying social degree, to say nothing of sex: Ikey Sanders; Saunders, a maid; Sir James Saunders; Mrs. Saunders, a housekeeper.[3])

Now, when Conan Doyle came to write *The Valley of Fear*, for publication in 1915, he once again felt compelled to use a name from the Galley trial that he had already used: *Jacobs*, who is a secretary in the 1905 story *The Second Stain*. "Jacobs" is obviously merely a cut-down version of JACOB'S WELL, just as Steve DIXIE *(The Three Gables)*, Jeremy DIXON *(The Missing Three-Quarter)*, and Mrs. DIXON, yet another housekeeper *(The Solitary Cyclist)*, all echo the name of Mrs. Carew's Yokohama lover, in their cut-down versions of Mr. Dickinson's name.

But to return to the need, ten years after he had used the name *Jacobs* in *The Second Stain*, Conan Doyle felt that curious compulsion to use the name again; but now he decided to use a variant.

In colloquial English usage, the words "well" and "shaft" are considered to be synonymous; and, indeed, as I checked in my old *Nuttall's Standard Pronouncing Dictionary* of 1873, the words were considered synonymous in something more than merely colloquial employment, as the following definitions plainly show:

SHAFT, *shäft*, s. An arrow; a missile weapon. – In *mining*, a deep entrance into a mine. *(Etc.)*

WELL, *wel*, s. A spring; a fountain; a pit, or cylindrical hole, sunk perpendicularly into the earth to reach a supply of water. . . . In *mining* and the *mil.* art, a hole or excavation in the earth . . .

Thus we see that Conan Doyle and his contemporaries had even standard dictionary authority for equating, semantically, "well" and "shaft."

So, to vary the name "Jacobs," itself a contraction of JACOB'S WELL, Conan Doyle replaced the "Well" of "Jacob's Well" by

---

[3]In polite English society, the names "Sanders" and "Saunders" have, despite the slight difference in spelling, identical pronunciation.

the synonymous "Shaft," and devised, for *The Valley of Fear*, the second variant on JACOB'S WELL – JACOB SHAFTER.

I have pointed out that Conan Doyle did not use the name *Galley* until 1910, thirty years after he had first encountered it, and then disguising the allusion to Edmund Galley by using his surname as a common, and not a proper, noun: "The Last Galley."

But that Galley's rejected evidence had been read by Conan Doyle in the newspaper accounts of Galley's trial is certain from Doyle's use of the many names there–the same or only slightly altered–but also in his use of the names of places either mentioned in Galley's evidence or known to Conan Doyle as typically Devonian. Galley, in his attempt to establish an alibi, said that "on the day this murder was committed, he was at Dartford,[4] where he remained till the 18th. He then went to Ryegate [*old spelling*] races." This part of Galley's evidence is remembered in the title of the June 1893 story *The Reigate Squires,* though the American title of the story, *The Reigate Puzzle,* recalls more accurately Galley's despairing plea to establish an alibi; it was, indeed, a puzzle for poor Galley: how he was to convince the court of his having been at "Ryegate" races when he was reputed to have been busy murdering Jonathan May.

I cannot account for Conan Doyle's having postponed his using the actual name of "Galley" until nearly thirty years had passed since Galley's belated vindication; but I would say that both Galley's name and the familiar name of Mrs. Bird's sulphate of copper–"blue-stone"–appear together in the story that Doyle (still at Plymouth) sold to *London Society* in 1882: "The Gully of Bluemansdyke." The slight change of "Galley" to "Gully" may be explained by the fascination that criminal medicos had for Conan Doyle: Dr. *Gully* had made himself notorious in the still

---

[4] It has occurred to me that Galley's troubles began just as he was about to be released from detention as a vagrant in Coldbath Fields Prison, not merely when, not suspecting a trap, Galley admitted to Sergeant Thomas McGill that he was sometimes nicknamed "Turpin," but when, in his ignorance and eagerness to find a "wanted" man, the Sergeant confused Dartford, in Kent, with Dartmouth, in Devon, a mere twenty-six miles south of Exeter.

vividly remembered Bravo case. Conan Doyle liked, not so much puns, as rather juvenile "hidden meanings"–what today are called "in" jokes–that he secured by the alteration of spelling or by the use of some word synonymous with the word to be hidden.

Typical of the more catachrestic of these verbal transformations is the manner in which "Amberley" has developed into "Bernstone."

Amberley is a village in Sussex, once the seat of a bishop; it provided the secondary peerage, Viscount Amberley, for the detested–by Conan Doyle, that is–Lord John Russell, on his being raised to the Lords. Conan Doyle uses the names Josiah and Mrs. Amberl(e)y in *The Retired Colourman*. "Amberley" is less instantly perceptible in "Bernstone" (*The Sign of the Four*); yet it is there–and this is how the former became the latter.

"Amber" in German–and Doyle was at school in Austria–is *Bernstein*. Englishing the "-stein" into "-stone" (for, as I shall explain below, Doyle seemed to have an obsession with not only the word "stone" but more, with the very idea of "stone"), he gets "Bernstone" from "Amberley."

As late as 1924, the acid memory of Lord Amberley was still vivid: "Lamberley," in *The Sussex Vampire*, is only a variant of "Amberley," as is "Maberley" in *The Three Gables* (1926).

Again and again, in his Sherlockian and other writings, the word "stone," either by itself or with prefix or suffix, perpetuates the memory of Mrs. Bird's "blue-stone." We have seen how an echo of that poisonous substance recurs both in *Blue*mansdyke and in *The Blue Carbuncle*–literally a blue stone–but observe Conan Doyle's apparent fascination (perhaps "obsession" would not be too forceful a word) by the word "stone" or its semantic equivalents. Carefully note the following:

1. Johnny Hones (*A Study in Scarlet,* 1887). *Nuttall's* 1873 dictionary defines: "HONE, A stone of a fine grit, used for sharpening instruments."

2. *Micah Clarke*[5] (novel, 1888). *Nuttall's:* "MICA-SCHIST, A schistose rock . . ."

---

[5] Of course, I am as aware as was Conan Doyle that Micah was a Hebrew prophet; but the semantic connection (and similarity of sound)

3. Captain Arthur and Mary Morstan (*The Sign of the Four,* 1890). "Morstan" is the phonetically spelt MOORSTONE, defined by *Nuttall's* as: "A species of granite, found in Cornwall and other parts of England."

4. Mrs. Bernstone (*The Sign of the Four,* 1890).

5. *The Firm of Girdlestone* (novel, 1890)

6. Wilhelm Gottsreich von Ormstein (*A Scandal in Bohemia,* 1892). (Note that he was "Grand Duke of Cassell-Fal*stein*.")

7. Helen and Julia Stoner (*The Speckled Band,* 1892). *Nuttall's:* "STONER, One who beats or kills with stones."

8. Hurlstone Manor (*The Musgrave Ritual,* 1893).

9. *Rodney Stone* (novel, 1894).

10. Patrick Cairns (*Black Peter,* 1904). *Nuttall's:* "CAIRN, A name given to rounded or conical heaps of stones . . ."

11. Hugo Oberstein (*The Second Stain,* 1905). German: *Stein,* "stone, rock."

12. Slater, a *stone*-mason (*Black Peter,* 1904).

13. Reverend Joshua Stone (*Wisteria Lodge,* 1908).

14. Mason, a plate-layer (*The Bruce-Partington Plans,* 1908).

15. White Mason (*The Valley of Fear,* 1915).

16. Birlstone Manor (*The Valley of Fear,* 1915).

17. Steiner (*His Last Bow,* 1917). German: *steinern,* "stony."

18. Mrs. Mason, a nurse (*The Sussex Vampire,* 1924).

19. John Mason (*Shoscombe Old Place,* 1927).

Petra is both Latin and Greek for "stone, rock," but even those who have not had the benefit of a Classical education, but who have been exposed to the basic instruction of a Christian upbringing, are aware of the semantic connection between the name "Peter" and the word "rock." The connection is made in *Matthew* XVI:18, where Christ says to Simon Peter: "And I say also unto thee, That thou art *Peter,* and upon this *rock* I will build my church . . ." As a pupil in a Jesuit school in mid-Victorian times, Conan Doyle, as I shall point out, was made completely familiar with his Holy Bible, in both the Old and New Testaments. And, taught both Latin and Greek at Stonyhurst, he was certainly in no doubt that the familiar name "Peter" was derived, through the Greek Testament, from the word *petra.* Why this equivalence should have impressed itself so strongly on Doyle's youthful mind, I cannot say—possibly, though, because youthful attention in Divinity classes is called to the fact of the pun on "Peter" and

---

between "Micah" and "mica" must have proved irresistible to punning Victorian schoolboys.

"rock"–much more apparent in the original Greek–is the only one in Holy Writ. But whatever the reason, the young Conan Doyle had the name "Peter" and its equivalents fixed so firmly in his mind that the consciousness of this name never left it. And because "Peter" does mean "rock, stone," then "Peter" and its recognizable variants will be seen to take their place among the "Stone" names, as thus:

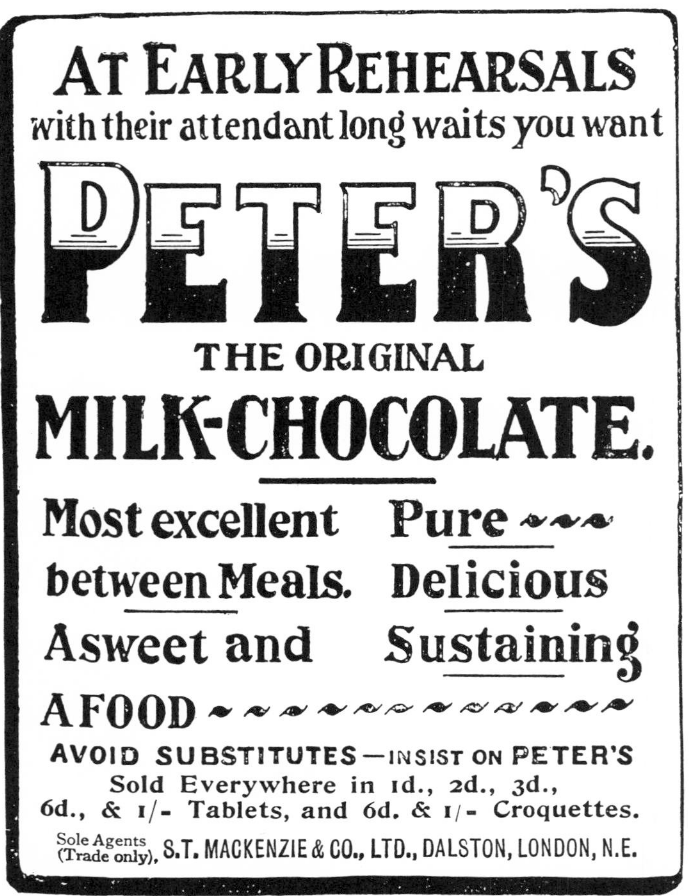

Was this, perhaps, the origin of Doyle's obsession with the name "Peter"? Victorian advertisement for Peter's Chocolate, then the most popular in Britain, especially with schoolboys, to whom the price of one penny a wrapped bar seemed as attractive as the chocolate itself.

20. Indian Pete (*A Study in Scarlet,* 1887).
21. Peter Jones (*The Red-Headed League,* 1891).
22. Petrarch[6] (pocket edition of) (*The Boscombe Valley Mystery,* 1891).
23. Peterson, commissionaire (*The Blue Carbuncle,* 1892).
24. Peter Steiler (*The Final Problem,* 1893).
25. Peter (*The Solitary Cyclist,* 1903).
26. Peter Carey (*Black Peter,* 1904) (note also that "Black Peter" seems to be a play upon "blue-stone": *Blue/Black–Stone/Peter*).[7]
27. Pietro Venucci (*The Six Napoleons,* 1904).
28. "The Tiger of San Pedro" (original *Collier's Weekly* title of *Wisteria Lodge,* 1908).
29. "Holy Peters" (*The Disappearance of Lady Frances Carfax,* 1911).
30. Simon Bird (*The Valley of Fear,* 1915) (there are two "lapidary" allusions here: "Simon" was St. *Peter's* other name, and Mrs. *Bird* was the innocent defendant in the Exeter "blue-stone" case).

We may *possibly* be justified in adding to the list the name:

31. Kratides (Paul and Sophy) (*The Greek Interpreter,* 1893).

The name–but especially Conan Doyle's reasons for choosing *(and inventing)* it–is, I feel, here well worth our examining.

Krates, in Greek, means, literally, "strength, might," and by

---

[6]The name of the great Italian poet means–if interpreted as coming from the Greek–literally "Lord of the Stone"–the exact semantic equivalent of the apparently Doyle-coined name for his spy: "Oberstein." But here, the name "Petrarch" must owe its inspiration less to the Italian poet than to the great scandal attaching to the swindling Lord Dupplin's scratching of his horse *Petrarch* from the Derby runners of 1876.

[7]But, concealed here (from us now, but not from the Victorians) is yet another pun, based on the enamelled showcard displayed everywhere in Britain: the showcard for "Stephens' Blue-Black Ink." No one travelling by rail in the Britain of the 'eighties and 'nineties could have failed to see and remember the advertisement for Stephens' Ink–perhaps (I say this as an experienced advertising man) one of the most effective advertisements ever designed. It should not be forgotten that in Britain, when men–especially footballers, and especially rugger players–foregather to drink, a coarse song is often heard; a song concerning the accidental begetting of a "blue-black child"–"They called the bastard Stephen."

extension, "rule, sway, sovereignty, master over, power," etc. But there is another word, undoubtedly derived from *kratos–krataiïs*–which occurs in *The Odyssey* (and there only) as the term for the *stone* of Sisyphus, when, as the Lexicon says, he had rolled it up the hill.

Krater was the large bowl in which the wine for the meal was mixed with water; but *krater* also means, by analogy, a basin in a *rock*–so that here again we meet the Doyle obsession with the notion of rock or stone.

Further, there is yet another word derived from *kratos: krataileōs,* defined by the Lexicon as "of hard stones, rocky."

I suggest, then, that we may confidently add the name *Kratides* to the list of "stone" or "stone-associated" names. May we add even "Muller" (*A Study in Scarlet*): "a hand-held *stone* for grinding colours" (*Nuttall's*)?

Thirty sure and two almost certain "lapidary" references!

So frequent a use of the "stone" theme in the Canon alone must rule out any suggestion of accidental use–though, of course, it does not rule out the theory that Conan Doyle's use of the stone-theme may have been completely subconscious. The fact is that he must have had an obsession with the idea of stones; and that this obsession is plainly demonstrated in his choice of names.

It would take a far better psychologist than I even to attempt an explanation–a fully acceptable explanation, that is to say–of this curious fascination, though I am about to suggest where the answer *might* be found.

Certainly the explanation will not be forthcoming in my pointing out that, both in Scotland and in Cornwall and Devon (especially, as regards the latter two, all over Dartmoor), Conan Doyle saw *cairns* by the dozen. For it was precisely because of his already fully-developed lithophilia[8] that he noticed and remembered the cairns of the North and West.

Why did the idea of *stone* so fascinate him?

May I tentatively advance the theory that the origin of this

---

[8]Lithophilia: a morbid love of stones. I have coined this word on regular principles, since it fills–at least in this context–an obvious need.

Arthur Conan Doyle's public school: Stonyhurst College, Lancashire, as it was when Doyle was a pupil there. The Jesuit masters gave him the best of educations, but it is now impossible to assert that, at Stonyhurst, Doyle spent "the happiest years of his life." *Contemporary engraving: courtesy of the Reverend Father F. J. Turner, Librarian, Stonyhurst College.*

enduring obsession–Conan Doyle was using "stone-names" over the extensive period of forty years–is to be found in the name of his unloved (even if not actually hated) school, *Stony*hurst–literally, "The Grove of Stones." That school, from the unwelcome religious influences of which Conan Doyle strove so desperately to free himself in the years which followed . . .

Nor, in advancing this theory–albeit tentatively–have I done here with Stonyhurst and its influence, as we shall see.

I trust that, when I shall have come to the end of this book, I shall have made it clear to the reader that much–perhaps even all–of the "suppressed" Conan Doyle may be revealed in a careful study and analysis of his choice of names, with, to be hoped, the deep-seated reasons for his choice.

Readers of the Canon will not have failed to notice the modest–mock-modest?–manner in which Conan Doyle's creation disclaims a close acquaintance with Holy Writ: "My Biblical knowledge is a trifle rusty . . ." It is, however, quite adequate to provide him with the exact historical precedent for Colonel Barclay's betrayal of Henry Wood in King David's lethal betrayal of Uriah the Hittite. I think, though, that the late D. Martin Dakin is guilty of exaggeration when he writes:

> We are told that Mrs. Barclay was a member of the Roman Catholic Church. She must also have been an accomplished Biblical scholar, to be so familiar with the details of King David's affair with Bathsheba as to have his name occur to her instantly as a term of reproach for her erring husband. It seems almost too recondite to come naturally to an angry woman, especially as the parallel, although close, is not quite exact . . . Holmes's own knowledge of the story shows that his Biblical scholarship, in spite of his disclaimer, was well above that of the average man.

Alas! a claim to "Biblical scholarship" would hardly be supported by a familiarity with the story of David and Bathsheba, which for long has been part of that corpus of familiar knowledge in which one may encounter the story of Pope Gregory and the Saxon slave ("Non Angli, sed angeli. . ."), of King Alfred and the burnt cakes, of King Henry and the White Ship ("He never smiled again"), of King Robert Bruce and the try-again spider, of Washington and the cherry tree, of the Boy Who Stood on the Burning Deck. . . and of so many others, all more familiar to the generality through oral tradition than from any great familiarity with the history books.

Whether or not we may accept Holmes's "Biblical scholarship" as established, there is no doubt of Conan Doyle's familiarity with the Bible–and especially with the Old Testament, rather than the New. Though Holmes quotes Shakespeare and others not quite accurately, we may overlook his misquoting *Matthew* VI:34 and Mistress Quickly in *King Henry V*, since misquotations are most often facetiously deliberate. However, apart from two misspellings–they can be no more than slips (and one is outside the Canon)–the fact that Conan Doyle uses no fewer than twenty-three Old Testament names for his characters throughout the Canon argues strongly an unsuppressed (indeed, one would say, unsuppressible) interest in Holy Writ not at all in keeping with that modest, "My Biblical knowledge is a trifle rusty . . ."

Here is the list–almost as long as that giving the "stone" names; but still impressively long for all that:

Abel
Elias
Enoch
Ezekiah
Heber
Hebron
Jabez
Jacob
Jephro (*sic;* but should be "Jethro")
Jeremiah
Jonas
Jonathan
Joshua
Josiah
Michael
Mordecai
Nathan
Rachel
Reuben
Samuel (as "Sam")
Sarah

and two extra-Canonical Biblical names:

Habakuk (*sic;* should be Habbakkuk)
Micah

Conan Doyle must not only have read his Bible with the deepest attention; it must have had a significance for him that I cannot hope to discover here. I may only note the fact, and leave the conclusions to others.

The case of Mrs. Bird and her blue-stone—but let us not overlook the important point that it prefaced, in the newspaper, Galley's trial—most certainly made the strongest impression upon Conan Doyle, who must have seen in the unjustly-charged woman yet another victim of legal irregularity.

It is interesting, and it may be psychologically significant, that though Conan Doyle never uses the term "blue-stone" unaltered, he gives Mrs. Bird's surname without change. Edwards, of *The Valley of Fear,* bears the same name as a familiar nickname; the association of "Birdy" and "Edwards" I shall explain in a note in Appendix III, explaining the use by Conan Doyle of names taken from various edible substances, or their manufacturers, still familiar to most British households. However, one striking instance, intimately connected with the Galley case, should be noted. To the British ear, certain double names, especially those of firms in profitable business, are so familiar that to say the first name is inevitably to provide that name with its complement: Dickins and Jones, Debenham and Freebody (Major Freebody is included in the *dramatis personae* of *The Five Orange Pips,* 1891), Marshall and Snelgrove, Swan and Edgar, and so on. These are the names of firms selling female apparel; others, equally familiar to any British household, sell food: McVitie and Price, Huntley and Palmer (both biscuits), Lea and Perrins (Worcestershire sauce); silverware, plated cutlery, and clocks from Mappin and Webb–and, perhaps most familiar of all: Crosse and Blackwell, still flourishing as "Preserved Provision Manufacturers." It would have been as impossible for the average Briton over the past century to hear or think of "Crosse" without adding, in his or her mind: ". . . and Blackwell." Conan Doyle does not use the name "Crosse," that of Assheton Cross, last-but-one and, next to Lord John Russell, most malignantly obstinate of all those who willingly denied mercy to Galley. But Doyle, in suppressing the "Crosse," does add ". . . and Blackwell"–for it is Lady Eva *Blackwell* who is being blackmailed by Charles Augustus Milverton, described by Holmes as "the worst man in London," a term that, one cannot help feeling, young Dr. Conan Doyle might have felt justified in applying, not to the fictional Charles Augustus Milverton, but rather to the real-life Richard Assheton Cross . . .

A study of the names used by Conan Doyle–better still, an imaginative analysis of the various sources of those names–ought, from the extent to which Conan Doyle extracts and uses the names from one particular set of facts, to afford us an *exact* measure of the importance that Conan Doyle attached to that particular set of facts. By this standard, the Galley case may be shown to have far exceeded in importance, and thus, for Conan Doyle, interest, even the two tragedies which (from his lavish use of the names associated with them), so fascinated him: the

Dr. Palmer-the-poisoner case, and the Mrs. Maybrick-like folly of Mrs. Carew.

By the name-use standard alone, the Galley case is unique in the attention that Conan Doyle gave to it, and one not only finds names extracted from the newspaper accounts of the Galley trial but also from those other cases (unconnected with either Oliver or Gàlley) to which Conan Doyle, having read the details of Galley's ordeal, turned to study in the large pages of *The Exeter Flying Post*.

Conan Doyle's obsession with names sometimes takes some curious forms–he will give the name of some inanimate object or of a place-name to a living person, and give the name of a living person to some inanimate object or place. "Jacob's Well," which had become a mere district-name by 1836, becomes the names of two persons: Jacobs and Jacob Shafter; whilst, conversely, the name of the murdered Jonathan May and of his witness nephew Walter is used to provide half a name for the steam packet *May Day,* on which James Browner (of *The Cardboard Box*) served as a steward (but then, "May" was also used to provide half a name for Lady Maynooth of *The Empty House*).

But of all the names encountered by Doyle in the accounts of the Galley trial, that of the town of Moreton held the greatest interest. Employing it as a personal surname, with a slight change of spelling but with none of pronunciation ("Moreton" to "Morton"), there are no fewer than five mentions of the name, covering ten years of Doyle's literary work, from the first mention, in 1903, in the adventure of *The Solitary Cyclist,* to the fifth, in 1913, in *The Dying Detective.* As mentioned in the evidence, the town of Moreton is often called by its longer (and more precise) name: Moretonhampstead. The "suffix," transferred by Conan Doyle to the Hampstead district in London, is mentioned in no fewer than three other stories. Thus eight mentions of Moreton (or Moretonhampstead) in all!

What I have not yet discovered, and what, in all probability–now that Conan Doyle is no longer with us–I shall never discover, is the principle (if there was a principle) on which he bestowed those names which had caught his attention. For there are some pretty problems involved here. For instance, how may we interpret Conan Doyle's use of the name *Latimer;* that, in real life, of the veriest hero of the pro-Galley crusade; that of Devon's most respected, most praised, most fêted son: "The Cobbett of the West"? To whom–to which of his characters, rather–does Conan Doyle assign the name Latimer? Why, to Harold Latimer, kidnapper and murderer of Paul Kratides, and close associate of Wilson Kemp, "a man of the foulest antecedents." And the other Canonical character to whom Conan Doyle gives the name *Latimer?*–why, a mere hotel menial: the boots in *The Disappearance of Lady Frances Carfax!*

The rule, of course, as with any other rule, may be reversed. On the page of the newspaper which reports the end of the Oliver–Galley trial, there is brief mention of a Charles Bradley, 39, who, though acquitted ("No Bill"), had been pulled in "on suspicion." Conan Doyle bestows his surname on a tobacconist in *The Hound of the Baskervilles*. And, again from the same page, a report of an action at law, brought by Sir Ralph Lopes, Baronet, against George Stone Baron, "gentleman," initiated the following distribution of the names involved:

Sir Ralph Lopes, Bart	1. *Ralph* Smith, died penniless in South Africa (*The Solitary Cyclist*, 1903)
	2. *Lopez*, a murderer (*Wisteria Lodge*, 1908)
George Stone Baron	1. *George* Tregennis–with sister Brenda and brother Owen, were victims of the Cornish Horror: "George and Owen were . . . gibbering like two great apes" (*The Devil's Foot*, 1910)
	2. The Reverend Joshua *Stone* (*Wisteria Lodge*, 1908)
	3. *Baron* Dowson, hanged for murder (*The Mazarin Stone*, 1921)
	4. *Baron* Maupertuis (*The Reigate Squires*, 1893)

And one more example of the curious in Conan Doyle's character-naming: Elizabeth Harris, who (perhaps understandably) perjured herself to escape seven years' transportation, was referred to, at various times during the Oliver–Galley trial, as the "paramour" of

George Avery–and sure enough, Conan Doyle converted this moderately derogatory term for a light-o'-love into a proper name: Paramore *(The Five Orange Pips)*.

In Appendix II, I have shown the results of a careful statistical analysis of the names found in the report of the Oliver–Galley trial, and, separately, of the names appearing elsewhere in the newspaper of the same date. I have decided that these two complementary analyses may be more conveniently set out as an Appendix than here introduced into the body of the text.

A word of explanation: since Conan Doyle was more inclined to use a name that he had encountered more than once, rather than one derived from a "singleton" encounter, the same name may appear in each of the two analyses. Thus, *Harriet Langbridge* (from the Galley trial) and *Harriet Stacey* (who got three months' "hard" for having been mixed up in a burglary with four men, all transported for life, at Witheridge) may each be considered as having individually given her name to the "name stock"; in combination, the two women strengthened the "memorability" of that shared name, so that Conan Doyle used it later–as the Christian name of Hatty (Harriet) Doran.

Now, let us examine the percentages of use.

THE OLIVER-GALLEY TRIAL

Surnames in report (or names of places)		*Christian names in report (where given)*	
Total: 64	%	Total: 52	%
Number used (exact names): 15	23.43	Number used (exact names): 18	34.61
Number of times used in Canon: 37	57.81	Number of times used in Canon: 93	178.77
Near or echoing surnames			
Total (from main name-total of 64)	26.55		

Sum of exact surnames and echoing names: 49.98 of a total of 64 trial names

A word, not so much of explanation, as of reminder, here: when I allude to "near-to" or "echoing" surnames, I have in mind slight changes in an original trial-name of this type:

Original trial-name:	*Changed or modified to:*	
George AVERY	AVELING	PRIO[9]
"BLACK Ann"	BLACK PETER	BLAC
"BLACK SOPH and her man"	BLACK JACK of Ballarat	BOSC
	SOPHY Kratides	GREE
Samuel CANN	Sam BREWER	SHOS
(draught beer was delivered to private houses in cans)		
John CAREW	Capt. Peter CAREY	BLAC
	(same pronunciation)	
Anne CARPENTER	Alice CHARPENTIER	STUD
Richard Assheton CROSS	(Crosse &) BLACKWELL	CHAS
Edward GIBBONS	Neil GIBSON	THOR
Mr. HORN	John HORNER	BLUE
Jonathan MAY	Lady MAYNOOTH	EMPT
(as one educated in a Roman Catholic school, the Seminary of MAYNOOTH, Kildare, Ireland, would be well known to Doyle)		
Grace & Nicholas TAVERNER	TAVERNIER (waxman)	MAZA
Grace TAVERNer	Grace DunBAR	THOR
(note the semantic association of TAVERN with BAR)		

Many more examples of this typically Doyleian word-changing will be seen in the full lists in Appendix II; but already I have, I trust, made it clear to what a large extent Conan Doyle drew upon the names mentioned in the Galley trial as names for his fictional characters. In respect of the cases, unconnected with that of Galley, which were heard in either the Crown Bar Court or the Nisi Prius Court of the Exeter Assizes, and of which Conan Doyle read in the 1836 newspapers, he modifies, after the fashion shown above, almost all the names that he encountered, with much more evidence of "analogical" change—for example, a Mr. CARLISLE becomes KESWICK (STUD), as the town of Keswick lies only twenty-three miles southwest of the ancient Celtic city of CARLISLE.

Now let us see how many names, both Christian names and surnames, Conan Doyle extracted and used from the accounts of the non-Galley court cases.

The total number of names to be found in Conan Doyle's reading through the "non-Galley" remainder of the newspaper's pages makes a total of seventy surnames, of which twenty-six

---

[9]The convenient four-letter code identifying all the stories in the Sherlockian Canon is explained in Appendix I.

carry Christian names. Here is the analysis of their employment in the Sherlockian Canon:

OTHER CASES IN THE CROWN BAR AND NISI PRIUS COURTS AT EXETER

Surnames (or place-names)		*Christian names (or titles)*	
Total: 70	%	Total: 26 (2 duplicated)	%
Names used unaltered: 16	22.85	Names used unaltered: 11	42.30
Times used in Canon: 32	45.71	Times used in Canon: 70	269.23
Names used altered: 31	44.28	Names used altered: 11	42.30

These figures are extraordinary–and extraordinarily convincing–especially when we consider, in both lists, the very high percentages, respectively 23.43% and 22.85%, of the surnames taken *without alteration* into the Canon. The percentages for the Christian names, though high and, indeed, impressive, are not, all the same, so impressive as the intake of names adopted from the surname lists–and taken into the Canon, as I have said, without the least alteration (save in some quite trivial detail, as when "Pyke" and "Lopes," from the Nisi Prius cases, become, respectively, "Langdale Pike" (3GAB) and "Lopez" (WIST). In both lists, surnames are of far greater variety than are Christian names, and it is this fact which makes the high percentages of the unaltered surnames so impressive.

True, some extremely common Christian names will be found in both lists, and there are some common surnames, too–Smith, Williams, Harris–in the "Galley" list; Johnson, Jones, and Robinson in the other list. But, these very common surnames excluded, the remaining surnames are by no means common, and some–quite a large number–are unusual indeed.

The testimony, then, that the extracts from the Galley trial and Nisi Prius names bear is that the use of all these names, *taken from a common source,* could have come about only through Conan Doyle's having read and (under the influence of an emotion-induced deep interest) absorbed all that he might learn of Galley's tragic history and of the gallant efforts that his friends had made to secure justice to a wronged man.

In these accounts, Conan Doyle found the inspiration to begin to create Sherlock Holmes, and to provide himself with at least the major part of the essential name stock that every author needs. At the end of that same year of 1882, in the reports of the St. Luke's Mystery, he would find the second Scherer, with added inspiration for both Conan Doyle and the immortal character which was slowly but surely taking shape in his mind. With the second Scherer would come the next instalment of names and places to be used; but it was not to be until 1884 that the third hero came into Conan Doyle's romantic, hero-worshipping consciousness. Here again was self-sacrificing charity in the voluntary service of others; here again was what Conan Doyle was always seeking: the pattern on which he was modelling himself, so that, one day in the not-too-distant future, he would have fitted himself to join the ranks of his heroes as an equal.

Who this hero was, who, so far, has gone unnoticed, even unsuspected, of even the most assiduous of Sherlockian scholars, we shall now see. In his rare character, in his wholly admirable life, and in his heroic death–or, rather, in the completely uncritical worship with which they inspired Conan Doyle–he added a smaller, but not less important (to us now, an indispensable) element in the accepted portrait of Sherlock Holmes, as Conan Doyle presented it to the world, for the first time, in 1887.

Thousands pass the bronze statue[10] of this hero every day, as they walk through and around Trafalgar Square. Above him is another great British hero–Lord Nelson. And above Nelson are the pigeons, so like gulls that their friendly presence seems most fitting of all for one of the greatest sea commanders of all time. *Our* modest hero–Conan Doyle's hero–stands, not on a tall Corinthian column, but on a modest granite plinth, hardly higher than a man. He seems, in his uncomplaining way, to be, not so much forgiving of the mean, seedy political necessities which betrayed him to death, as contemptuous, though in no bitter fashion, of the men whose descendants and heirs still play their nasty little games at the bottom of Whitehall, which he could have seen from his stand in Trafalgar Square. If he could have looked ahead, I think that he would have been greatly moved by the tribute that Conan Doyle was to render to him; a tribute which will endure as long as books endure . . .

---

[10]The statue is the work of the well-known sculptor Hamo Thorneycroft. That this fact was known to Conan Doyle is evident from his use of Thorneycroft's unusual surname as the forename of Dr. Thorneycroft Huxtable of *The Priory School.*

9

GENERAL GORDON: GODFATHER OF THE BAKER STREET IRREGULARS

MILLAIS'S "Girl in a Yellow Jacket" is wearing the jacket which, with the right to wear the Peacock's Feather, gave the honoured recipient not only the highest rank in the army of the Chinese Empire but, with his being given the title of "Ti-Tu," brought him to the highest rank to which a subject had ever been raised. "The Yellow Jacket and the Peacock's Feather," wrote one of his many biographers, ". . . are the Chinese equivalents for [the Orders of] the Garter and the Bath. Addresses were likewise presented to him in considerable numbers, but he would accept no substantial rewards, and he returned from China in 1864, as poor as when he entered it–being, probably, the only person who had failed to profit by his own brilliant deeds"–and, in this mildly expressed tribute, there is not one word of exaggeration.

Prince Ti-Tu, disdaining all rewards save the approbation of his somewhat eccentric morality and of his own far-too-scrupulous conscience–as incorruptible as De Gaulle, but without the orthodox-Catholic Frenchman's sense of humour–became, through no effort on his part–indeed, to his embarrassment and often genuine mortification–one of the most popular of Britain's heroes in a century in which discovering heroes to worship was an epidemic preoccupation. This was a man of whom the biographer quoted above remarks that

> for the mere acquisition of facts or rules [he] had never any taste; he was not cut out after the ordinary pattern; and even the drudgery necessary

Major-General Charles Gordon, the warm-hearted humanitarian: "Through him, more than one youth was spared the consequences of having yielded to a momentary temptation. . . . The rescued youth grew up into a man of excellent character, thanks to his benefactor . . ."

to obtain admission into the ranks of the senior arm of the service was distasteful to him. Once he was severely rebuked, and told that "he would never make an officer." The rebuke does not seem to have been altogether merited, and the spirited cadet, who felt it keenly, "tore his epaulets from his shoulders, and cast them at his superior's feet."

Nevertheless, this son of a lieutenant-general and younger brother of a major-general passed his examinations successfully and was gazetted subaltern in the Corps of Royal Engineers, a regiment long distinguished as a forcing-house, not only of military brilliance, but of military and personal eccentricity. The two other great military heroes of Queen Victoria's very own century were also Royal Engineers–"Sappers," as we call them, and as they are proud to call themselves: Field Marshal Earl Roberts, V.C. and Field Marshal Earl Kitchener, though neither, for all his oddity, approached, in his ambivalence which seems sometimes to be schizophrenia, the most ambivalent Prince Ti-Tu.

His name was Charles George Gordon, and he died in a manner which so touched the hearts of his countrymen that he lived on, ennobled far beyond the trivial earthly honours which had made him a major-general and a Companion of the Most Honourable Order of the Bath.

That end which ennobled, almost apotheosized, him has been told with exceptional skill in a fairly recent motion picture, *Khartoum* (1966), in which the part of Gordon was taken by that fine actor Charlton Heston. None save the most trivial liberties were taken, in this picture, with historical fact; especially in the careful, loving interpretation of Gordon's complex character. It is a pity that Dr. Watson did not live long enough to see Heston's fine performance–for it was "your picture of General Gordon"

General Gordon, the sternly inflexible, ruthless empire-builder: "England was made by adventurers, not by its Government, and I believe it will hold its place only by adventurers . . ."

that Watson imported into Baker Street and hung on the wall of "our large sitting-room" at 221B.

That display of petulant insubordination which found its most alarming climax in the tearing-off of Gordon's epaulets and in his casting them to the ground should be taken without losing sight of the fact that he entered the Royal Military College at Woolwich –"The Shop"–at the age of fifteen and that he grew from boyhood to young manhood in a discipline which concerned itself even more with the development of the mind than it did with that of the body. The training that Sapper cadets received was unique –at least, in the modern world. They emerged, not only as fully trained and essentially *practical* engineers–Gordon's first official appointment, in 1854, at the age of *twenty-one,* was in connection with the fortifications then being erected for the protection of the new docks at Pembroke, Wales–but as soldiers whose sound instruction in the purely military art made so many of them demonstrably brilliant masters of strategy and tactics. Not since the days when the legions of Rome conquered the Western world –building as they conquered–had that perfect fusion of the engineer with the military commander been effected, as it was effected, over many generations, at Woolwich (where, one recalls, the blueprints of the most jealously-guarded of all Government secrets were kept: those of the Bruce-Partington submarine).

This chapter has for its purpose the answering of that puzzling question–puzzling to the present writer, at any rate: why, so far, has not even the most dedicated of Sherlockian exegetists posed and satisfactorily answered the question: *why* did the picture of General Gordon hang on a wall at 221B? Why was it bought in the first place? What was there in the character of "Chinese Gordon" to merit, not merely the emotional response to a Hero whose heroic qualities had, justly but not without conscious political motivation, been trumpeted by journalists, biographers, and popular lecturers throughout the immensity of the British Empire, but a more lasting respect, emphasized by the symbolism of Watson's buying Gordon's picture and hanging it on the wall?

In trying to answer this question, we shall not only examine the more obvious of Gordon's qualities and achievements; we may come to know more of the qualities of the two men of Baker

Street, in whose daily life Gordon was to have a deep and lasting influence—an influence so far unsuspected, as I have said, by even the most meticulous of Sherlockian researchers.

That Conan Doyle was familiar with every detail of Gordon's history is made plain by the use that he makes, in the Canon, of names from that history. Newspaper accounts of Gordon had not sufficed to tell him what he wished to know about the greatest British hero of late Victorian times; it is obvious that Conan Doyle had read many of the biographies available only a short while after the news of Gordon's death had reached London.

Again, we have the still unexplained use of the names for persons of decidedly unheroic cast. At the conclusion of the Crimean War, from which Gordon had emerged with a reputation for reckless bravery and for that which actively fighting men always respect: an almost miraculous ability to expose his person, without hurt, to enemy fire, he was ordered to join Major (afterwards Lieutenant-General) Sir Edward Stanton, "to assist in laying down the new frontiers of Turkey, Russia and Roumania." In April 1857—he was still only twenty-four, remember!—he was instructed to join Colonel (afterwards General) Sir Lintorn Simmons, "in the important work connected with the delimitation of the boundary in Asia."

Pausing here only to observe that the names of Sir Edward Stanton and Sir Lintorn Simmons both duly appear in the Canonical text—the former in *The Missing Three-Quarter* in no very complimentary context; the latter (slightly altered, as "Simon Bird," "Lord Robert St. Simon," and the three "Simpsons" of *Silver Blaze, The Blanched Soldier,* and *The Crooked Man*) again in no heroic cast—we pass on to the uninterrupted success of that very strange young officer, Charles Gordon.

Now, I wish to point out the existence, at this formative period of Gordon's life, of a striking parallel between Gordon's experience and that of Sherlock Holmes (the latter at an age, however, some thirteen years older):

> Gordon [says the biographer] was engaged for some time in Armenia, and visited Erzeroum, Kars, Erivan and other places. He also ascended Little and Great Ararat with the object of personally ascertaining their

respective heights . . . Summoned after a stay of six months in these distant regions to a Conference of the Commission at Constantinople, he was detained for some time in the Turkish capital in consequence of the illness of his chief. . .

I was struck by the resemblance of this hegira of Gordon's to the general pattern of what A. Carson Simpson calls Holmes's *Wanderjahre*–for, in each, the man turned his face resolutely toward the East. In Holmes's case, of course, his intentions took him beyond Armenia. Gordon twice reached more distant China, but not until he had returned home on long-postponed leave. As for Holmes's *Wanderjahre*, this is what he himself had to tell Watson concerning the wanderings, though Holmes still reserved some information for himself: he certainly did not tell Watson everything. But what he did tell was significant enough, and strangely reminiscent of Gordon's travels in the first stage of *his* wanderings:

"I travelled for two years in Tibet, therefore, and amused myself by visiting Lhassa, and spending some days with the head lama. You may have read of the remarkable explorations of a Norwegian named Sigerson, but I am sure that it never occurred to you that you were receiving news of your friend. . ."

On his way back from distant Lhasa, Holmes, as William S. Baring-Gould points out, "passed through Persia, looked in at Mecca"–then, as now, a city barred to all save the Faithful– "[and] visited the Khalifa at Omdurman" four years before Lord Kitchener began to move against the Khalifa, whom he was to defeat utterly in the great battle of Omdurman in 1898.

The parallels between Gordon's life and that of Holmes's are remarkable indeed, as are the parallels between the characters of the two men.

All of us are ambivalent; Man is an ambivalent animal. We all live out our lives, swayed this way and that by the opposing yet complementary tugs of two contrasted sets of impulses. It is only when the contrast between these opposing impulses is more than usually striking that we recognize and call attention to the ambivalence of another–and perhaps no men more startlingly displayed their ambivalence than did Charles Gordon and Sherlock Holmes (which means, of course, Conan Doyle).

Many years ago, the talented novelist Pamela Hansford-Johnson remarked to me in conversation upon the streak of cruelty to be observed in Conan Doyle through his writings, and this streak of cruelty—almost, at times, inhumanity—is to be observed also in Charles Gordon. What makes their characters seem so startlingly ambivalent is that each contrasted his cruelty (in Gordon's case, permitted active expression; in Doyle's, expression through imagined scenes of horror) with the most sentimental tenderness.

There is no need here to describe how Gordon was given command of "The Ever-Victorious Army" of China, opposing a serious threat to the Imperial throne by the "Tai-Pings," led by a Chinese named Hung Hsia-Ch'wan, a rebel who, like so many other rebels against the central authority, claimed to act under Divine inspiration. Hung wished to change the religion of the Empire and overthrow the ruling Manchu dynasty. He established independent communities called "Churches of God," and his communications had been, he said, revealed to him by the Heavenly Father and by Hung's "Heavenly Elder Brother," Jesus Christ. Gordon's task was to restore order among the "loyal" Chinese troops, and, having established his command over them, to proceed to thrash Hung soundly. That he succeeded brilliantly is why Gordon was loaded with the highest honours of the Celestial Empire. However, his methods of establishing discipline offended the Liberals at home, and it was they who, in the end, contrived his death. When, at one stage of his attempt to restore discipline to the rebellious troops under his command, "the artillery refused to fall in, [threatening] to blow the officers to pieces, both European and Chinese," Gordon issued a proclamation, ordering all the non-commissioned officers to attend on him; reluctantly they did so, and when they had sullenly assembled to hear what Gordon had to say, he told them that one in every five would be shot—"an announcement which they received with groans."

During this manifestation, the Commander, with great shrewdness, determined in his own mind that the man whose groans were the most prolonged and emphatic was the ringleader. This man was a corporal:

Gordon approached him, dragged him out of the rank with his own hand, and ordered two of the infantry standing by to shoot him on the spot. The order was instantly obeyed . . .

There were never any half measures in Gordon's approach to the solution of any problem; yet this was the man who, already a Colonel, commanding the Royal Engineers at Gravesend, would spend hours visiting the aged sick in the Gravesend workhouse infirmary, reading the Scriptures to lonely and otherwise neglected old women and in other ways showing them compassion and practical kindness. This contrast of harshness and compassion we notice, too, in Sherlock Holmes: the quite indefensible insulting of the Negro, Steve Dixie, in *The Three Gables* stands out in remarkable contrast to his treatment of Eugenia Ronder in *The Veiled Lodger,* in which he seeks to comfort the mutilated woman in words which are no less applicable to him than to the woman whom he is trying to help: "The ways of Fate are indeed hard to understand. If there is not some compensation hereafter, then the world is a cruel jest."

Gordon spent several years at Gravesend, and all the time which was not taken up with his military duties, he spent in noble works of philanthropy. He devoted himself to relieving the want and misery of the poor, visiting the sick, teaching, feeding and clothing the many waifs and strays among the destitute boys of the town, and providing employment for them on board ship. He presided over evening classes which he instituted for boys whom he had rescued from the gutter, and his house was school, hospital and almshouse in turn . . . He was never satisfied till he could place his "boys" in the way of getting an honest living, or could obtain for them berths on board ship . . .

From this well-organized work to rescue Gravesend's underprivileged youth from hunger and cold, prison and worse, came the Ragged School, which long continued under that typically Victorian title and which still exists under a less blunt name.

And this is the legacy that he not only left to Gravesend, not only to his admirers throughout the world of hero-worshippers, but, in particular, to Sherlock Holmes and Dr. Watson, who paid Gordon the tribute of imitation. For the inspiration behind

Colonel (later Major-General) Gordon takes time off from his military duties to give the pupils of his "Ragged School" a lesson in geography. To Gordon's practical care for the homeless, often petty-criminal lads of Gravesend, Conan Doyle certainly owed the idea of Holmes's "Baker Street Irregulars."

Holmes's recruiting and training of the Baker Street Irregulars we recognize as that of Major-General Charles George Gordon.

Now, just as Sherlock Holmes is a synthesis of so many inspirations encountered in Conan Doyle's earlier years, so the Baker Street Irregulars have no single origin in General Gordon's Ragged School. As I pointed out in my original essay of (now) ten years ago, one possible element in the conception of Holmes's

The raw material of General Gordon's–and Sherlock Holmes's–boy-rescuing philanthropy. In this Victorian "drawing from life," a policeman and a Board School inspector have joined forces to flush the homeless, school-dodging lads out of their grim hiding places.

Is this how Conan Doyle found the name "Wiggins" for the commander of Holmes's Baker Street Irregulars? John Wiggins, one of the last of the British murderers to be hanged in public, was long remembered for the fierce struggle that he put up on the scaffold whilst loudly protesting his innocence.

own band of "Irregulars" (a type of fighting man with which Gordon had always great military success) could have been the gangs of the Skeleton Army, which were raising hell for the "soldiers" of the Salvation Army all over Britain–one of the worst riots of the gangs of mischief-makers parodying military discipline having taken place in Gravesend itself–Gordon's "territory"–a riot of such violence that the military had to be called in to back up the efforts of the regular police.

But, as I said in that original essay, what may have been the much more remote origin of the Baker Street Irregulars is to be found in what I then called the most unexpected place of all: in a passing comment in the pages of Sir William Smith's *A Smaller Latin–English Dictionary,* which first appeared when Conan Doyle was eleven but which, as the Father Librarian of Doyle's old school kindly informs me, was *not* available at Stonyhurst to the schoolboy Doyle. If one look up the Latin word *paniceus,* this is what one finds:

> **paniceus**, a, um, *adj.* (panis) *made of bread:* milites panicei, apparently a pun, as one might say, *the Baker-street brigade.*

At Stonyhurst, Father Turner tells me, only the larger Smith's was available in the school.

"Here," Father Turner explains, " 'paniceus' is given, and the reference to Plautus, *Captivi,* 'milites panicei,' but there is no translation. The syllabus [at Stonyhurst in the 1870s] was strictly confined to the more 'classical' authors, Caesar, Sallust, Ovid in the lower classes, Vergil, Horace, Cicero, Livy in the higher."

So that, if Conan Doyle did not study Plautus, and there was no reference to the pun of "milites panicei" in the Latin dictionary available to him at school, he must have encountered the entry in his independent reading—a sign that the "detectival" interest had been aroused at an early age.

Had this innocent little pun—"as one might say, *the Baker-street brigade*"—remained in Conan Doyle's head all through the years of adolescence and early manhood, to be recollected, happily apposite, when he needed a name for the band of ragged "Irregulars" that he had recruited and organized in conscious and admiring imitation of General Gordon's own?

10

DR. BELL AND DR. WATSON

And what of Dr. Joseph Bell, accepted these many years as the "official" original of Sherlock Holmes?

On the face of it, there seem to be small grounds for rejecting the identification which has the impressive authority of Conan Doyle's own statement that Sherlock Holmes was a character inspired by Dr. Joseph Bell, professor at the Edinburgh Medical School when Conan Doyle was a student there. Indeed, Conan Doyle, in an article in the *Strand* magazine which was "subbed" to serve as a preface for later editions of *A Study in Scarlet* (Ward, Lock), described Dr. Bell's method of snap diagnosis, based on highly trained powers of observation, in terms which, superficially at least, are convincing testimony to the justice of an identification of Dr. Bell of real life with the fictional Sherlock Holmes. And, furthermore, the article ends with these quite unambiguous words:

> . . . [W]hen I took my degree and went to Africa, the remarkable individuality and discriminating tact of my old master made a deep and lasting impression on me, though I had not the faintest idea that it would one day lead me to forsake medicine for story-writing.

This handsome and unequivocal tribute is reinforced and confirmed in an article by Dr. Bell himself which appeared in the pages of *The Bookman* and was reprinted as a preface to the fourth reissue of *A Study in Scarlet* (1893), though it must be observed that Dr. Bell modestly claims for his predecessor, Syme, not only a skill in medical diagnosis superior to that of Bell, but a *direct* influence on Conan Doyle, through Syme's having made his method a "tradition of the school."[1]

Now, what are we to make of all this? Were George Scherer, Wendel Scherer, and General Charles Gordon the composite original of Sherlock Holmes?–or must that honour be reserved, as Conan Doyle obviously invited us to believe, to Dr. Joseph Bell? (But surely it is relevant that Conan Doyle, in using the so-called "honoured" Christian name "Joseph" in the Canon, awards it to the sneak and traitor Joseph Harrison, after having bestowed it on the infamous Joseph Stangerson?)

The answer would seem to be that the *persona*–or, more precisely, a striking virtuosity–of Dr. Joseph Bell did play its part in building up the many-elemented figure of the sleuth of Baker Street; but, apart from that one highly-advertised parlour trick of Dr. Bell's, he has not contributed anything more important to the make-up of Holmes.

However, as Conan Doyle himself records–giving an example of Dr. Bell's diagnostic and off-the-cuff character reading–the snap deductions of Holmes, which always so astonish Watson and are intended, no less, to astonish the reader, are cleverly based on Dr. Bell's similar tricks:

> "Dr. Watson, Mr. Sherlock Holmes," said Stamford, introducing us.
> "How are you?" he said cordially . . . "You have been in Afghanistan, I perceive."
> "How on earth did you know that?" I asked in astonishment.
> "Never mind," said he, chuckling to himself.

It is in this one respect–a most important respect, of course–but *only* in this one respect, that Holmes owes something of his origin to the notable idiosyncrasy of Dr. Joseph Bell. Why, then, did Conan Doyle, who had built up the character of Sherlock Holmes from many admired heroes and near-heroes, voluntarily ascribe a *single* origin to his most famous creation, and positively state that Holmes had his origin in Dr. Bell?

Well, we must not forget how swiftly the years pass; how

---

[1] But see Appendix III.

fugitive is the public interest in even the most startling of events. Not only had the average newspaper reader forgotten, by 1892, the St. Luke's Mystery, already ten years in the past, but, as the fourth reissue of the third edition of *A Study in Scarlet* was being prepared for publication, the Stanger–Stumm case was, legally, still *sub judice*. In 1892 or 1893, there would have been no point in Conan Doyle's reminding the readers of the *Strand* magazine that an important element in the creation of the most popular detective in fiction had been an obscure, unsuccessful real-life detective whom the youthful Conan Doyle had admired a decade before, and who had gained the author's admiration in a now-forgotten case of unexplained disappearance. What would Wendel Scherer—or George Scherer, for that matter—have meant, ten years after the successful conclusion of the Galley case, and the unsuccessful conclusion of the St. Luke's Mystery, to the readers of the *Strand?* Both cases, and the men associated with them, were forgotten—were well in the past.

Whereas Dr. Bell was living, respected, and certainly not unsuccessful. And Dr. Bell's detective powers were certainly impressive. It is easy to understand why Dr. Bell should have been nominated for the honour of having been Sherlock Holmes's "onlie begetter." (It saved a lot of argument . . .)

And what of Dr. Watson? What were *his* origins?

Well, we have learned that a Dr. James Watson was a leading member of the Portsmouth Literary and Scientific Society when Conan Doyle was trying to build up a medical practice locally. It has been suggested that Conan Doyle changed the doctor's first name to "John" (adding the middle initial "H"), but there may have been a nearer inspiration, not only for the name "Watson" but for the fuller form of "John Watson."

The reader may recall that, on coming down from the University, Holmes took rooms, he said, in Montague Street, by the British Museum (the "Montague," of course, being originally the "Montague" of Montague Smith's name). Now, in 1878 and later, No. 26 Montague Street was a lodging house, conducted by a Mrs. *Holmes,* who held a seven-year tenancy of the house from the Duke of Bedford's estate. Her name-plate, of then well-polished brass, must have inspired Conan Doyle to place Holmes's first lodgings in this street.

Well, now, if one left Montague Street in those years, turned slightly left, and crossed Great Russell Street into Bloomsbury Square, and walked through the Square into Southampton Street (now Southampton Place), one could not have failed to see the nameplate, on the front door of No. 6, of a medical man whom I have already mentioned: JOHN WATSON, M.D.

We should note that Conan Doyle makes *his* Dr. Watson recall, of "young Stamford," that he "had been a dresser under me at Barts"; and the choice of St. Bartholomew's is curious. It was not Conan Doyle's teaching hospital but that of Dr. William Palmer of Rugeley, the mass poisoner who, as I have already pointed out, held a strange fascination for Conan Doyle. It is not easy–nor have I attempted in this book–to find the reasons behind Conan Doyle's apparent contradictory assignment of names; an assignment which seems to imply that his real opinion of certain persons was not by any means the declared one.

Before I go on to examine this question further, in relation to Doyle's choosing the name "Watson," I must observe that there occurred, in a decisively formative year of Conan Doyle's life–1882–an event which would have added to his stock of names and ideas, the names both of "Watson" and "St. Bartholomew's" ("Bart's"): on 11 December 1882, a most eminent member of Dr. Conan Doyle's profession died at the great age of ninety.

The Times obituary, recording, "with the deepest regret," the death of Sir Thomas Watson, "an eminent physician," was as lengthy and as respectful as the eminence of the deceased amply justified. As I have pointed out elsewhere, Sir Thomas had been one of St. Bartholomew's most distinguished Governors; M.D., D.C.L., LL.D., he had been President of the Royal College of Physicians, the first representative of the Royal College of Physicians on the Medical Council, and a Physician-in-Ordinary to Her Majesty the Queen. For his distinguished services both to the Crown and to the medical art, he was created a baronet in 1866. If ever a more likely "Watson" were to impress itself on Conan Doyle's consciousness, I cannot think of one.

As a still professionally active medical practitioner, though it was not until three years later that he was to graduate as M.D., Conan Doyle took in not only *The Times* but also, as we know,

In this carefully-restored Georgian house on the right of the photograph, No. 6 Southampton Street (now Southampton Place), Bloomsbury Square, London, a John Watson, M.D. conducted his medical practice in 1878. A few yards from Montague Street, where Holmes first lodged on leaving the University, the house must often have been passed by Conan Doyle. *Specially commissioned photograph by Mann Brothers, Victoria, London.*

The Lancet and the *British Medical Journal*, as well as *The Daily Telegraph*. He would not–could not–have missed the (at least) four glowing obituaries with which the most respectable in British journalism paid Sir Thomas Watson his last tributes.

Have we here, then, a break with the tradition, established by Conan Doyle in his name-selection, that a certain name in real life should be bestowed on, at worst, the villainous; at best, the incompetent or merely unfortunate? One cannot help but be struck by the fact that, once a certain name had been impressed upon both the subconscious and the just-below-the-surface consciousness of Conan Doyle, the name *must* be used–and never, so far as one may see, in any but the most unheroic context. (The name "Hope" is encountered yet again, in any life of General Gordon, as that of the Admiral commanding the naval squadron supporting Gordon's attack on the Taku Forts in 1860–and if there were any doubt that Doyle was ignorant of the details of his hero, Gordon's, career, the doubt would be effectively banished in the fact that Doyle alludes to the Taku Forts in his nearly-forgotten novel of 1892, *Beyond the City*.)

In this "downgrading" of a real-life character, it must be said for Conan Doyle–or Conan Doyle's very wayward subconscious? –that he (or it) is most consistent. In a late (1926), poor, and most uncharacteristic short story, *The Three Gables,* we meet "Langdale Pike," a gossip-monger for, in Watson's contemptuously disapproving words, a "garbage paper." Pike's profession and Watson's (that is, Doyle's) language in describing it, are certainly not calculated to present this character in an attractive light. In the name "Pike"–or, rather, in Conan Doyle's choice of that name for the dubious gossip-monger, we may see both the literal and the metaphorical: the metaphorical allusion to that voracious freshwater fish, the pike, which is also popularly regarded as a "dirty eater," and the literal, in which the name or names of real-life persons have been recalled.

At least twice did Conan Doyle encounter the name; the more important of the two being, of course, Doyle's Southsea fellow practitioner and *friendly* neighbour, Dr. Pyke; the less important, the defendant in a Nisi Prius Court case of 1836: Webber *vs*. Pyke.

Dr. Pyke it was who brought together Miss Louise Hawkins ("Touie") and young Dr. Conan Doyle, who married her as his first wife. The other Pyke "registered" in Conan Doyle's memory when he noted it in the case that Webber brought against the Devonian Pyke, in 1836, before Baron Alderson. The contemporary newspaper reports that, in this action, "the record in this case was withdrawn"–so that Pyke had been unjustly or merely unfairly brought to court. Neither Pyke was unworthy; so that, always consistent, Conan Doyle gave their name to the less than admirable "Langdale Pike." Strange . . .

Is, then, Conan Doyle offering us another exception to the "downgrading rule" in giving the respectable and respected name of "Watson" to the sub-hero of the Sherlockian Saga? Were that question seriously to be posed, it would imply that, in Conan Doyle's estimation, the Dr. Watson of 221B Baker Street is a hero –or, at least, has something heroic in him.

Conan Doyle thought nothing of the sort; and because this was so, his creation, Sherlock Holmes, has no higher an opinion –and why (one may hear Conan Doyle asking his readers) should Holmes have had a higher opinion of the man who was permitted to share his "diggings" only because he was the one man prepared to split the rent? Watson is introduced to Holmes, and to us, as an idle toper; a self-confessed, and obviously unsuccessful, backer of racehorses (half his miserable pension of eleven-and-six a day went, he tells us, to the bookies); he is a self-confessed womanizer (". . . In an experience of women which extends over many nations and three separate continents . . ."), and, by his own companion's reference to something that Watson had told him, addicted perhaps to irregularities even more grave ("Your morals don't improve, Watson. You have added fibbing to your other vices . . ."). Watson admits to a neurotic–alcoholic?– temperament; grants that he is lazy; and readily confirms Holmes's allusions to his weaknesses: "I have another set of vices when I'm well, but these are the principal ones at present."

That Holmes–at least at the beginning of their association– had a poor opinion of the man who was enabling him to live in the "diggings" of *his* choice, there may be no doubt; but Holmes's pleasure in treating the wretched Watson as a butt worsens, far too often, into petty and not-so-petty spite. How, for instance, if Holmes had felt for Watson no more than the sentiments of an ordinary, unemotional friendship, could he have permitted himself to interpret the scratches around the keyhole of Watson's dead brother's watch as the literally aimless attempts by a hopeless drunkard to let the watch-key eventually find the hole that the tosspot himself couldn't?

That, in "deducing" the scratches around the watch's keyhole as the clues to the *facilis descensus* of the dead Watson is less an exercise in deduction than an hypocritical indulgence of mere neighbourly nosiness, is as clear to us, the readers, as it must have been to the embarrassed Watson. Holmes merely used the scratches—or his theory as to their origin—to extract from his "friend" the dismal family secret: that Watson's brother, living in a poverty lightened only by occasional and progressively rarer accessions of money, had finally, in despair, turned for solace and oblivion to the bottle, and so died.

And in thus letting Holmes "deduce" all this from scratches around a watch's keyhole, Dr. Conan Doyle—not yet the specialist ophthalmologist that he would become, but already (1889) a Doctor of Medicine of Edinburgh, is being less than honest with us, his readers. He appears to be suppressing—and, at that, deliberately suppressing—what he knows to be at least probable, if not altogether certain: that a simple difference in the power of the eyes is enough to inhibit the parallactic displacement whereby the human being, with his binocular vision, is enabled to judge distance precisely, and to "aim"—especially watch-keys—with accuracy. And even with the best of vision, how many of us have not "missed" at first trial, when fitting a key into a keyhole—whether of a watch or of a front door?—and this must have been even more common in the poor lighting of Victorian streets and of Victorian domestic interiors.

This "explanation" on Holmes's part is the act of an enemy, no less; nor is it an isolated example of spite in the forty years of the Holmes–Watson companionship. Those indefatigable Sherlockian exegetists, Michael and Mollie Hardwick, refer to Holmes's pleasure in teasing, taunting, even openly insulting Watson, but in an oblique manner which seeks to lay most of the blame for Holmes's unpleasantness on the shoulders of Watson, quoting Watson himself in Holmes's defense:

I was a whetstone for his mind. I stimulated him. He liked to think aloud in my presence. . . . If I irritated him by a certain methodical slowness in my mentality, that irritation served only to make his own flame-like intuitions and impressions flash up the more vividly and swiftly.

So the self-abnegating, the self-effacing John Watson, M.D.! The Hardwicks, evidently agreeing with this self-condemnation, add: "Sometimes Holmes was irritated by Watson's slowness of mind; sometimes he laughed at him, though kindly. 'Excellent, Watson! Compound of the Busy Bee and Excelsior!' "

Holmes never laughed at Watson in a "kindly" manner; and if the relationship between the two men–"they complemented each other perfectly" is the opinion of the Hardwicks–mellows over the sixty books of the Canon, that is because, as every writer of fiction knows, the children of his or her imagination share, with our children of physical procreation, the ability to grow up, to change, to seek and contrive to develop a character and behaviour of their own. In the beginning, however, Conan Doyle planned that Watson should be shown to be in every way inferior to Holmes; to be Holmes's butt, Holmes's unpaid servant, even Holmes's cringing and fawning dog.

This, then, must be the question of this chapter: who, then, was Watson?

I had asked Father Turner, of Stonyhurst College, if there had been boys, contemporary with Conan Doyle at school, who had borne the names *Scherer, Holmes, Sherlock,* and *Watson*. I have already quoted what Father Turner had to tell me about Patrick Sherlock. As regards the other three names, this is what Father Turner wrote:

Names: No SCHERER–however spelt–and no HOLMES.

WATSON–perhaps the only period [1869–75] in which there was no-one named Watson at Stonyhurst. But I think the name was chosen because it was common and ordinary. To check this I counted the names WATSON in the Blackburn Telephone Directory in current use. To my amazement there were 400! Doyle wanted an ordinary name, but he had too much taste to write Smith, Brown or Robinson . . .

Perhaps those other common names were not suitable for the entity that Conan Doyle eventually named "Watson," but they were perfectly suitable for use in naming other characters in the Canon: *Brown* is used four times, *Robinson* only once, but *Smith* (as one might expect with so common a name) is used no fewer than eight times–"Joseph Smith" I do not count, since the great Mormon prophet was a real person.

Father Turner's remarks about the name "Watson" left me curiously dissatisfied. I could not reasonably account for the feeling, but I did feel convinced that Conan Doyle's choice of the name was not at all because "it was common and ordinary." I felt that, at some time in Doyle's life–perhaps in the earlier part–the name had become familiar to him and that the "reappearance" of the name, as I have mentioned, merely "reinforced" the recollection of that early-encountered surname in Conan Doyle's mind, conscious or subconscious. Perhaps it was my seeing a re-run of that superb motion picture *Citizen Kane* which urged me to continue the search for an important "Watson," most likely in Conan Doyle's earlier years. In the film, Charles Foster Kane's puzzling reference to "Rosebud" is never explained to those who hear the word–the name–though it is explained to the viewer: a name from the very infancy of the dying man . . .

The searcher not only always needs a little luck; he has, if he have devoted his whole life to research, the right to *expect* it. The required luck came my way–by chance, as all such bits of luck seem to do–on Easter Sunday, 11 April 1982.

I was watching the BBC television programme *The Antiques Road Show* without any great interest when my attention was sharply caught by the sight of a grandfather's clock around which the "experts" were pontificating. It was the painted dial of this late Georgian clock which interested me–no, which filled me with excitement, rather.

The clock had been made in Blackburn, Lancashire, around 1824–and it is just outside Blackburn that Conan Doyle's school, Stonyhurst, is situated. The painted clock-face clearly bore the name of the town: *Blackburn*. But, far more to the point, it also clearly bore the name of the maker:

Jno Watson

Had Conan Doyle, in the school walks through the still lovely Lancashire countryside and in permitted *exeats* to the neighbouring villages and towns, seen the name "John Watson" above the clockmaker's shop?—had gazed, in the fascination that clocks and watches always exert upon boys, at the display of timepieces in John Watson's shop window?

Spurred to renewed endeavour by that accidental sighting of a clock-face bearing "Jno Watson's" name, and originating in the big town nearest to Conan Doyle's school, I wrote at once to the District Librarian—I learned afterward that Mr. J. B. Darbyshire holds this position—at Blackburn, asking him:

> . . . Have you local directories of the period between, say, 1820 and 1875—directories which *might* shew that "Jno Watson" or the trade-name was still current when Doyle visited Blackburn as a boy?
>
> I should be very grateful if you would make a search for me. If you should find Watson's clockmaking shop, would you give me all the details that you can? Small boys are fascinated by clocks.

It is my practice, when making enquiries of this sort, no matter of what potential source of information, to explain, not only what I wish to know, but *why* the information sought is important to me. So in this case; though, for the reason that I did not wish to "lead" the District Librarian, I refrained from mentioning that, in the Canon, there is a direct and important association of a watch with the name "Watson"—that watch which had once belonged to Dr. Watson's brother, and into the condition of which the percipient, "ratiocinating" (as Poe would have said) Sherlock Holmes read far too much. But I did mention in my letter that watches are mentioned importantly in *The Sign of the Four, The Five Orange Pips,* and *The Yellow Face*.

I did not mention my opinion that, examined in a word-association test, Conan Doyle, given the name "Watson," would almost certainly have snapped out the word "watches."

My letter, as they say in Western novels, hit pay-dirt—and of a richness beyond my expectations. In writing my letter, I had, it was now clear, gone to sympathetic as well as informed sources of information, for, in addition to facts from the Blackburn town records, Mr. Darbyshire and his assistant, Mrs. N. Yuill, added, as a bonus, a distinctly original theory of their own, for which they deserve, and shall have here, all the credit.

But, first of all, let me say that my "hunch" paid off: if, as Father Turner assured me, Conan Doyle encountered no Watsons at Stonyhurst College itself, he could hardly have avoided the name as he came to know the district around and, at least by repute, many of its inhabitants.

The suggestions from Blackburn begin with a possibility–no more:

1. There may have been a clock by John Watson in the village of Stonyhurst or the neighbouring Hurst Green.

But, from a possibility–even a probability–we pass on to ascertainable *fact:*

2. [Conan Doyle] may have seen the name, John Watson, on a list of former ministers of Osbaldeston Chapel, for it is quite likely that Conan Doyle visited the chapel, since the village is close to Stonyhurst . . .

It is more than likely that Conan Doyle visited Osbaldeston Chapel; it is certain. As an English county, Lancashire of the Red Rose remained steadfastly Roman Catholic both during and after the Reformation; and Roman Catholic chapels sprang up in most of even its smaller villages (and, of course, its principal towns) before and after the passing of the Catholic Emancipation Act in 1829. St. Mary's at Osbaldeston is a Roman Catholic chapel, built in 1836, and is one that the boys of Stonyhurst would have been permitted to visit. Within the chancel, brilliantly yet softly lit by the stained glass filling the tall windows, is the list of past ministers; among them, impossible to miss, the name of the Reverend John Watson.

In a contemporary guidebook to Lancashire, which must have been seen and read by young Conan Doyle, the "Landowners" of the village of Osbaldeston are given as "H. Ward, Esq. (lord of the manor), W. B. Slater, Esq., and Miss Hargreaves." "The other principal inhabitants" are also listed. Is it entirely coincidental that, of the three names of landowners–Ward, Slater, and Hargreaves–two should appear in the Canon: Slater (*Black Peter*) and Hargreaves ("Hargreave" in *The Dancing Men*) . . . or that, of the four members of the Barnes family appearing in the list of "the other principal inhabitants," the Canon should use their common surname, Barnes (*Shoscombe Old Place*) and their three Christian names: Joshua, Thomas, and William? In *Shoscombe Old Place,* the real Joshua Barnes is recalled in memory as the hardly altered "Josiah Barnes."

But there is another nearby village which, I feel, might have had a strong influence in shaping, not so much Sherlock Holmes as Conan Doyle. This is Pleasington, which had a population of just over three hundred when Doyle knew it in the 1870s. Of it, the guidebook says:

> It is famed for quarries of building stone and good spring water, and it commands fine views of the surrounding country. The only place of worship is a *Catholic Church,* which is dedicated in honour of the Blessed Virgin and St. John the Baptist, and was opened 24th August 1819. This sacred ediface is in the florid Gothic style of architecture. . . . *The windows are filled with various coats of arms, richly emblazoned* . . . It was erected at the expense of the late John Francis Butler. . . [Emphasis added]

Noting, in passing, that Butler's three names are all used in the Canon–in, respectively, three cases; in *The Noble Bachelor* and *The Beryl Coronet;* and in *The Musgrave Ritual,* where "butler" is employed as a common, rather than a proper, noun–we must see, in the "richly emblazoned" armorial windows of Pleasington Catholic Church, a mere anticipation of that window in the new house, *Undershaw,* that Conan Doyle built as the first important material expression of his literary success. In John Dickson Carr's description, "In the hall at Undershaw, the great window sparkled with panel after panel of coats-of-arms . . ." And that the boyhood memories of both Osbaldeston and Pleasington were never effaced from his recollection is obvious from the fact that, using the surname *Slater* from memories of Osbaldeston, he gives the name (in *Black Peter*) to a *stonemason:* one who would have been at home in Pleasington, "famed for quarries of building-stone."

Let us return to the letter from Blackburn.

3. [Conan Doyle] may have met some of the employees of the *Watson* travelling-drapers–[that is, "tally-men"; house-to-house salesmen who sold clothes and other necessities on small weekly payments]–who would visit Stonyhurst village to shew their stock and collect the weekly payments.

But the most impressive of all the suggestions from Blackburn is:

4. [Conan Doyle] may have got the name [of Watson] from the branch of the family at Eanam Smithy. When travelling to Stonyhurst by railway, the windmill was a prominent landmark which was visible immediately on leaving Daisyfield Tunnel at Blackburn. The windmill was demolished by Houlker Watson, who wanted the site for an improved smithy and wheelwright's shop. Conan Doyle may have been in Blackburn around the time that the sails and tower disappeared, and heard that the Watsons demolished it. Combining the names of John Watson and Houlker Watson gives us John H. Watson. I also enclose a description of Osbaldeston and a drawing of the old windmill. The clockmaker's shop [*i.e.*, of John Watson] has long since disappeared, and, unfortunately, we have no illustration.

Now I find that suggestion, that the "H." of "John H. Watson" recalls the initial of the windmill-destroyer, significant and not at all implausible; certainly when we consider certain well-displayed and well-recorded aspects of Conan Doyle's character. All his life, he hated and always loudly denounced wilful destruction—especially when done for a profit which, to his uncommercial mind, he saw only as sordid. I have quoted part of the poem in which his indignation at the threatened sale of Nelson's old flagship erupted into vitriolic stanzas: "Ye hucksters, have ye still to learn the things that money will not buy!"

He can have been no different as a boy—doubtless even less restrained in his indignation—and that he not only deplored the old windmill's destruction but had learned more about it than might come from seeing it as he entered or emerged from Daisyfield Tunnel is apparent from his use of the distinctly unusual name *Derbyshire* in the tale of *Silver Blaze*.

For the windmill—the only one ever to be erected in Blackburn—was built by Samuel *Derbyshire,* of Audley Hall, on the canal bank at Eanam in 1822, the canal itself having been opened to traffic in 1816.

The comment, in a local guidebook of later date, that "as much of the land round about consisted of open fields, and [thus] the windmill must have been a conspicuous object" brings vividly to the mind the lovely open Lancashire countryside in which Conan Doyle spent the formative years of his youth. He not only became familiar with that "conspicuous object," the Eanam windmill; he sought out its history and nursed, we may well

The only windmill ever built in Blackburn, and familiar to Conan Doyle as he travelled to and from Stonyhurst by train. Pulled down by Houlker Watson–note the name!–the "vandalism" must have greatly prejudiced Doyle against Houlker Watson and, perhaps, some other Watsons as well. *Contemporary drawing by F. S. Watson, kindly supplied by the Blackburn District Library.*

believe, a fierce resentment against the vandal who destroyed it for mere monetary gain. It is interesting to note that the sketch reproduced here, made whilst the windmill was still standing, is signed, "F. S. Watson"–again introducing that already well-introduced name into the nomenclature of Conan Doyle's boyhood.

If there were no Watsons at Stonyhurst itself, there were certainly Watsons enough in Stonyhurst's surroundings. The name, so frequently encountered outside the actual limits of the school, must have impressed itself deeply and ineradicably on Doyle's name-responsive memory.

The resurgence of that already familiar name in the years after schooldays would have strengthened the hold that the name Watson had already gained on him. It was Dr. *James* Watson who, as President of the Portsmouth Literary and Scientific Society, "did the honours" at the banquet given by the society to bid farewell to the Conan Doyles as they left financially unprofitable Southsea for the still-untried hazards of London.[2]

I think that we may now concede that the awareness of that name "Watson" came early to Conan Doyle; and the recurrence of that by-no-means-uncommon name, in the years after he left school, would have served only to deepen the already deep-etched consciousness of that early-learned name and its half-bitter, half-pleasant associations. It is not difficult to see, in the Canon's frequent references to horses, to the men and objects associated with horses–the "freemasonry among horsy men" (*A Scandal in Bohemia*), the "curious horseshoes" mentioned in *The Priory School*–the memory of boyhood hours spent, a fascinated spectator, outside the open door of Houlker Watson's smithy.

Well, thanks to that "hunch" which impelled me to look outside the strict limits of Stonyhurst College and revealed to me, through the good offices of the librarians at Blackburn, the presence, in Conan Doyle's boyhood, of an ineradicable "Watson consciousness," I had accounted for the name, if not altogether for the *persona*, of that Dr. Watson who is an indispensable element in the *design* of Sherlock Holmes.

But there remained, I felt, yet another most powerful influence in the making of Conan Doyle, and so, inevitably, in the making of Sherlock Holmes. I refer to Edgar Allan Poe.

The influence of Edgar Allan Poe on Conan Doyle has been long debated; and though Doyle (through the mouth of Holmes) tried to minimize that influence, as depriving Conan Doyle of much of the credit for his own creative work, it is clear that, at the beginning of his authorship, Doyle was strongly influenced by Poe. Why not? If one be about to embark on a detective story, what better tutor than the genius who, as Dorothy Sayers said in discussing "The Murders in the Rue Morgue," wrote what "constitutes in itself a complete manual of detective theory"?

Where the assessment of Poe's influence on Conan Doyle has gone wrong is in the assessors' concentrating on the influence of

---

[2] In *The Man with the Twisted Lip*, Mrs. *John* Watson calls her husband *James*.

Poe, *the inventor of the detective story,* to the ignoring of Poe's influence as the author of so much fiction of a different kind. For instance–and, as an instance of the most shameless plagiarism, this could hardly be excelled–compare Conan Doyle's short story "The New Catacomb" with its most polished original, "The Cask of Amontillado": here we have available both the impressive original and the blurred carbon-copy that the young Conan Doyle made of it.

But there is another short story of Poe's–a long short story, to be sure–which had, I maintain, the most profound influence on Doyle's thinking (rather than on his writing alone); and this tale of Poe's has never yet been suspected as one of the prime influences among the many influences which went into the shaping of Conan Doyle. This was that strange story of the man, "William Wilson," haunted by his double–his Doppelgänger–whom, in a rage of terror, he eventually kills . . . and, in so doing, kills himself.

A most curious point that Poe makes in the telling of this plainly autobiographical story is that the surname "Wilson" is of that kind which, in England, extends to cover the whole social spectrum (Poe said it in slightly less modern terms!) from the humblest labourer to the landed aristocrat or even the belted earl. This, as a glance at the current telephone directory and my Debrett makes clear, applied equally to the name "Watson."

"Watson," then, is to Conan Doyle what "Wilson" was to Poe: his "other half," his Doppelgänger, his uneasy conscience and constant reproach.

Conan Doyle, to go back to what I hinted earlier in this book, was not only a failure as a doctor; worse: he was tormented by the knowledge that he had so failed. That he had gained a fairly rapid and, as it turned out, an assured success as a writer did not rid him of that sense of guilt in considering how he had "treacherously" (so his far too scrupulous conscience saw it) abandoned his true vocation for the quicker profits of an inferior substitute.

For the "abandonment" of Medicine for Literature had been, for him, no simple choice. Had he accepted the urgings of his wealthy and influential London relatives and permitted them to make him an established *Catholic* medical practitioner, he would have been assured of both success in his vocation and of rewards not less than those that even great success as a writer promised. He had not merely "failed" in medicine, to the extent that he had failed to achieve a medical practice worth more than £300 ($1,500) a year; he had *rejected* the promise of success, so as not to be indebted to a religious discipline to which he was not prepared to pay even lip service.

That he was, in the early days of his writing, after he had given up his medical practice and had come to rely entirely on his writing to support himself and his family, not at all convinced that he had behaved correctly–let alone wisely–is evident. Even after he had gained great popularity as a writer and had reaped the financial rewards commensurate with that literary success, he still tried to "make amends" in respect of his lapse from grace. His visit to Vienna and his attempt to set himself up as an ophthalmological specialist in London shows well his desire to "make amends" for the dereliction of his duty toward that vocation for which he had worked so hard to fit himself. We know that the pressures that success creates made it impossible for him to neglect, let alone abandon, his literary work. But he did make one further attempt to turn back to his true vocation, to ease his conscience in so doing: that is when, as a doctor of medicine, and

The sobering smell of Success. The thoughtful face of the suddenly best-selling Dr. Conan Doyle seems to be regarding, not so much the astonishingly successful present as a future promising. . . what?. . . for both Conan Doyle and his unique creation, Sherlock Holmes.

not—oh, most certainly not (for all the books and pamphlets and short stories which followed)—as a writer, he took his field hospital to the war in South Africa.

It is ironic that this belated and final move to reconcile himself to his abandoned profession should have earned him the offer of a knighthood; and it must have been his clear knowledge of his own impulses which made him, in the first place, decline the honour.

The compulsion under which Conan Doyle laboured, once his writing, from having been a welcome financial help whilst he was building up his medical practice, became, almost without his volition, a substitute for it, was to force himself to believe that he had done wisely, done well, in making the change from unsuccessful doctor to successful author. But he needed—all the time he needed!—assurance that he had not done the wrong thing; and if what Queen Gertrude observed of Ophelia's protesting too much applied in equal force to Conan Doyle, the over-protestation was the expression of a genuine agony of conscience.

The creation of Watson was an exercise, then, not so much in self-deception as in self-justification—for the most imperfect Watson (a fully qualified Doctor of Medicine, be it remembered!) was what, Conan Doyle could tell himself, that successful but conscience-stricken Conan Doyle might have been, had he "done the right thing," as his family, especially his influential Roman Catholic relatives, would have wished him to do. But, in the image of the idle, ineffectual Watson, *unemployed, for all his good medical degrees,* Conan Doyle could see, with a shudder, an alternative to what his family assured him that *he* would be. A Harley Street specialist? A ladies' hand-holder, of the comforting bedside manner? But what if it had not turned out like that, for all the help that he was promised among the tight-knit, rabidly exclusive colony of "Romans"? What he *might* have been; what he feared to express, save by what so many have considered the most obscure symbolism; he has pictured, with harsh, pitiless accuracy, in his introductory portrait of Dr. Watson—the alternative self which fascinated as much as it frightened and repelled the sadly insecure Conan Doyle.

No wonder, then, that the Heroic Conan Doyle—Holmes—despises and mocks and treats as a servant the aimless hanger-on: Watson, the Unheroic Doyle.

Sherlock Holmes, then, is Conan Doyle as he wished to be; as what he very nearly became. Watson is what Conan Doyle feared that, taking a different path in the forked road of life, he might have become.

Edgar Allan Poe, in that strange story of the Haunted Man and his ever-present, tireless "other self," "William Wilson," as surely provided the pattern for the association and the delineation of Holmes and Watson as Poe's tale "The Cask of Amontillado" offered a pattern for Conan Doyle's copying in "The New Catacomb." Consciously or subconsciously, Conan Doyle responded, with all the fervour of his emotional being, not only to the concept of the personified self-reproach, the personified voice of conscience which is the theme of "William Wilson" but also, and thankfully, to the *solution* of his own perplexities that that strange story offered.

For the solution offered was this: If, in the *persona* of Watson, Conan Doyle was symbolizing the reproachful reminder of duties neglected, he might still, in the *persona* of Sherlock Holmes, offer a defense of Conan Doyle. He never quite succeeded in either dismissing the reproachful Watson in his life, nor yet achieving a total triumph for his defender, Holmes. But he came very near to victory . . .

11

THE ENGLISH OPIUM-EATER

I WROTE, at the end of Chapter 8, that I had not yet done with my examination of the influence of Stonyhurst on Conan Doyle; and now it is time to return, not so much to Stonyhurst itself as to a perhaps fully equal influence–but one which would never have come to affect Conan Doyle so profoundly had not Stonyhurst come to dominate his conscious and subconscious, so that the very name "Stonyhurst" triggered off for him (as, indeed, it did for me) a train of association leading to an awareness that I shall now discuss. This, in truth, is the strong influence of Stonyhurst still, but the influence exerted by association; exerted, as it were, indirectly; at second-hand.

As the writing of this present book progressed, my mental ears were growing ever more sensitive to the "echoes" to be found in Conan Doyle's name-choices: "echoes" of a thousand past experiences, fixed in his awareness by the never-to-be forgotten names associated with those experiences, and names which, with that strange, essentially idiosyncratic frugality of Doyle's, were never to be wasted, never not-to-be-used. It was in 1896, on his return from a visit to Egypt, where he had been entertained by yet another famous British hero, Kitchener, that he was pleased to know how well his book *The Exploits of Brigadier Gerard* had been received by the public. The success was deserved; next to Holmes, Gerard, as I have already said, was Conan Doyle's most felicitous invention. The name . . . ? Again as I have said, the choice of any name used by Conan Doyle seems to have become "eligible by reinforcement": once encountered in memorable circumstances, the name became securely fixed in the "name list" by a second encounter.

So with Gerard—though which Gerard-encounter came first, I cannot say. But I would suggest that the first Gerard was encountered personally; the second, in Doyle's historical reading. The first, in my opinion, was Father John Gerard, who joined the staff of Stonyhurst in 1870 and in 1887—the year which saw the appearance of Sherlock Holmes in *A Study in Scarlet*—published a Latin grammar, and whose influence we see in the Canon's four Latin quotations.[1] The second Gérard is that famous French general who, in rallying to the returned Napoleon, seems, in his dedication to the Emperor, no less than a prefiguration of the fictional Gerard of Conan Doyle.

Now for another "echo". . .

The name of "Stonyhurst" was familiar to me as being one of England's principal public schools—not merely one of the principal Roman Catholic public schools—but in that name "Stonyhurst" the echo of something different, of something "long ago and far away," persisted in troubling the inner ear of memory. *What* was it in that name which haunted me with the sense of something which had once been so familiar—something quite apart from the name "Stonyhurst" as that of a school? It was a most fugitive memory, and many days had to pass until I might account for the vague familiarity of the name.

But at last it "came back," as the saying goes, and I got up from my chair at my writing table and went to one of my many bookcases; happy to find that the little volume that I sought was still to be found among my books. I opened the book and, within a few seconds, had found what I sought: the passage which had seemed to echo (certainly for Conan Doyle, as it had for me) something in the name "Stonyhurst." Yes . . . here it was:

---

[1] This information was kindly supplied by the Reverend Father F. J. Turner, S.J.

So then, Oxford-street, stony-hearted stepmother!

"Stonyhurst"..."stony-hearted stepmother"... The link had been broken for me, and restored after so many years. I could not believe that Conan Doyle, reading that line from one of the most moving passages in all the world's literature, had not heard the echo: *Stonyhurst . . . stony-hearted stepmother*. But here, with the little Victorian volume in my hand, it was the easiest task to check my theory. And, oh yes! the proof that I was right was readily forthcoming...

In 1886, the year in which, so Conan Doyle tells us, he wrote *A Study in Scarlet,* the London publishing house of Walter Scott added to their list *Confessions of an English Opium-Eater, by Thomas De Quincey. With Introductory Note by William Sharp*. The volume itself–"pocket-size"–is a charming little production, in the highest tradition of Victorian publishing: intelligent in criticism, elegant in format, and astonishingly modest in price. There may be not the least doubt that, whether Conan Doyle or "Touie" bought the book (and its pretty decorative gold-stamped cover might have appealed more to a woman than to a man), De Quincey's *Opium-Eater* came into the small library of the small house at No. 1, Bush Villas, Southsea–but not, I think, for the first time in Conan Doyle's life.

The Conan Doyles had yet to be married a full year, and the late John Dickson Carr has drawn aside the veil for a brief glimpse at their modestly happy married life:

> "Shall we read aloud together, my dear," [Conan Doyle] would suggest, "and improve our minds? Say Gordon's *Tacitus?* Or perhaps, in a lighter vein, Boswell's *Johnson* or Pepys's Diary?"
>
> "Oh, do!" cried Touie, who would have been just as eager to hear him read in Sanskrit if he had possessed that accomplishment.

To Tacitus and Boswell and Pepys, we may confidently add a better writer than any of them: Thomas De Quincey, the English Opium-Eater.

But whether or not Conan Doyle read the *Opium-Eater* aloud to Touie, it is certain that he read it–and read all of it; and all of it with unflagging interest and attention. Here, as printed on the reverse of the title page, is the table of contents:

Confessions of an English Opium-eater
The Pleasures of Opium
Introduction to the Pains of Opium
Levana and our Ladies of Sorrow
Unwinding the Accursed Chain
Notes from the Pocket-book of a Late Opium-eater
On the Knocking at the Gate in Macbeth
On Suicide
Rosicrucians and Freemasons
Kant on National Character
Analects from Richter

And there is not one of these chapters–indeed, we must take care to include William Sharp's biographical Introductory Note–which has not provided Conan Doyle with a name, a thought, a philosophical reflection, whilst the totality of this slim book's influence on his thinking is such that we now could not imagine Sherlock Holmes without that still unexplained self-indulgence in which, as Conan Doyle made him do, he copied De Quincey, and became the Opium-Eater of Baker Street.

I have, I hope, plausibly demonstrated the influence on Conan Doyle–specifically on Doyle as he slowly puts together the jigsaw-picture which finished as the portrait of Sherlock Holmes–of many an element that he was to encounter until he, as did the young Byron, woke to find himself famous. There was the Houlker Watson who pulled down the windmill; there were the two fighting Scherers–the first fighting to get justice for Galley, the second fighting against the mean prejudice of yet another attorney; there was Poe, who not only gave him his earliest idea-models, but showed, in "William Wilson," how the Hero Holmes might be separated from his lesser self by making that other self, Watson, his Doppelgänger . . . But most potent of all the many influences going to make up both Conan Doyle *and* Sherlock Holmes was De Quincey: the man *and* his book.

I had forgotten what, apparently, others have never seen: that Conan Doyle must have grown up in Edinburgh in the very lively consciousness of that most eccentric of all literary geniuses, Thomas De Quincey.

How? Why . . . ?

Because, next to Walter Scott, Thomas De Quincey was Edinburgh's most famous literary man, who had lived, an unforgettable character even to the inhabitants of a city with more than its share of eccentrics, for more than the last twenty years of his life in "Old Reekie" and who had died at No. 42 Lothian Street, just around the corner from any of the Doyles' five Edinburgh addresses, but nearest of all to Picardy Place, where Arthur Conan Doyle was born in 1859, the year in which De Quincey died.

As a boy, I grew up in a Kent to which Charles Dickens was what De Quincey had been to mid-Victorian Edinburgh; the Rochester of my youth was not only full of the memories and associations of "Boz" but full, too, of people who had known him. Yet, when I came to an awareness of this local hero, he had been dead for over forty years. Whereas Conan Doyle must have grown up even more aware of a De Quincey who had died less than twenty years before than I was of a Dickens who had died over forty years earlier. Indeed, as Conan Doyle lived in the Edinburgh family house until he was well past twenty, he could not have grown up save in a constant awareness of De Quincey.

Conan Doyle, then, must have bought De Quincey's little volume, not because Doyle was unfamiliar with either De Quincey or his works, but because he *was* familiar with them, and had been so since early boyhood.

We have not long to wait to see how deeply Conan Doyle was influenced by that re-reading of Edinburgh's second greatest literary lion. In Sharp's brief biographical preface to the book, up come the names which are to be so familiar to us in the Canon: Miss Blake, Lady Erroll's sister, whom De Quincey met on his way to visit his young friend in Ireland, Lord Westport—"Blake" and "Westport" being echoed in "Blaker" (*The Valley of Fear*) and "Westport" in a double-echo: "Arthur Cadogan West" (*The Bruce-Partington Plans*) and Mrs. Porter (*The Devil's Foot*), but also —as regards the first part of the split name—in Westaway's (*The Copper Beeches*), Violet Westbury (*The Bruce-Partington Plans*),

Westhouse & Marbank (*A Case of Identity*), and Honoria Westphail (*The Speckled Band*).

De Quincey's mother, Sharp tells us, having got tired of Bath, had moved to a house in Chester "called the Priory," and, sure enough, up comes the name of that Chester house in *The Priory School.* That most heart-rending episode of the "famishing scholar and the neglected child," cold and hungry in the unfurnished room in Greek Street, is not the only mention of the word "Greek" to be echoed in *The Greek Interpreter;* earlier in his autobiographical narrative, De Quincey tells us that he "was very early distinguished for my classical attainments, especially for my knowledge of Greek. At thirteen I wrote Greek with ease; and at fifteen my command of that language was so great that I not only composed Greek verses in lyric metres, but could converse in Greek fluently, and without embarrassment"–so that Conan Doyle, reading De Quincey, had the word "Greek" well impressed upon his consciousness.

So, too, from this same narrative come the names of Keswick, where he stayed with Southey (Keswick–*A Study in Scarlet*); of his wife Margaret (Maggie Oakshott–*The Blue Carbuncle*); and of her brother Horace (Horace Harker–*The Six Napoleons*); and of his friend and constant companion, John Wilson–"Christopher North"–"of tremendous physique, who played Titan to De Quincey's pygmy" (a name which appears no fewer than *nine* times in the Canon!).

And here again, in this multiple use of his great friend's surname, we strike the curious paradox almost always inherent in, not so much Conan Doyle's *choice* of name, as in his *award* of name. Bearing in mind that John Wilson ("Christopher North") was De Quincey's constant and greatly loved friend, see how the "Wilsons" of the Canon have been distributed: a chaplain, a constable, a sergeant, four Wilsons in *The Valley of Fear,* a messenger-office firm, and the name in an undescribed case noted by Watson as "the arrest of Wilson, the notorious canary-trainer"–the strangest name-award of all, since here "canary" is not the little yellow bird which warns coal-miners of the presence of lethal methane, but (as *A Dictionary of Historical Slang* informs us) "a gaol-bird, a mistress, a harlot or a thief's female assistant," the last sense obviously being the one intended here.

"Landor," says Sharp, "utters a fine and true saying when . . .

he makes Vittoria Colonna remark that 'the human heart is a world of poetry; the imagination is only its atmosphere.'" Conan Doyle evidently agreed with this, for he uses the name "Colonna" unaltered (as the "Prince of Colonna") in *The Six Napoleons.*

But the most striking use of a name from the De Quincey volume is that of a man who has left us a detailed description of De Quincey in his last Edinburgh days: "One of these accounts, from the pen of the late *Hill Burton,* may be given as an especially vivid presentment of the Opium-Eater . . ."

In *The Illustrious Client* (1924), when Dr. Watson has to adopt an *alias,* it is *Hill Barton* that he chooses, or that Holmes chooses for him. This could not possibly be coincidence.

Turning now to the portion of the De Quincey volume entitled "Analects from Richter," we find this short passage set out separately from the main text of the section:

The GRANDEUR OF MAN IN HIS LITTLENESS

Man upon this earth would be vanity and hollowness, dust and ashes, vapour, and a bubble, were it not that he felt himself to be so. That it is possible for him to harbour such a feeling–*this,* by implying a comparison of himself with something higher in himself, *this* it is which makes him the immortal creature that he is.

In *The Sign of the Four* (1890), Holmes synopsizes, paraphrases, and generally simplifies this for his friend, the simple-minded military man, Dr. Watson:

"He [Richter] makes one curious but profound remark. It is that the chief proof of man's real greatness lies in his perception of his own smallness. It argues, you see, a power of comparison and of appreciation which is in itself a proof of nobility."

Another section of the De Quincey volume deals with "Kant on National Character in Relation to the Sense of the Sublime and Beautiful," and here again we find something that not only has Conan Doyle read but which has greatly impressed him. One example of this influence will suffice:

Kant has written:

The Italian genius has distinguished itself especially in Music, Painting, Sculpture, and Architecture. All these fine arts meet with an equally refined culture in France . . .

and Kant goes on at length to examine and define the French attitude toward, and idiosyncratic handling of, art in its various forms.

But with this opinion of the French and their art, De Quincey does not agree, and makes his own opinion clear in this footnote:

To the judicious reader it need not be said how strikingly in opposition to facts is Kant's judgment on the French taste in the Fine Arts. What the French poetry is, most men know: ***the French music is the jest of Europe:*** and if we except the single name of Poussin, there is no other in any of the Fine Arts which can impress our ear with much reverence. [Emphasis added]

This grotesque evaluation of the most gifted race in the modern world—or, rather, of that gifted race's incredibly versatile creative talent—deserves nothing more than to be dismissed with contempt, as being an opinion disregarding fact and springing only from the most childish xenophobia. But . . . we cannot so dismiss it; for Conan Doyle, despite his "French connections," obviously approves the sentiment sufficiently to make it the sentiment of Holmes, too; though Holmes rather praises the German than denounces the French when he remarks to Watson in *The Red-Headed League:* "I observe that there is a good deal of German music on the programme, which is rather more to my taste than Italian or French."

More mildly expressed, it is yet the pure De Quincey francophobia.

The De Quincey volume includes the famous essay on an "Historico-critical Inquiry into the Origin of the Rosicrucians and the Freemasons," and the Freemasons are referred to, both literally and metaphorically (the "freemasonry among horsy men" —*A Scandal in Bohemia*), several times in the Canon; the infamous Enoch Drebber of *A Study in Scarlet* is a Mason; *The Red-Headed League* lets us examine an "arc-and-compass breastpin"—what we call now a tie-pin. And there are other references to the Craft and its traditional symbols.

But by far the most important echo of De Quincey, not merely in the Canon but in the very essentials of Holmes's character, are those vivid descriptions of drug-taking which give

De Quincey's volume its always most memorable title: *Confessions of an English Opium-Eater*.

It hardly matters that there are references to opium in the Canon which concern, but do not actually include, Holmes: *The Man with the Twisted Lip*, Hugh Boone, who is really Neville St. Clair, is first seen by the reader in a Thames-side opium den; there is opium again in *Wisteria Lodge;* and there are other mentions.

But what is most important of all, in the making of Sherlock Holmes, is that Conan Doyle has endowed Holmes with–I was about to say, De Quincey's admitted vice; but "vice" is hardly the correct term for the drug-taking of either De Quincey or Holmes. Both drug-takers plead necessity: in De Quincey's case, the necessity first to combat the pain of hunger and, after, the need to combat what we may call a "secondary" pain–a pain arising out of the acquired habit of drug-taking ("opium-eating"); the real, even though psychosomatic, pain induced by the fear of the "withdrawal symptoms"; in short, the well-known "tiger by the tail" syndrome.

Holmes only *appears* to offer a different explanation of his addiction to Watson: "I suppose that its influence is physically a bad one. I find it, however, so transcendently stimulating and clarifying to the mind that its secondary action is of small moment."

Watson–the ordinary (and not at all successful) general practitioner, and never the specialist–protests:

"But consider! Count the cost! Your brain may, as you say, be roused and excited, but it is a pathological and morbid process which involves increased tissue-change . . . You know, too, what a black reaction comes upon you. Surely the game is hardly worth the candle. Why should you, for a mere passing pleasure, risk the loss of those great powers with which you have been endowed?"

Holmes is not offended; he has his answers ready:

"My mind rebels at stagnation. Give me problems, give me work, give me the most abstruse cryptogram, or the most intricate analysis, and I am in my own proper atmosphere. I can dispense with artificial stimulants. But I abhor the dull routine of existence. I crave for mental exaltation."

And, as De Quincey points out, with opium one does obtain that desired "mental exaltation":

. . . [F]or ten years, during which I took opium at intervals, the day succeeding to that on which I allowed myself this luxury was always a day of unusually good spirits.

With respect to the torpor supposed to follow, or rather (if we were to credit the numerous pictures of Turkish opium-eaters) to accompany the practice of opium-eating, I deny that also. Certainly opium is classed under the head of narcotics; and some such effect it may produce in the end; *but the primary effects of opium are always, and in the highest degree, to excite and stimulate the system* . . . [Emphasis added]

If a reader now were to exclaim, "But this surely is Sherlock Holmes talking!" that reader would be quite correct–for, indeed, it *is* Holmes who speaks, though the words and phrases that he uses, the arguments (some consciously specious, others not) that he presents, are those of De Quincey, the English Opium-Eater, put into Holmes's mouth by Conan Doyle.

There is no need further to seek and display the many points of identity between De Quincey's detailed account of his drug addiction and Conan Doyle's re-presentation of it, though in a highly synopsized form, in *The Sign of the Four* and elsewhere throughout the Canon.

No other book, no other single source of inspiration for Conan Doyle, had so creative an influence in the Making of Sherlock Holmes . . .

But, I can hear so many protesting, Conan Doyle did not give us Holmes as an "opium-eater"–he is presented as a cocaine addict!

I refer the makers of such protest to the source: *The Sign of the Four,* which begins with what must surely be the most famous passage in the Canon:

Sherlock Holmes took his bottle from the corner of the mantelpiece, and his hypodermic syringe from its neat morocco case. With his long, white, nervous fingers he adjusted the delicate needle and rolled back his left shirtcuff. For some little time his eyes rested thoughtfully upon the sinewy forearm and wrist, all dotted and scarred with innumerable puncture-marks. Finally, he thrust the sharp[2] point home, pressed

---

[2]One would say that the needles of *all* hypodermic syringes are sharp (save in the Army), but the selection of this particular adjective surely echoes William *Sharp,* writer of the prefatory note to the De Quincey volume.

down the tiny piston, and sank back into the velvet-lined armchair with a long sigh of satisfaction.

With what had he just injected himself? Certainly, nine out of ten, asked that question, would reply: "Cocaine"–and in this particular instance that nine-tenths of the questioned would be right. But it is a fact which was not at all "obvious" to Dr. Watson, watching the injection with disapproval; and it needed a question from Holmes's critical friend to establish the nature of the drug subcutaneously injected before him:

> "Which is it to-day," I asked, "morphine or cocaine?"
> He raised his eyes languidly from the old black-letter volume which he had opened.
> "It is cocaine," he said, "a seven-per-cent. solution. Would you care to try it?"

Now, through the influence of such successful books as Nicholas Meyer's *The Seven-Per-Cent Solution*, the image of Holmes as a *cocaine* addict has been, I think ineradicably, fixed in the public mind.

"Pass the cocaine, Watson!" has now become the instantly-comprehended facetious reference to Sherlock Holmes.

Yet from the very commencement of, not the record of the Holmes–Watson association, but of the revelation of Holmes as a self-confessed drug addict, there is no question that at least *two* drugs are concerned in Holmes's addiction, and Watson, who remarks sadly that, "Three times a day for many months I had witnessed this performance," still has to enquire which of the preferred drugs it is that Holmes is taking at present.

That Holmes is using a hypodermic syringe does not provide the information; but that Holmes could use a hypodermic needle for the administration of either morphine or cocaine does tell *us* the probable form in which he is taking his *opium*.

Opium . . . ?

Here is the relevant entry in *The British Pharmacopoeia:*

MORPHINAE HYDROCHLORIDUM

[Morph. Hydrochlor.]

Morphine Hydrochloride

$C_{17}H_{19}O_3N,HC1,3H_2O$ . . . Mol. Wt. 375·7

Morphine Hydrochloride is the hydrochloride of an alkaloid, morphine, obtained from opium. . . .

DOSES

Metric	Imperial
0.008 to 0.02 gramme	1/8 to 1/3 grain

Well, Holmes did take opium–in the form of morphine–as Watson states with his quite unambiguous question: "Which is it to-day, morphine or cocaine?"

I think that Holmes's facetious question to Watson, when the two men met in the Bar of Gold opium den may have been read by too many people with insufficient attention, with a consequent misunderstanding of what Holmes said and meant: "I suppose, Watson, that you imagine that I have added opium-smoking to cocaine injections, and all the other little weaknesses on which you have favoured me with your medical views."

What Holmes specifically denied here was that he *smoked* opium. Of course he didn't: he *injected* it, as morphine hydrochloride.

But here, as in other places in the Canon, there is more than the mere implication that indulgence in opium (morphine) and cocaine by no means exhausts the total of Holmes's vices–if we are justified in calling them that (De Quincey would not so have described them).

For what were "all the other little weaknesses" which had called forth Watson's medical condemnation? To add morphine to the cocaine injections would simply have given admission to *two* "little weaknesses"–what, then, were the rest? Certain of Watson's references to Holmes's "weaknesses" are not so much ambiguous as obscure–and one may consider them deliberately so. For instance, in *The Devil's Foot,* Watson tells us that Holmes's illness was caused not only by hard work but had been "aggravated, perhaps, by occasional indiscretions of his own." What could these have been? As Watson had already stated, in *The Sign of the Four,* which was published in 1890, that Holmes took both morphine and cocaine, there must be a graver significance in that reference to "occasional indiscretions" made with the publication of *The Devil's Foot* in 1910. As Watson has already told us about the morphine and cocaine, these "indiscretions" must be something else; and, one assumes, something graver. One might suspect that opium derivative at second hand: heroin, the drug prepared from morphia and ignorantly prescribed at the turn of this century as a *non-addictive* substitute for morphine!

What, even if we admit the addiction of heroin to the list of "vices," were the other "indiscretions" which had called forth Watson's criticisms as a doctor? Watson is most severe in his choice of phrase: he refers to Holmes's "drug *mania*," and he expresses his fears that Holmes might return to his seemingly conquered indulgences in the gloomy opinion that "the fiend was not dead but sleeping, and the waking near."

Holmes's "opium-eating" is derived directly from Conan Doyle's knowledge of De Quincey, the Edinburgh "great man," and an admiration of his writings; Doyle obviously having read with the greatest attention *The Confessions of an English Opium-Eater*. Even the introduction to the volume by William Sharp had not been skipped, for not only did the title page of the book yield the to-be-used-in-the-Canon names "Walter" and "Scott" but the introduction itself yielded, as I have said, "The Priory," "Keswick," "Colonna," and "Hill Burton," whilst, in De Quincey's essay on "Rosicrucians and Freemasons," there is a reference to "the late Mr. Von Born," in which name it is hard not to see the original of the "Von Bork"[3] of *His Last Bow*.

No matter what Conan Doyle, *as a doctor*, makes Watson, *as a doctor*, say in condemnation of Holmes's drug-taking, it must be noted with the sharpest attention that it is to cocaine specifically that Watson objects—as, presumably, did Conan Doyle. But what is certain is that, just as De Quincey did not regard his opium-eating as a vice to be condemned, so neither did Conan Doyle regard Holmes's opium-eating—his morphine-taking—as a vice. The grave warnings against indulgence in drugs with which Watson attempts, like the Fat Boy in *Pickwick*, to make Holmes's flesh creep, are directed against cocaine, and against cocaine only. At no point in the Canon is opium condemned, and, in this defense-by-silence, Conan Doyle is warmly supported by a

---

[3] De Quincey's reference is to Ignaz von Born (1742–1791), Austrian mineralogist and metallurgist. It was he who invented the process of extracting silver from ores by amalgamation and also introduced improvements in mining, salt-working, and bleaching.

famous doctor who was also a famous writer–I have mentioned him before–and in every way a hero to Conan Doyle: Dr. Oliver Wendell Holmes, who gave more than his surname to the making of Sherlock Holmes.

Dr. Oliver Wendell Holmes not only does not disapprove of wine, he doesn't disapprove of opium either; he . . . but read what is probably the most famous passage from the soundly common-sense side of medical thinking:

> Throw out opium, which the Creator himself seems to prescribe, for we often see the scarlet poppy growing in the cornfields, as if it were foreseen that wherever there is hunger to be fed there must also be pain to be soothed; . . . throw out wine, which is a food, and the vapours which produce the miracle of anaesthesia–and I firmly believe that if the whole *materia medica,* as now used, could be sunk to the bottom of the sea, it would be all the better for mankind–and all the worse for the fishes.

So that, whatever assurance that he had received from De Quincey that opium's benefits far outweighed its disadvantages, Conan Doyle had his hero, Wendell Holmes, supporting De Quincey . . . though possibly not altogether for the same reasons. Judging by the number of names encountered in the De Quincey writings which have been used in the Canon, one might confidently assign the major influence to De Quincey in the matter of Conan Doyle's making Holmes an opium-eater, save for the fact that, as Doyle's encountering the name of Wendel Scherer instantly put him in mind of Wendell Holmes, we must accept that Wendell Holmes was no minor influence over Conan Doyle's thinking.

The making of Sherlock Holmes was like the making of a patchwork quilt: an assembling of the most diverse scraps, gathered from a hundred sources, as each scrap caught and held the attention of the gatherer. Yet, sewn together, each scrap contributes not only to the complete design but to the strength which makes and maintains the whole. I would not claim ever that, for all my minute research into the sources of Conan Doyle's numberless names, I have traced every one to that eye-catching origin which earned it inexclusable inclusion within the Conan Doyle name store.

I cannot explain many things about this selection and use of names; for instance, why does Conan Doyle sometimes alter the name only slightly; sometimes greatly; sometimes not at all? An example of the last: I have mentioned Doyle's Latin master at Stonyhurst–Father John Gerard, probably the prime source of that name that Conan Doyle gave to his dashing Brigadier. But I also suggested, as a possible "reinforcing" source, the equally dashing French cavalry general who rallied to Napoleon for the Hundred Days and, two days before Waterloo, repelled Blücher's Prussians at Ligny, thus winning the last French victory of the Napoleonic twilight: Etienne-Maurice, Count Gérard, marshal of France.

And what did the Brigadier get as a name from Conan Doyle? Why, the unaltered name of Napoleon's victorious general: *Etienne Gérard!*

But if, in this instance, the actual name of the original appeared in Conan Doyle's "echo," the presence of yet another French Gérard must not be overlooked: François Gérard, the renowned historical artist, made a baron of the Empire by Napoleon I for having painted "The Battle of Austerlitz" to the greater glory of his Imperial Master. But, given these completely "open" uses of the name of Gérard–derived, I suggest, primarily from that of Father Gerard of Stonyhurst; secondarily from that of the French cavalry general, victor of Ligny; and thirdly, but to a much lesser degree, from that of the artist who recorded Napoleon's "Battle of the Three Emperors," his most famous victory–there were other derived names, not so "open."

As with so many of Conan Doyle's name-usings, there were two facets to name-use: the "open," the evident, the obvious–and the use hidden behind pun and analogy, not always the easiest thing in the world to discover and interpret.

For there is, as any biographical dictionary will confirm, yet another famous Gerard, and in one's seeing the name of both the general and the artist, one could not avoid the sight of this third "Gerard" name.

The use of this name is in the "concealed" class; and one has had to learn the means of detecting and exposing it for what it truly is. It would take too long that I should explain how I came to understand Conan Doyle's somewhat boyish love of secrecy for its own sake, so that he felt himself often under a compulsion to hide what to him (though possibly not to us) seemed to demand concealment.

I refer now to Balthazar Gerard (1558–1584), the fanatic who assassinated William of Orange and suffered on the scaffold in punishment.

This criminal, though never named in the Canon, is the "inspiration" from which Conan Doyle derived both the unreported "delicate affair of the reigning family of Holland"–the house of *Orange,* a derivation still fairly close to the original–and, very much removed, the title of *The Five Orange Pips,* of which Holmes remarked to Watson: "I think that, of all our cases, we have had none more fantastic than this."

Over the luncheon table, Conan Doyle's daughter, Dame Jean, was giving me her views on the several recent biographers of her distinguished father. One she picked out for her special disapproval, but there were others who had irritated her (though in a lesser degree) by the same fault as that with which the chief offender had earned her disapproval: a hope–a promise–that "the whole story" of Conan Doyle would be known and told as and when his "private papers" would be made available to historians.

"What nonsense!" Dame Jean commented, with some warmth; "they keep on about these so-called 'private papers,' and imply that they would reveal Heaven-knows-what dark secrets. But the fact is that there simply *aren't* any 'hidden archives' that they all keep on about. Why do they insist on hinting at them, when they simply don't exist?"

"They keep on *hoping,*" I said, "that there are such 'archives' –though they'd be in for much disappointment if they went looking for dark secrets. I can't think of any man in the public eye who lived a more open, a less secret, life than did your father . . ."

This was and is true, of course; but both Dame Jean and I were wrong in denying the existence of a concealed record of Conan Doyle's interests, hopes, plans, disappointments, affections, dislikes–all, in short, that we group under the general heading of "emotional response." Conan Doyle, as did Samuel

Pepys, left a record of what had deeply interested him; in particular, what had most intimately involved his most inward sentiments. Pepys, as is so often, and so erroneously, stated, did not leave a diary "in cypher"; he wrote his famous diary in what, by 1800, had become a quite obsolete shorthand. Had the shorthand been recognized as such from the beginning, a "decypherment" would have been an easier task—but it is obvious that Pepys's concealment, such as it was, was designed to do no more than hide his personal record from the eyes of his wife and her servants. The code with which Conan Doyle has concealed his more private interests, speculations, and conclusions, his affections and dislikes, is one far more difficult to crack, but, as Sir Thomas Browne observed: "What Songs the *Syrens* sang, or what Name *Achilles* assumed when he hid himself among Women, though puzzling questions, are not beyond all Conjecture."

And, indeed, did we know nothing of Conan Doyle save from what we may find in his writings, careful study of the names that he uses would tell us much. We know, from John Dickson Carr's *Life,* of the "Ma'am's" somewhat excessive interest in genealogy and heraldry; an interest that Conan Doyle acquired from her, putting it to practical use in both *The White Company* and *Sir Nigel.* But if we had been ignorant of this family interest in heraldry, we might reasonably have surmised the existence of such interest in our observing Conan Doyle's use of the name "Fairbairn" in *The Cardboard Box,* for *Fairbairn* was the standard Victorian (illustrated) guide to the crests of the British armigerous families.

But too often, one may trace the origin of a name, yet still find oneself unable to explain why the name, or the event to which the name belongs, attracted Conan Doyle's attention in the first place.

For example, in *The Five Orange Pips,* Watson alludes to an undescribed "adventure of the Paradol Chamber." I may well have missed the explanation of this curious title, but in all the thousands of words of Sherlockian exegesis that I have read, I cannot find one. Am I the first to explain how Conan Doyle came to think up the phrase "Paradol Chamber"? Well, here is the correct explanation of how he came to encounter the name; though I cannot—yet—explain how it had a special significance for him.

A century ago, Prévôt Paradol, whilst France's ambassador to

Washington, committed suicide there. So much for the unusual name "Paradol." How, then, did the word "chamber" come to be attached to "Paradol"? The answer lies in the French dictionary, and here, be it noticed, only one of the many French dictionaries at which I looked. So that we know that, *in all probability,* Conan Doyle owned or consulted the very popular Victorian *Bellows' French Dictionary,* the one that my father, who was educated in France, bought for me, the second pocket edition, 1876.

If one turn up the word *prévôt* in the *Bellows*[4] (and not, say, *Larousse*), this is what one finds:

PRÉVÔT• • provost (de *salle*) assistant fencing-master

The italicized word, *salle,* is the first to catch anyone's eye who turns up *prévôt* in *Bellows;* and it certainly caught Conan Doyle's eye.

So, then, he translated *salle* into English. *Salle:* "hall, room, chamber." Neither *salle* nor "chamber" has anything to connect it with *prévôt,* save loosely in the phrase *prévôt de salle.* But Conan Doyle knew his own code; knew his very boyish system of mnemonics–and I give this most typical "Conandrum" in some detail because, if we understand how Conan Doyle set down the fact of Prévôt Paradol's suicide as a reference (perfectly comprehensible to Doyle, though quite incomprehensible to his reading public) to the "adventure of the Paradol Chamber," we may be well on the way to decypher and interpret all the other hidden allusions.

I have blazed the trail to discovery. I now invite others to take up the search where I leave off. . .

And lastly, a most important question: why, to complete the finishing touch to that multi-origined character, Sherlock Holmes, did Conan Doyle make his so carefully and lovingly put-together Superman Detective. . . an opium-eater?

---

[4] I refer, of course, to the *Bellows* available before *The Five Orange Pips* was written in 1891: the 1876 edition. The entry in my more modern Fourth Edition (1951) varies slightly from earlier versions.

That he did must assure us of one irrefutable conclusion: that, in doing so, Conan Doyle was not bestowing a "vice" on his hero. It has been said to me that this endowment of Holmes with a drug addiction shows, not so much Conan Doyle's tolerant attitude toward human weakness, as his masterly understanding that the reading public doesn't like its heroes to be too heroic; that they prefer the most majestic to have at least one foot of clay.

I cannot agree; Holmes's opium-eating is not presented to the reader as a fault, for all that Watson insists that it is. Though Poe, to whom Doyle owed so much, merely *hints* that his detective hero, the Chevalier C. Auguste Dupin, takes drugs, De Quincey (to whom Conan Doyle owes little less) states plainly, not merely that he has taken drugs but that in so doing he has been but one of a large and notable company of men sharing the same addiction. Here is a passage which must have impressed Conan Doyle greatly:

> Guilt, therefore, I do not acknowledge; and if I did, it is possible that I might still resolve on the present act of confession, in consideration of the service which I may render to the whole class of opium-eaters. But who are they? Reader, I am sorry to say, a very numerous class indeed. Of this I became convinced some years ago, by computing, at that time, the number of those in one small class of English society *(the class of men distinguished for talents, or of eminent station)*, who were known to me, directly or indirectly, as opium-eaters; such for instance as the eloquent and benevolent —, the late dean of —; Lord —; Mr. —, the philosopher; a late under-secretary of state (who described to me the sensation which first drove him to the use of opium, in the very same words as the dean of —, viz, "that he felt as though rats were gnawing and abrading the coats of his stomach"); Mr. —; and many others hardly less known, whom it would be tedious to mention. [Emphasis added]

One might well dignify this passage as Conan Doyle's authority—his plenary authority—to confer the distinction of opium-eating on his master sleuth; opium-eating which not only did relatively little harm, and kept the intestinal rodents quiet, but which generated no feelings of guilt in the addict, and which was the indulgence—if one might use even so harsh a term to describe it—of "the class of men distinguished for talents, or of eminent station," a class to which Sherlock Holmes, with or without drug-taking, so obviously belonged.

And Conan Doyle needed to give his hero some notable characteristics. "Ratiocination"–the ability to solve a knotty problem–wasn't enough; Poe's Dupin could rival that; so could Gaboriau's Lecoq. Arrogance wasn't enough–Dupin could be pretty arrogant on occasion. Something else–some other striking quality–was needed to make Sherlock Holmes instantly memorable. And this was, as Conan Doyle saw it, to make Holmes a *controlled* drug addict.

"Indeed," says De Quincey, "the fascinating powers of opium are admitted even by medical writers . . ." De Quincey certainly had an important say in the making of Sherlock Holmes.

Thomas De Quincey (1785–1859), "The English Opium-Eater"–superb essayist and critic; for many years the near-neighbour of the Doyle family in Edinburgh; friend of Wordsworth, Coleridge, and Southey. His influence on Arthur Conan Doyle–and thus on the Making of Sherlock Holmes–may never be over-estimated.

Appendix I

THE CODE OF THE CANON

For convenience of reference, Sherlockians long ago reduced the often lengthy original titles of the Sherlock Holmes stories and novels to a standard four-letter (or numeral-and-three-letter) code. I did not use this code in the book just finished, for it seemed that many outside the strict confines of Sherlockianism might find it too unfamiliar to be comprehensible. But now that, I trust, both Sherlock Holmes and his creator have been presented to the reader in some detail, that reader ought to be made acquainted with the code by which all true *aficionados* of the Master refer to the elements of the Sacred Writings. Some Sherlockians write the code in upper-and-lower case; others in capital letters throughout. I prefer the latter method. Here is the complete code:

ABBE	The Abbey Grange
BERY	The Beryl Coronet
BLAC	Black Peter
BLAN	The Blanched Soldier
BLUE	The Blue Carbuncle
BOSC	The Boscombe Valley Mystery
BRUC	The Bruce-Partington Plans
CARD	The Cardboard Box
CHAS	Charles Augustus Milverton
COPP	The Copper Beeches
CREE	The Creeping Man
CROO	The Crooked Man
DANC	The Dancing Men
DEVI	The Devil's Foot
DYIN	The Dying Detective
EMPT	The Empty House
ENGR	The Engineer's Thumb
FINA	The Final Problem
FIVE	The Five Orange Pips
GLOR	The Gloria Scott
GOLD	The Golden Pince-Nez
GREE	The Greek Interpreter
HOUN	The Hound of the Baskervilles
IDEN	A Case of Identity
ILLU	The Illustrious Client

LADY	The Disappearance of Lady Frances Carfax
LAST	His Last Bow
LION	The Lion's Mane
MAZA	The Mazarin Stone
MISS	The Missing Three-Quarter
MUSG	The Musgrave Ritual
NAVA	The Naval Treaty
NOBL	The Noble Bachelor
NORW	The Norwood Builder
PRIO	The Priory School
REDC	The Red Circle
REDH	The Red-Headed League
REIG	The Reigate Squires
RESI	The Resident Patient
RETI	The Retired Colourman
SCAN	A Scandal in Bohemia
SECO	The Second Stain
SHOS	Shoscombe Old Place
SIGN	The Sign of the Four
SILV	Silver Blaze
SIXN	The Six Napoleons
SOLI	The Solitary Cyclist
SPEC	The Speckled Band
STOC	The Stockbroker's Clerk
STUD	A Study in Scarlet
SUSS	The Sussex Vampire
THOR	The Problem of Thor Bridge
3GAB	The Three Gables
3GAR	The Three Garridebs
3STU	The Three Students
TWIS	The Man with the Twisted Lip
VALL	The Valley of Fear
VEIL	The Veiled Lodger
WIST	Wisteria Lodge
YELL	The Yellow Face

Appendix II

CONANICAL NOMENCLATURE

1. NAMES FROM THE NEWSPAPER REPORT OF THE OLIVER-GALLEY TRIAL

List A. *Unaltered surnames or placenames*

Name from newspaper	*Name in Canon*	*Story*
Bennett, Ann	Bennett, Trevor	CREE
Crocker	Crocker, Capt. Jack	ABBE
Gregory, Rev. George	Gregory, Inspector	SILV
Harris, Elizabeth	Harris (S.H.)[1]	STOC
Harvey, M. Woolland (attorney)	Harvey —	SHOS
Jackson, Mr.	Jackson, Dr.	RESI
	Jackson, General	FIVE
Latimer, Thomas ("The Cobbett of the West")	Latimer, Harold	GREE
	— Latimer (boots)	LADY

[1]This is certainly the most puzzling name-allocation in the whole of the Canon, for, as an *alias* to be adopted by Holmes in the case of *The Stockbroker's Clerk,* Conan Doyle may find no better choice of name than "Harris"–the surname of the perjured harlot encountered by Doyle in his reading of the Oliver–Galley trial. Watson's *alias,* for use in *The Illustrious Client,* exhibited quite the reverse tendency: as the false "Dr. Hill Barton," Dr. Watson was allocated the name of a respectable Exeter attorney of the firm of Messrs. Terrell, Barton and Smale, "their" Mr. Terrell prosecuting Mrs. Bird in the *blue-stone* attempted-murder case (on the other hand, would Conan Doyle have seen the prosecutors–persecutors, rather–of an innocent woman as anything but despicable?). But see the much more proximate source of "Dr. Hill Barton" on p. 201.

Moreton (town in Devon)	Morton, Cyril	SOLI
	Morton, Inspector	MISS
	Morton (Oxford Rugby player)	MISS
	Morton & Kennedy	SOLI
	Morton & Waylight	REDC
Moreton*hampstead* Fair	Hampstead, London	VALL
	Hampstead, London	CHAS
	Hampstead, London	REDC
May, Jonathan (murder victim)	*May Day* (ship name)	CARD
"Paramour" (Harris so called in court)	Paramore	FIVE
Sanders, Ralph (County Clerk)	Sanders, Ikey	MAZA
	Saunders (a maid)	DANC
	Saunders, Sir James	BLAN
	Saunders, Mrs.	3GAR
Smith, Mary (witness in court)	Smith, Culverton	DYIN
Smith, Montague (prosecuting counsel)	Smith, Jack	SIGN
	Smith, James	SOLI
	Smith, Jim	SIGN
	Smith, Mordecai	SIGN
	Smith, Ralph	SOLI
	Smith, Violet	SOLI
	Smith, Willoughby	GOLD
Stone	Stone, Rev. Joshua	WIST
Turner, George William (attorney)	Turner, Alice, John	BOSC
	Turner, Mrs. (?Hudson)	SCAN
White, Thomas	White, Abel	VALL
Williams, Mr. Justice (John)	Williams, Charlie	VALL
(This surname also appears in the "Altered" List B)	Williams, James (baker)	WIST
	Williams	SIGN

List B. *Surnames altered (including by pun or "echo")*

Name from newspaper	*Name in Canon*	*Story*
Avery, George	Aveling	PRIO
Cann, Samuel	Brewer, Sam (Pun linking "[beer]-*can*" with "brewer")	SHOS
Cannon, Constable Thomas McGill, Police-Sergeant (arrested Galley)	MacKinnon, Inspector (But there are also *Constable* MacPherson, Bodymaster John McGinty – and eleven other "Mac-" or "Mc-" names)	RETI
Carpenter, Anne, Jane	Charpentier,[2] Alice, Arthur	STUD
Crocker (unaltered in List A)	Crowder, William	BOSC
Cross, Richard Assheton (Home Secretary)	Blackwell, Lady Eva (Punning allusion to the familiar name of the well-known food purveyors, Crosse & Blackwell. But the use of "Blackwell" has obviously generated:)	CHAS
	Blackwater, Earl of	PRIO
	Backwater, Lord	SILV
	Backwater, Lord	NOBL
Galley, Edmund	"The Gully of Bluemansdyke" (short story)	
	"The Last Galley" (short story)	
Gibbons, Edmund	Gibson, J. Neil	THOR
Horn, Mr. (Clerk of Arraigns)	Horner, John	BLUE
Kekewich, Mr. (prosecuting counsel)	Keswick	STUD
May, Jonathan (name unaltered in List A)	Maynooth, Lady	EMPT
	May Day (ship)	CARD
Stone	Stoner, Helen, Julia	SPEC
Tallamy, John, Mary (witnesses)	Bellamy, Maud, Tom, William ("Bellamy" then generating:)	LION
	Bellinger, Lord	SECO
	Belminster, Duke of	SECO

[2] Slight as is the change of "Carpenter" to "Charpentier," it is still rather a change of spelling than a change of meaning, since *charpentier*, in French, signifies a ship's carpenter.

*Tavern*er, Grace (witness)	Dun*bar*, Grace (Pun on semantic link between "tavern" and "bar")	THOR
Taverner, Nicholas and Grace	Tavernier (waxman)	MAZA
Williams, Mr. Justice (John) (unaltered in List A)	Williamson, Mr.	SOLI
	Wilson (chaplain)	GLOR
	Wilson (constable)	GOLD
	Wilson, Bartholomew	VALL
	Wilson, Jabez	REDH
	Wilson (messenger office)	HOUN
	Wilson, Sergeant	VALL
	Wilson, Steve	VALL
	Wilson (Scowrer)	VALL
"Young Hero" (one of the "real" Turpin's nicknames)	Young, Brigham (Brigham Young was, of course, a real person, but his name was suggested to Conan Doyle by the latter's thinking of "The Young Hero" as a "young brigand")	STUD

List C. *Unaltered Christian or other forenames*

Name from newspaper	*Name in Canon*	*Story*
Ann Bennett (witness)	Anna Coram	GOLD
Anne Carpenter (witness)	Annie Fraser	LADY
"Black Ann" (vagrant)	Annie Harrison	NAVA
	Annie Morrison	REIG
Arthur Pardew (prisoner on bail)	Arthur Cadogan West	BRUC
	Arthur Charpentier	STUD
	Arthur Holder	BERY
	Arthur, Lord Saltire	PRIO
	Arthur Morstan	SIGN
	Arthur Willaby	VALL
"Black Soph" (vagrant)	Sophy Kratides	GREE
Catherine Gaffney (witness)	Catherine Cusack	BLUE
	Kate Whitney	TWIS
	Kate Winter ("Kitty")	ILLU
Rev. George Gregory (magistrate)	George Burnwell	BERY
George William Turner (attorney)	George Tregennis	DEVI

Grace Taverner (witness)	Grace Dunbar	THOR
Harriet Langbridge (witness)	Hatty Doran ("Hatty" was the normal Victorian contraction of "Harriet")	NOBL
Henry Luscombe (witness)	Henry Baker	BLUE
	Henry ("Holy") Peters	LADY
	Henry Staunton	MISS
	Henry Wood	CROO
Jacob's Well (where May was killed)	Jacob Shafter (Pun: here "shaft" is used as a synonym for "well")	VALL
	"Jacobs" also used as surname:	SECO
James Gardner (turnkey at gaol) James Salter (witness) James Terrell (attorney)	29 characters in the Canon bear the names "James," "Jim," or "Jimmy"	
Jane Carpenter	Jane Stewart	CROO
	Jane Tregellis	MUSG
John Hiscox	34 characters in the Canon bear this Christian name	
Jonathan May (murder victim)	Jonathan Small	SIGN
Mary Marengo (lodging-house owner)	Mary Brackenstall (Fraser)	ABBE
	Mary Cushing	CARD
	Mary Holder	BERY
	Mary Maberley	3GAB
	Mary Morstan	SIGN
	Mary Sutherland	REDH
	Mary Sutherland	IDEN
	Mary	FIVE
	Mary	3GAB
	Mary Jane	SCAN
Montague Smith (defending Oliver)	Montague (Street), London	STUD
Ralph Sanders (County Clerk)	Ralph Smith	SOLI
Samuel Cann (innkeeper)	Sam Brewer	SHOS
	Sam Merton	MAZA
Thomas Archer (farmer) Thomas Cannon (constable)	Tom Bellamy	LION
William Cole (Governor of County Prisons)	William Bellamy	LION
William Crocker (labourer)	William Crowder	BOSC
	William Darbyshire	SILV

William Taylor (gaol-bird)	William Hales	VALL
William Rowe (innkeeper)	William Kirwan	REIG
William Rattenbury (uncalled witness)	William Morris (Ross)	REDH

NOTE: It is apparent that not only proper names supplied source material for the Canonical nomenclature, though there is no space to permit me to pursue here this line of enquiry. However, as a guide to (another scholar's) possibly fruitful area of research, I might point out that both the names of towns and the names of taverns appear frequently in the Canon: Appledore (certainly the Devonian rather than the Kentish town of that name) appears both as a personal name–Edith Appledore (PRIO)–and the name of Charles Augustus Milverton's Hampstead mansion; the then most important naval base and Royal dockyards of *Devonport,* adjoining Plymouth, one encounters in the Canon as "Davenport" (GREE); and Colonel Dorking (CHAS) bears the name of a pleasant Surrey town. As for tavern names, one might not unreasonably see, in the name of Galley trial witness Harriet Langbridge's tavern, The Golden Lion, the "triggering" of two stories written long afterward: the adventures of *The Golden Pince-Nez* (1904) and *The Lion's Mane* (1926–forty-five years after Galley's official vindication).

2. NAMES FROM THE NEWSPAPER REPORT OF OTHER CASES IN THE CROWN BAR AND NISI PRIUS COURTS AT EXETER

List D. *Unaltered surnames or placenames*

Name from newspaper	*Name in Canon*	*Story*
Barton, Mr. (attorney)	Barton, Hill	ILLU
	Barton, Inspector	TWIS
Bird, Daniel (accuser of wife)	Bird, Simon	VALL
Bird, Elizabeth (defendant)	"Birdy" Edwards	VALL
Bird, Mr. (attorney)		
"Blue-stone" (supposed poison)	*The Blue Carbuncle* "The Gully of Bluemansdyke" (stories)	
Bradley, Charles (acquitted)	Bradley (tobacconist)	HOUN
Crowder, Mr. (barrister)	Crowder, William	BOSC
Edwards, Mr. (attorney)	Edwards, Birdy[3]	VALL

[3]Here again (as in the reference to "Crosse & Blackwell") is a hidden allusion to two food products then widely advertised in Britain and to be found in the majority of British middle-class homes: *Bird's* custard and *Edwards'* desiccated soup. That "Birdy" and "Edwards" are joined in one name argues that Conan Doyle had the two well-known culinary products in

Johnson, Samuel (transported burglar)	Johnson (Oxford Rugby player)	MISS
	Johnson, Shinwell ("Porky")	ILLU
	Johnson, Sidney	BRUC
	Johnson, Theophilus	HOUN
	Johnston (Mormon elder) (same pronunciation)	STUD
Jones, Robin (acquitted)	Jones, Inspector Athelney	SIGN
	Jones, Billy	VALL
	Jones, Inspector Peter	REDH
Lopes, Sir Ralph (baronet)	Lopez (Lucas)	WIST
Pyke (defendant)	Pike, Langdale	3GAB
Richards, Mr. (attorney)	Richards, Dr.	DEVI
Robinson, Mr. (M.P.)	Robinson, John (Ryder)	BLUE
Scott (ejected tenant)	Scott, James H.	VALL
	Scott Eccles, John	WIST
Smith, Nicholas (labourer)	8 characters in the Canon bear the name "Smith," as in List A	
Waldron, Mr. (attorney)	Waldron (Prescott)	3GAR
Walter, Mr. (Member of Parliament)	Walter, Colonel Valentine	BRUC
	Walter, Sir James	BRUC

List E. *Altered surnames or placenames*

Name from newspaper	*Name in Canon*	*Story*
*Alder*son, Baron (judge)	*Apple*dore, Edith	PRIO
	(Pun on tree names: *alder* and *apple*)	
	Dowson, *Baron*	MAZA
	(The "tree-motif" *may* be further exploited in the use, twice, of an unusual name:	
	Oakshott, Sir Leslie	ILLU
	Oakshott, Mrs. Maggie	BLUE
	both echoing the "Alder" of "Alderson")	
Baron, George Stone (attorney)	He has obviously given all three of his names—unaltered—to the Canon's name-list, but his sur-	

mind, the surname of "Birdy Edwards" both suggested by, and "reinforcing," that of the Exeter attorney. *Hudson's* popular soap inspired "Mrs. Hudson."

	name may have "reinforced" the selection (see List D) of the two unaltered names:	
	Barton, Dr. Hill	ILLU
	Barton, Inspector	TWIS
Barstow, Mr. (attorney)	Baxter, Edith	SILV
Benmore (plaintiff)	Oldmore, Mrs.	HOUN
	Sutherland, Mary	IDEN
	Sutherland, Mary	REDH
	(The latter is a striking example of Conan Doyle's more "catachrestic" puns: Ben More is a mountain in the county of *Sutherland*, northern Scotland)	
Butchers, John (witness)	A most unusual name, suggesting and perpetuated in:	
	Butcher's shop: Allardyce's	BLAC
Butter (plaintiff)	Butter, parsley sunk in (as vital clue)	SIXN
Cann, Abraham (witness)	Brewer, Sam	SHOS
	(Same explanation as for Samuel Cann, in List C)	
Carlisle (defendant)	Keswick	STUD
	(*Keswick* is a small town 22 miles southwest of the city of *Carlisle*, both in the county of Cumbria, England)	
Cousens, Thomas (plaintiff)	Cusack, Catherine	BLUE
	Cushing, Mary, Sarah, Susan	CARD
Erle, Mr. (barrister; later Lord Chief Justice of the Common Pleas)	*Earl* of Dovercourt	CHAS
	Earl of Backwater	PRIO
	(and possibly echoed in:)	
	*Hurl*stone Manor	MUSG
Farwell, Mr. (attorney)	Farquhar (physician)	STOC
Furlong, Mr. B. (attorney)	Miles, Hon. Miss	CHAS
Furlong, William Hobson (attorney)	McLaren, Miles	3STU
	(Once more the altered surname used as a forename: both "Miles" names being, of course, punning on "furlong" as a measure of distance)	

Furneaux (defendant)	Fournaye, Mme. Henri (as the English name *Furneaux* was, in the 1880s, more commonly pronounced "Ferney," the factual name may also have been the inspiration for:)	SECO
	Verner, Dr.	NORW
	Vernet, Horace	GREE
Grater (defendant)	Greathed, Colonel	SIGN
Gurney, Mr. (barrister, afterward Baron Gurney, High Court judge)	Gruner, *Baron* Adelbert (The derivation of "Gruner" from "Gurney" is made the more likely by the fact that, shortly after the Exeter cases, Mr. Gurney was raised to the Bench as Mr. *Baron* Gurney. There is a further point of interest: "Gruner" is not the *exact* anagram of "Gurney"–but "gurner" is. Mr. Baron Gurney was a judge of the utmost harshness, a professional intimidator of both counsel and witnesses; "he had," Ballantine wrote, "earned the reputation of being a very pitiless judge, and his manner at times was almost brutal." Ballantine does not add that Gurney's face was often twisted into a mask of menace. In England, at country fairs, prizes are awarded for "gurning" a *gurner* being one who can contort his face into the ugliest shape possible. Mr. Baron Gurney on the Bench could have won prizes as a champion *gurner*.)	ILLU
Hawkes, Mr. (attorney)	Fowler, Mr. (The ornithological flavour of the pun owes something to the appearance, in the court calendar, of both the names "Bird" (three times) and "Pidgeon," q.v.)	COPP

Herwood, Thomas (convicted burglar)	Hayward — (crook) (Surname to forename once more – a rare example of suitability of name-giving: here a fictional crook bears a real crook's only slightly altered surname, and, again, a name "reinforced" from another source: a familiar standby of the Victorian "cold collation" [cold meat and pickles] was the still-popular *Hayward's Military Pickle*.)	RESI
Hurrell, William (horse thief)	Harold, Mrs.	MAZA
	Latimer, Harold	GREE
	Stackhurst, Harold	LION
Lavers (party to process-at-law)	*Lever*stoke, Lord (The inspiration for this name did not come wholly from that of *Lavers*, who made an appearance in the Nisi Prius Court. It seems evident to me that Conan Doyle was also not unaware that the 1st Baron *Revel*stoke ["Lever" being an anagram of "Revel"] was raised to the peerage in 1885 as Baron Revelstoke of Membland, county *Devon*, and that his lady was the daughter of *John Crocker* [cf. Captain "Jack" Crocker: ABBE] Bulteel, of Flete, Devon. In regard to the manufactured name "Leverstoke," we may note that the first element of the name was supplied by "Lavers," whilst the second element, "Stoke," came, as we shall see, from another name mentioned in a case heard in a different court.)	PRIO

In order that the reader may follow clearly the semantic linking behind the name-conversion next considered, it is necessary to point out that the report of the cases in the *Exeter Flying Post* prints the following two cases, the upper, as here given, directly above the lower:

Benmore v. *Neck*. – In this case there was no issue.

Webber v. *Pike*. – The record in this case was withdrawn. Attorneys: Symes for plaintiff; Waldron for defendant.

As has been noted, the names *Symes* (as "Soames") and *Waldron* (unaltered) have been used in, respectively, PRIO and 3STU, and 3GAR. *Benmore* and *Pyke* have also been used, and before we go on to consider what use Conan Doyle made of the two remaining names, *Neck* and *Webber*, we must agree that, for a number of reasons, he found this close association of six names quite fascinating–and quite unforgettable.

Of what did the very rare surname *Neck* instantly remind him? Of what he had just read on page 4 of the *Exeter Flying Post:* the dreadful words that Mr. Justice Williams had addressed to the prisoners, after he had assumed the Black Cap:

"...that you, Edmund Galley, and you, Thomas Oliver, be taken...to the place of execution; there to be hung respectively *by the neck*..."

Of what else, reading the newspaper account of long-past but still unamended horror, could that strange name, *Neck*, remind him: of men hanged "until your bodies are dead"?

Then Conan Doyle must have recalled that the last man to be hanged in public was the Irishman, Michael Barratt, and that Conan Doyle might have seen that grim sight (in which nineteen persons were crushed to death by the crowd), for the last hanging had taken place in the year in which Doyle joined his Jesuit preparatory school, Hodder House. Barratt was hanged outside Newgate Gaol, in Old Bailey, and so Conan Doyle recalled some odd expressions from his wide reading: criminals' slang–"Newman's Hotel" for Newgate Prison and "Newman's Lift" for the gallows in Old Bailey, outside the prison. And he must have recalled, too, that even that burial-ground within the prison, in which the bodies of the hanged were interred anonymously, was still called, by the pious, "God's Acre." So, out of all this semantic linkage, the following name-conversion took place:

Neck (defendant)	*Old*acre, Jonas	NORW
*New*man, Mr. (attorney)	(By inversion, *Old* puns on *New;* "Newman's Hotel" is Newgate Prison,[4] where they hanged	

[4]Here is the most important evidence of Conan Doyle's knowledge of what, in Victorian opinion, was regarded as "improper" reading: the 1811 updating of Francis Grose's *Classical Dictionary of the Vulgar Tongue* (1785). The 1811 up-dating was published in London by C. Chappel, of Pall Mall, under the title *Lexicon Balatronicum: A Dictionary of Buckish Slang, University Wit, and Pickpocket Eloquence*–a work on which, by the way, the Reverend Charles Lutwidge Dodgson ("Lewis Carroll") drew heavily for, especially, the so-called nonsense-words of *Jabberwocky*. But what must most interest us here is the fact that, on the title page of the *Lexicon Balatronicum,* three revising authors are given as "Hell-Fire Dick, and James Gordon, Esqrs. of Cambridge; and William *Soames,* Esq. of the Hon. Society of Newman's Hotel"–an attribution which brings both "Newman's Hotel" (Newgate Prison) and the

	felons and then buried them in the prison's "God's Acre." Thus *Newman* becomes *Oldacre*.)	
Pidgeon, William (convicted burglar transported for life)	*Culver*ton Smith (Probably a double surname, rather than a forename and surname. The conversion is not as far-fetched as might be thought at first sight: *culver* is the old yet still not obsolete name for *pigeon*–especially *wood pigeon*. So: "W. Pigeon = *wood pigeon* = *Culver*[ton Smith])	DYIN
Presswell, George (party in law-case)	Prescott, Rodger (A choice of conversion of name certainly greatly influenced by the fact that Conan Doyle, a boxer when young and a notable patron of [and successful writer on] the Fistic Art later, had in mind Colonel *Prescott*, the banker-chairman of the National Sporting Club)	3GAR
Pring (plaintiff)	Pringle, Mrs.	SECO
Smale, Mr. (attorney) Smalridge (defendant)	Small, Jonathan	SIGN
Stenlake (defendant)	Stendall — (Surname into forename)	VALL
Stoke Damerel (a village near Exeter) "Nicholas Smith is a labourer at Stoke Damerel, and received a paper from Daniel Bird [in the	Stoke D'Abernon (The real name of that "Stoke Moran," in Surrey, where the evil Dr. Grimesby Roylott lived with his two step-daughters)	SPEC

surname "Soames" (used both in *The Priory School* and *The Three Students*) into immediate association. In the list on p. 229, I have suggested that the name of Symes, the Exeter attorney, may have suggested the two "Soames" names. This contention may still stand; as I have several times pointed out, name-inspiration could affect Conan Doyle from two or more sources. That Conan Doyle must have read *at least* the title page of the *Lexicon Balatronicum* is certain. We must not overlook the fact that, still on the *Lexicon's* title page, is the surname "Gordon," which would have "reinforced" the inspiration which eventually gave the name, the *persona*, and the heroic stature of General Charles George Gordon to the Canon (see Chapter 9).

"blue-stone" alleged poisoning] . . . which he took to Mr. May, druggist . . ."	The "blue-stone" case so impressed Conan Doyle that "Stoke Damerel" yielded yet another name for the Canon:	
	Damery, Sir James	ILLU
Stuart, Mary (acquitted)	Stewart, Jane	CROO
Symes, Mr. (attorney)	Soames, Sir Cathcart	PRIO
	Soames, Hilton	3STU
Walter, Mr. (Member of Parliament)	Walker Brothers	VALL
	Walters,[5] Constable	WIST
Whiteford, Mr. (attorney)	White, Abel	SIGN
	Whyte, William	STUD
	(As forename:)	
	White Mason	VALL

List E. *Unaltered Christian names, forenames, or titles*

Names from newspaper	*Name in Canon*	*Story*
Alexander Cockburn (defense counsel)	Alec Cunningham	REIG
	Alec Fairbairn	CARD
	Alec MacDonald	VALL
	Alexander H. Garrideb	3GAR
	Alexander Holder	BERY
Baron Alderson (judge)	Baron Adelbert Gruner	ILLU
	Baron Dowson	MAZA
	Baron Maupertuis	REIG
Blue-stone, or sulphate of copper (alleged poison)	*The Blue Carbuncle*	
Charles Bradley (acquitted)	Charles Gorot	NAVA
	Charles McCarthy	BOSC
	Charles Williams	VALL
George Stone Baron (attorney)	George Burnwell	BERY
	George Tregennis	DEVI
Harriet Stacey (convicted burglars' accomplice)	Hatty Doran	NOBL
	("Hatty" was the conventional	

[5] The name "Walters"–unchanged–may, in fact, recall the dim-witted Mrs. Annie *Walters* of the 1903 "baby-farming" case (see footnote, p. 144), a case which brought the name "Galley" to Conan Doyle's attention for the second time. Constable Walters appears in *Wisteria Lodge*, written a mere five years after the "baby-farming" case.

	Victorian contraction of the name "Harriet")	
Henry Fullen (burgled house-owner)	Henry Baker	BLUE
	Henry Staunton	MISS
	Henry Wood	CROO
	Henry ("Holy") Peters	LADY
John Butchers (witness) John Loosemore (attorney)	34 characters in the Canon bear the name "John"	
Mary Stuart (acquitted)	11 characters in the Canon bear the name "Mary"	
(Sir) Ralph Lopes, Bart. (landowner)	Ralph —	BLAN
	Ralph Smith	SOLI
	–and seven names in the Canon prefaced by "Sir"	
Samuel Johnson (convicted burglar)	Sam Brewer	MAZA
	Sam Merton	BLUE
Thomas Cousens (witness) Thomas Herwood (convicted burglar)	Tom Bellamy	LION
William Hurrell (convicted horse thief)	William Bellamy	LION
	William Crowder	BOSC
William Pidgeon (convicted burglar)	William Derbyshire	SILV
	William Hales	VALL
William Rowe (convicted burglar)	William Kirwan	REIG
	William Morris (Ross)	REDH

Appendix III

DR. SAM JOHNSON: CRIMINOLOGIST AND DETECTIVE

In his slight (I talk here only of its length) but deeply penetrating *Holmes and Watson: A Miscellany,*[1] the late Sir Sidney Roberts, with that assurance of opinion, clarity of expression, and economy of thought that we had come to expect from one of Britain's most distinguished academics, managed not only to touch on an astonishing number of subjects in his little volume but also to introduce some novelties into a general study of Holmes and Watson, both individually and as an inseparably joined pair.

Sir Sidney acquired eminence in "the groves of Academe" as Vice-Chancellor of Cambridge University and Master of Pembroke College, one of the oldest of Cambridge's foundations, dating from 1347, in the reign of King Edward III. To Sherlockians, however, whether or not "Cantabs," Sir Sidney will always be revered as one of the Founding Fathers of Sherlockian Exegesis, most learned in his knowledge of the Sacred Texts and a worthily creative critic of the earliest attempts at Sherlockian commentary. He praised when praise was deserved but could be sharp in rebuke of those errors which owe themselves principally to the laziness of "not verifying one's references"–"sloppiness," he called it. He was particularly sharp with his Oxonian contemporary (and somewhat earlier Sherlockian), Monsignor Ronald Knox, S.J., when rebuking Father Knox for quoting from his own faulty memory rather than from the Canon itself, though Sir Sidney does pay generous tribute to the Jesuit Sherlockian in affirming, in the Preface to *Holmes*

[1] S. C. Roberts, *Holmes and Watson: A Miscellany* (Oxford: Geoffrey Cumberlege, Oxford University Press), 1953.

and Watson, that "it was Monsignor Knox's famous essay[2] that first beckoned me to Baker Street." Still, Sir Sidney was almost–though not quite!–as sharp in correcting some theories of that lady early-Sherlockian, the late Miss Dorothy Sayers.

I mention, and emphasize, this strict critical attitude of Sir Sidney's, both to the Canonical text and to those who, before him, had speculated upon it, because he is one of the few who have ventured into such criticism armed with, and invulnerably secure in, the conscious infallibility which is the gift of a scholastic probity for which the happy possessor has striven so single-mindedly so long. It is in no spirit of denigration that I say that it is impossible, especially in his Sherlockian exegesis, to fault the sometime Master of Pembroke College, Cambridge. The one error into which he did fall–and, being human, he is surely entitled to *one* error, as Man's Best Friend is commonly held to be entitled to his one legal bite–was to assert that Dr. Watson, as a young man, had played three-quarter for Blackheath. In admitting and correcting this error–"The author regrets that this place in the [Rugger] field was assigned to [Watson] on insufficient evidence"–Sir Sidney paid warm tribute to the Sherlockian who really could pontificate on Watson's sporting past: "the reader," Sir Sidney advises, "should consult the authoritative monograph of Mr. Bernard Darwin."

But, after that one small and, in my opinion, unimportant lapse from a total authority in Sherlockian matters, Sir Sidney made no more mistakes; and, since that Watsonian stumble from grace, Sir Sidney may be followed in his comments and his theories, with every confidence in the soundness of his views.

A Johnson to His Boswell

Sir Sidney commences a well-known essay in his *Miscellany* with this passage:

> Holmes's famous remark that he was lost without his Boswell has naturally led commentators to draw a comparison between the Holmes–Watson and the Johnson–Boswell association.

I don't think that we need to follow Sir Sidney into his consideration of a relationship in which "At first sight, the contrasts seem more striking than any resemblances." To me, the important part of this very brief–far too brief–paper lies in Sir Sidney's consideration, not of "the

---

[2] Ronald Knox, *Essays in Satire* (London: Sheed and Ward), 1928.

Johnson–Boswell association," but of the character of the "Great Cham of Literature" himself. If I have a fault to find with this little essay, it is that the author, in calling our attention, for the first time, to the significance of Johnson in the "mix" from which, in the end, the fully-rounded character of Holmes emerged, gives us far too little of Johnson.

To what extent, if any, may we justly include the "Sage of Lichfield" –Dr. Samuel Johnson, LL.D., the first great lexicographer of the English tongue; hero, not only to James Boswell, barrister-at-law, but also, no less, to that artistic and sadly-abused monarch, King George III, who expressed his admiration for Johnson in the most practical way, by granting the Sage a pension of £300 a year–in that medley of characters who, earlier in this book, I have credited as influences in the making of Sherlock Holmes?

That Conan Doyle (most probably in his younger years) read Boswell's *Life of Johnson* goes without saying. We might confidently assume as much, even had we not that half-humorous, half-affectionate allusion of Holmes's to "his Boswell." "Way down South" in this small island of ours, the intense nationalistic pride of the sister kingdom to the north of the Tweed is too often forgotten in the Southrons' assessment of the Scottish character.

The Scots are proud of their "Jamie" Boswell, Laird of Auchinleck, and they overlook the irritating fact that Boswell's immortal work is no less than the glorification of a somewhat irritating old Sassenach in the pride that all true Scots feel in the fact that a Scotsman has achieved literary fame of the most enduring kind. I have already mentioned my belief that Conan Doyle read the works of Thomas De Quincey because De Quincey was already known to him–as he was to every literate inhabitant of Edinburgh–as one of Edinburgh's earlier residents and as one of her more brilliant ornaments. So, too, I believe that Doyle–a Scotsman by birth, upbringing, education, and residence, even though of Irish descent–came naturally to Boswell as to one of the books which would have graced the shelves of all middle-class Scottish homes with any pretense both to literacy and to that "national feeling" of which the Scots have almost more than their rightful share.

Anticipating Dr. Bell . . . and Sherlock Holmes

By the autumn of 1876, when young Arthur Conan Doyle had been first entered on the register of the Edinburgh Medical School, Boswell's *Life of Johnson* had already been available to the public for eighty-four years; and, unlike some later bestsellers, such as *The Lord of the Flies, The Way of All Flesh,* and–to come a little closer to our subject–both *A Study in Scarlet* and *The Sign of the Four,* which "got off to a slow start," Boswell's tremendous work gained the immediate recognition of the British (and American) public and ran into six large (and constantly revised) editions by the year 1811, nineteen years after the appearance of the first. We may then confidently assert that, by the time of Conan Doyle's boyhood —say, by the year 1871 or 1872—the already eighty-year-old classic was as well known to him as to most other educated families of his day.

Perhaps the most famous of all Sherlock Holmes's utterances—as it is also his first in the Canon—is that remark with which he greeted Dr. Watson after the latter had been introduced by "young Stamford": "You have been in Afghanistan, I perceive!"[3] an observation now as famous, if not indeed more so, than that other succinctly historical observation: "Dr. Livingstone, I presume?"

Here, Conan Doyle shows a fine dramatic sense, and lets Holmes take the stage with an explosive entrance which startles and is intended to startle the victim of this pyrotechnic display of deduction. And in this brilliantly-conceived entrance, Conan Doyle, the adroit stage-manager, uses a never-forgotten real-life experience which once impressed *him* as greatly as he has made Holmes impress Dr. Watson.

Dr. Joseph Bell, an Edinburgh University professor, is lecturing to a class of medical students, of which Arthur Conan Doyle is one:

> "This man," Dr. Bell would declare in rich Scots, "is a left-handed cobbler." Then he would wait, with carefully concealed glee, for the puzzled looks of the students.
>
> "You'll obsairve, gentlemen, the worn places on the corduroy breeks where a cobbler rests his lapstone? The right-hand side, you'll note, is far-r more worn than the left. He uses his left hand for hammering the leather."
>
> Or again, with finger-tips together:
>
> "This man is a French-polisher." Then, opening his eyes and rolling it out: "Come now. Can't you smel-l-l him?"

This is John Dickson Carr's retelling of Conan Doyle's own account; but when, years later, Conan Doyle (for reasons that I have suggested earlier) cited, with fulsome praise, his old professor as the principal, if not the only, model on which the novelist had based his Sherlock

---

[3]Now given material as well as literary immortality by means of a bronze plaque in the pathological laboratory of St. Bartholomew's Hospital, which commemorates the meeting on New Year's Day 1881. The plaque bears the dedicatory inscription: "The Baker Street Irregulars—1953 / By the Amateur Mendicants at the Caucus Club."

Holmes, Dr. Bell (obviously somewhat confused and embarrassed) protested modestly that, not only was this deductive trick no invention of his but was copied from that of his own instructor at Edinburgh, Professor Syme; Dr. Bell asserted that Syme was more proficient even than he in the art of deducing facts of character and employment from a patient's general appearance.

The fact is that not only did Dr. Bell, the deducing-from-a-glance professor, have a distinguished predecessor in the deductive art, but *that* predecessor also had a predecessor, not at all less proficient a deducer-at-a-glance. Sir Sidney Roberts names him for us, calling our attention to his detective skill for the first time in Sherlockian criticism. He was the famous Boswell-revealed Dr. Johnson, and what Dr. Johnson had to say in this connection certainly deserves our closest attention: "It is easy to guess the trade of an artizan by his knees, his fingers or his shoulders."

Sir Sidney adds: "That is a quotation, not from *A Study in Scarlet*, but from *The Rambler* (No. 173) [the literary journal that Johnson wrote almost wholly by himself and published between 20 March 1750 and 17 March 1752], and may serve to demonstrate that a comparison of Sherlock Holmes with Dr. Johnson is not a wholly fanciful exercise."

True. . . but, as I said above, I wish that Sir Sidney had taken his analogy further. I am now about to suggest that there is a different and (to my way of thinking) much more realistic view of Johnson's "anticipation" of both the Edinburgh professors and, through the attentive student, Conan Doyle, of Doyle's creation, Sherlock Holmes.

A Matter of Conscious Allusion

We should keep one important fact in mind: that all the medical students of Edinburgh University in mid-Victorian times were young men who had received an excellent general education; Conan Doyle, product of a famous Jesuit public school, in particular. And, to come to the essential point, it is unlikely that even one of those well-educated students was unfamiliar with Boswell's *Life of Johnson*, and many of them would have been familiar with much of Dr. Johnson's own writing, including his articles in *The Rambler*.

Thus, far from their regarding Johnson's remark about the ease with which one might "guess the trade of an artizan by his knees, his fingers or his shoulders" as having been an "anticipation" of the remarks, in a similar context, of a pair of Edinburgh Medical School professors, they considered–rightly–those last remarks as being no more than apposite references to *Dr. Johnson's* original statement. And we may be sure that, in making Sherlock Holmes burst into the world's consciousness with that remark about Afghanistan, Conan Doyle was well aware of the Johnsonian inspiration of Dr. Bell and his predecessor.

What Sir Sidney should have done was to go on to point out Dr. Johnson as not merely a criminological theorist but as a practical, *operative* investigator, no less. He not only theorized, he went to the scene of the puzzle, to view with his own eyes.

Boswell, always excellent reading, is especially so in his account of "Scratching Fanny, the Cock Lane Ghost," a supposed supernatural

Dr. Samuel Johnson, poet, essayist, lexicographer, philosopher–and both theoretical and practical criminologist. In one most important observation on the Art of Detection, he anticipates not only Dr. Joseph Bell but also Dr. Bell's distinguished and even more observant predecessor, Dr. Syme, and thus contributes, even if remotely, to the making of Sherlock Holmes.

phenomenon which, in Boswell's words, "in the year 1762, had gained very general credit in London." But, as Boswell adds, of all those taken in by the fraud (or was it?–a young girl was involved, and "Fanny" could have been a "normal" poltergeist manifestation, centring about a female adolescent), Dr. Johnson was not one: "he was one of those by whom the imposture was detected." He examined the room in Cock Lane (not a stone's throw from that Bart's where "young Stamford" was Dr. Watson's dresser), examined the girl and her parents, assembled a respectable company of the eminent, and laid the ghost. Johnson, perhaps not unjustly, took great credit for his action in the Cock Lane affair: "He expressed great indignation at the imposture of the Cock Lane ghost, and related with much satisfaction, how he had assisted in detecting the cheat, and had published an account of it in the newspapers."

Do we then justifiably include Dr. Samuel Johnson among those real characters who have gone into the making of that fictional character, Sherlock Holmes?

I think that we may, and ought to, do so. The *direct* influence of Johnson in the formation of Holmes may be slight; but his *indirect* influence, as the inspirer of both Dr. Joseph Bell and of Professor Syme, is powerful indeed. And if, as we should, we regard Dr. Joseph Bell as the echoer and expositor of the Johnsonian idea, then we see Dr. Johnson as a most important factor in the making of Sherlock Holmes.

Appendix IV

THE TRAGEDY OF MRS. FLORENCE CHANDLER MAYBRICK

A question of mistaken identity was the single cause from which sprang all Edmund Galley's sufferings—and those sufferings continued for forty-three years (if, indeed, they may be said to have ceased save with his death), not so much because his innocence of the crime with which he had been charged was unprovable, as that, in his case as in so many others, Authority was unwilling to confess itself mistaken.

They did not hang Edmund Galley in 1836; nor did they hang Mrs. Maybrick in 1889—though there must have been despairing moments in the long agony of each when the original sentence of death must have seemed preferable to the living death to which the reprieve of each had led.

Different in background, sex, nationality—but curiously alike in age (both were twenty-six when they stood trial for a crime of which they were innocent)—Edmund Galley and Florence Maybrick each found a tireless champion, though, in the lady's case, that champion was unable to effect her salvation.

In both cases, the obvious injustice of the sentence—hanging, commuted to life imprisonment—aroused the most violent indignation, the judge in the Maybrick trial needing a police escort to take him through the hissing, menacing Liverpool crowds, even before he had delivered judgment.

In all the long record of inexplicable injustice—injustice intentionally embarked upon and as obstinately persisted in—there is probably no more scandalous an example than is to be found in the trial and conviction of the unhappy woman against whom every malign influence, accidental and planned, operated with unchecked force.

Many a criminologist has studied and commented upon the case of

Mrs. Maybrick; and, possibly uniquely, here there is not one opinion differing from all the others: that no one was ever more unjustly charged, unjustly tried, and unjustly condemned. Medical evidence, proferred by some of the most respected names in England, was ignored; the admitted insanity of the trial judge was ignored; plain hearsay—that supposedly outlawed element of evidence in English law—was admitted and treated with the same respect as the wildest surmise, based equally on racial discrimination (though, as Mrs. Maybrick "was the descendant of notable ancestors and the daughter of a highly-respected, staunchly Confederate banking family," "xenophobic" is probably the more precise adjective) and the jealousy of servants in a household resentful of change. That James Maybrick was forty-two when he married Florrie Chandler in London on 27 July 1881, and that she was a pretty, "foreign" girl of only eighteen, expensively educated in her native country and "finished" at Madame Henriques's fashionable school in Paris, was enough to arouse critical comment in a Liverpool notable, even more than in the majority of English provincial cities, for its narrow conservatism. And that Florrie's mamma had taken, as her second husband, a German baron, Adolf von Roques, though it might have softened the animosity of the more snobbish element in what passed for "Society" in Liverpool, was yet one more unacceptability in the opinion of the servants' hall at Battlecrease House, Aigburth.

They watched her, day and night; they gossiped about her; they criticized her (though rarely to her face); they obeyed her with what the British Army calls "dumb insolence"; they talked of her—never kindly—to her "dearest friends"; they stole her letters and brought them to those "dearest friends". . .and one letter in particular was almost to hang her; it certainly brought her fifteen years' penal servitude and effectively ruined what was to be, by the most ironic decision of Destiny, a singularly long life (she was born in the year of Gettysburg; she died as Hitler's armies were converging on Moscow).

As her counsel, Sir Charles Russell, Q.C., who fought for his betrayed client until his death, said bitterly: Florence Maybrick had gone to prison "for the commission of a crime of which she had never been convicted." He was addressing himself to the then Home Secretary, who was to prove himself as deaf to Russell's plea as had the previous Home Secretaries, even though (this was in 1898) Charles Russell had been, for the past four years, no less than Lord Chief Justice of England, and elevated to the peerage as Lord Russell of Killowen. Even more bitterly, the Lord Chief Justice added: "The foundation on which the whole case for the Crown rested was rotten, *for there was in fact no murder;* on the contrary, the deceased [James Maybrick] had died from natural causes."

As I said, none of the many criminologists and historians of crime who have studied and commented upon the Maybrick case differ in their opinion, save only in the warmth expressed in their several denunciations of judge, Crown counsel, witnesses for the prosecution (including the inept Liverpool police), and, in fact, anyone at all not on the side of the persecuted defendant. The eminent American criminologist and novelist, Q. Patrick, concentrated his most acid remarks on the judge, Sir James Stephen: "a two-day harangue of impassioned malignity and misogyny. . . one of the most biassed speeches ever to come from the English bench." Biassed . . . ? In his summing-up, the judge had lamented from the bench that it must be a thought as horrible as it was incredible "that a woman should be plotting the death of her husband in order that she might be left at liberty to follow her own degrading vices"–the "vices" in question being a week's clandestine stay at a London hotel with her lover, Arthur Brierley.

Another noted British criminologist, Nigel Morland, tells us how Russell "hammered and battered like the genius he was; he called up his own witnesses, triumphantly refuting the other side, and as *Verdict in Dispute*[1] sums it up: 'There was, in fact, *no murder at all;* the chronic arsenic-eater had met his death from natural causes. That, in a nutshell, was the case for the defense.' "

It certainly was the case for Russell's defense, but to talk of Russell's having triumphantly refuted the other side is, in the context, rubbish: he did nothing of the sort, brilliantly though he may have tried to rebut the biassed and often perjured evidence for the prosecution. Had he "triumphantly refuted the other side," his unhappy client would not have had to listen to the pronouncement of the death sentence nor, on remission of that sentence, to endure fifteen years of a Victorian women's prison.

Judge Williams was guilty of flagrant errors of summing-up when he was directing the jury to find Buckingham Joe and Edmund Galley guilty–but in his memorandum to the Home Secretary, "praying" for a free pardon for Mrs. Maybrick, Charles Russell (now, let us not forget, writing from the almost supreme eminence of a Lord Chief Justice) listed no fewer than *one hundred and thirty* misdirections in Mr. Justice Stephen's summing-up. The errors were of so patent a nature that they were scandalously apparent even to the layman; and whereas it had been poor Mrs. Maybrick who had been hissed by the crowd–"hissed,"

[1] By yet another talented British historian of crime, Edgar Lustgarten.

A tragic victim of the Mad Judge: Mrs. Florence Chandler Maybrick, young American widow of an elderly Liverpool cotton merchant, the victim of his family's disapproval, racial prejudice, and servants' malicious intrigue, meets an undeserved fate at the hands of Sir James Fitzjames Stephen, insane father of the even more deranged "Jack the Ripper."

writes Mr. Lustgarten, "by a gathering of ladies who, in dignity and moral sense, must be historically regarded as rivals of the harlots who danced in the streets at the trial of Oscar Wilde"–now it was the judge who, in his journeys to and from the court, had to be protected from the violent indignation of the populace.

Though what Q. Patrick calls, and rightly calls, the insane judge's "impassioned malignity and misogyny" has been noted by all the other criminologists who have studied the Maybrick case–noting, unfortunately, that this misogyny seems to be a *consistent* element in English judicial opinion–not one of these criminologists has followed his own hints to their logical conclusion: which is, that Mrs. Maybrick was not condemned for having "administered arsenic" to an habitual arsenic-as-aphrodisiac taker but because she was a self-convicted adulteress. Indeed, even after Mrs. Maybrick had been reprieved on the grounds that, as the Home Secretary said, "the evidence . . . does not wholly exclude a reasonable doubt whether his death was in fact caused by the administration of arsenic," then why was she not set free? ask all the criminologists. Because she had committed adultery, and that *was* proven . . .

So that, for all the doubt concerning Maybrick's death, Lord Salisbury, a pious humbug and worthy representative of a family which had latched on to the body politic since the first Cecil had gained power by boot-licking the first Queen Elizabeth, could still refuse the Lord Chief Justice's plea for Mrs. Maybrick's freedom by stating that "the case of [Mrs. Maybrick] was that of an adulteress attempting to poison her husband under the most cruel circumstances. . . . The Secretary of State regrets that he has been unable to find any grounds for recommending to the Queen any further act of clemency towards the prisoner." Two years later, Russell was dead, and the influential *Liverpool Daily Post* of 13 August 1900 had this to say of Mr. Justice Stephen–without comment or contradiction from any other member of the ambitious Stephen family:

> In fancy one still hears the distant fanfare of the trumpets as the judges with quaint pageantry passed down the hall, and still with the mind's eye sees the stately crimson-clad figure of *the great mad judge* as he sat down to try his last case . . . It was shocking to think that a human life depended upon the direction of this wreck of what was once a great judge . . . [Emphasis added]

Let us pass over the fact that, despite this just but (in English law) libellous condemnation of a trial judge–for which the editor and proprietors of the *Post* were never prosecuted–Mrs. Maybrick was to remain in prison for a further four years, because, since 1889, successive Home Secretaries of both political parties had maintained the verdict imposed on the simple-minded jury by the "mad judge."[2]

One might have thought that the injustice dealt out to Mrs. Maybrick would have moved that vigorous denouncer of injustice, Dr. Conan Doyle, to fresh transports of indignation; but it was not so. Perhaps, as Charles Russell's agitation on Mrs. Maybrick's behalf was so vigorous and untiring, and as, even by 1900, the social authority of a Lord Chief Justice was still superior to that of a novelist, however successful and famous, one may suppose that Conan Doyle felt that Mrs. Maybrick could not have found a worthier or more powerful champion.

Perhaps. . .but there may have been other factors at work to prevent Mrs. Maybrick from gaining Doyle's usually so-ready sympathy. He may well, as he was more than a little of a classic-type Victorian prude, have disapproved of the lady's sexual waywardness. . .or (more likely, I think) he may have found himself out of sympathy with the lady's stout champion, ***since Charles Russell was not only a Roman Catholic*** but one whose religion was widely publicized: he being the first Roman Catholic Lord Chief Justice since the Reformation. And that, at this period of his life, Doyle was very anti-Roman Catholic may hardly be denied: a prejudice on his part deriving from his dislike of his Roman Catholic school, his resentment at his having been forced to break with his uncles and aunts, and, in view of his new beliefs, the Church's inflexible opposition to that Spiritualism which had already begun to fascinate him.

I have already said, many times, that the proof of Conan Doyle's interest in any case from real life is his use of the names occurring in that case; and certainly the non-use of any name from the Maybrick case would seem to prove that, in the decades following the trial, the case held no interest for him.

But in two stories published at the end of his life–in 1924 and 1926–two names do occur, of which the first provides a positive mnemonic link with the case, and the second almost certainly so.

---

[2] Simple-minded? This particular jury was composed of three plumbers, two farmers, one provision-dealer, one grocer, one iron-monger, one house-painter, and one baker. And this was a jury asked to reach their verdict on evidence that only professional toxicologists might have comprehended!

Mrs. Maybrick had a close friend, in whom "Florrie" confided far beyond the limit of a reasonable discretion. In the anxiety of that illness of her husband's which was to terminate fatally, Mrs. Maybrick, asking the Great Friend what she should do, received the advice to communicate with her lover, Arthur Brierley. The advice was later presented as a piece of sarcasm; but the obviously naïve Mrs. Maybrick, taking it literally, *did* write the letter which nearly hanged her. A servant intercepted the letter, and it was carefully preserved for later evidence at the trial. The first opportunity that Mr. Brierley had to read its contents was when it was read out in court.

The name of the Great Friend whose evidence was given, as Oscar Wilde said in another context, "with all the bitterness of an old friend," was. . . *Mrs. Matilda Briggs*–exactly the name that we encounter as one of the "unreported cases," linked so curiously (and, until now, inexplicabily) with a "giant rat of Sumatra."

The other Maybrick-linked name (used in a story published by Doyle in 1926) is "Kent"–to which I shall return shortly. "Matilda Briggs" and "Kent" are the only names which apparently echo the Maybrick case. We must now ask ourselves why, *thirty-five* years after her conviction for murder and *twenty* years after her release from prison and return to her native America, Mrs. Maybrick should suddenly have become so much an object of interest to Arthur Conan Doyle–and, it would appear, of *sympathetic* interest–that, by implication (the close association of the name of Mrs. Maybrick's venomous betrayer[3] with

---

[3]Mrs. Matilda Briggs. A curious phenomenon is apparent in even the most superficial study of the history of crime: the presence of the same name in cases often greatly differentiated in their nature and their date. Edwin James, Q.C. was one of Palmer's prosecutors; Sir Henry James, Q.C., the lawyer (soon to be Solicitor-General) who adroitly suggested the compromise by which the plea for Galley's pardon was "sent upstairs." And the name Briggs was not only that of the nasty lady who betrayed Mrs. Maybrick but also that of the innocent railway traveller, Mr. Briggs, who was murdered during a train journey by a young German, Franz Müller, in 1864. The inevitable "ballad," on sale the night of Müller's conviction, begins thus:

"That fatal night, I was determined
Poor Thomas Briggs to rob and slay:
And in the fatal railway-carriage,
That night, I took his life away.
His crimson gore did stain the carriage,
I threw him from the same, alack!
I of his golden watch relieved him,
And left him bleeding on the track!"

the nauseating image of a Giant Rat), he comes belatedly to declare her innocence?

Here I would suggest that the dates are of paramount importance and should be most carefully evaluated.

In 1923, Sir Arthur and Lady Conan Doyle visited the United States. For him, it was not the first time; but now, in the spring of that year, he had come as a man with a different, but still clearly defined, mission: as the prophet of (not so much the still vaguely-understood "Spiritualism" but) the proof of life after death. On the earlier occasions of his visiting America, he had been closely identified with Sherlock Holmes. Now, no longer. On this journey, he had been a long time travelling–it was as much before as 4 January 1893 that Conan Doyle took the chair at a lecture on "Psychical Research" delivered by Sir Arthur Barrett–and now, following on the very mixed reception awarded by a Sherlock-hungry public to his book *The New Revelation*, published in the last year of World War I, he had gone out "into the highways and byways" to preach his long-matured gospel. The year, please remember, was 1923 . . .

In 1924, after having bravely (the less generous would say "defiantly") stuck to her married name among the few friends and more unfriendly neighbours in, first, Florida, and then Illinois, Mrs. Maybrick decided to revert to her maiden name of Chandler; and it was as Mrs. Florence Chandler, of a tiny cottage near South *Kent*, Connecticut, that she at last found peace in obscurity.

In 1924–the story, as it was published in the *Strand* magazine and *Hearst's International* in January 1924, was certainly written at the end of 1923–appeared the adventure of *The Sussex Vampire*, in which allusion is made to the *Matilda Briggs* and the giant rat of Sumatra. And in 1926, in the tale of *The Blanched Soldier*, the name of Mrs. Maybrick's nearest town–South *Kent*–supplied a name for the surgeon in that tale.

Why the interest in Mrs. Maybrick? Had she, knowing that the great *rival* of Holmes was in America–the saviour of Edalji and Slater–written to him, as had that distressed hospital nurse, twenty years before; written to Doyle with her account of the Maybrick tragedy . . . with a plea for either his solution or (at least) his understanding? And did he realize that, for all his tenderness toward the dead, some compassion might still be spared for the sadly wronged living?

On the Spoor of the Giant Rat

In the search for Conan Doyle–or, to be more precise, in the search for the hidden, deeply reflective, Conan Doyle–the dictionary is the one indispensable tool. What the hazel-twig is to the dowser searching for water; what the aluminum coat-hanger was to the men of the U.S. Corps of Engineers "dowsing" for non-metallic mines in the jungles of Vietnam; so has the dictionary been to me in my search for the explanation of Doyle's name-choices: specifically, in that "unreported" case of the *Matilda Briggs* and the giant rat of Sumatra.

Without a dictionary–notably *The Standard Pronouncing Dictionary of the English Language,* "compiled and edited by P. Austin Nuttall, LL.D."–the origin and significance of that strange reference to, not only the Giant Rat, but, even more strangely, the East Indian island of Sumatra would never, I feel, have been discovered by me. (I specify Nuttall's *Dictionary*–in particular, the edition of 1871–as it is clear that this was the principal, if indeed not the only, dictionary of the English language habitually consulted by Conan Doyle throughout his life. It is not only the *meaning,* as found in *Nuttall,* but also the *phrasing,* which have inspired those flights of catachrestic fancy which have sprung from Conan Doyle's consideration of a word's many possible significances.)

Let me now explain how, first, I came to explain that esoteric reference to Sumatra, and, after that, how I came to identify and track down the Giant Rat.

I have no doubt that it was Conan Doyle's friend H. B. Irving, the then noted criminologist, who aroused or, may be, merely revived Doyle's interest in Mrs. Maybrick. Irving was the son of the great Sir Henry Irving, who, acting the name-part of Corporal Gregory Brewster in *Waterloo,* had given Conan Doyle his first stage success. It is understandable that Conan Doyle felt for Sir Henry Irving both respect and gratitude, and that Irving's criminologist son became one of Conan Doyle's most steadfast friends.

Having by 1911 already achieved considerable reputation as a writer on crime, H. B. Irving was commissioned by the Edinburgh publishers, William Hodge & Company, to contribute a volume to the firm's "Famous British Trials" series, and in 1912 appeared Irving's *The Trial of Mrs. Maybrick.* It is unthinkable that H. B. Irving did not present a signed copy to his friend Sir Arthur Conan Doyle. In any case, it seems clear that Doyle read it.

I have no doubt that the first puzzling matter to catch Doyle's interest, as he leafed through the *Trial,* was that curious name that the dead Maybrick's house bore: "Battlecrease House." What an extraordinary name! What on earth *was* a "battlecrease"? One knew what a "battle" was; but what, then, was a "crease"? What was defined by the dictionary as "A line or mark made by folding or doubling anything; a hollow streak, like a groove"? But *that* didn't seem to make sense. And then Doyle remembered (as I myself remembered) a word which, in his younger days, was spelled "crease" but had come to have its spelling slightly changed, as he checked with his *Nuttall's:*

> **Kris**, *n.* kreece, creece: a Malay dagger with a wavy blade.

And there were so many ways in which the word "Malay" would then have been familiar to Conan Doyle. In the first place, there is the mysterious Malay who knocked at the door of De Quincey's cottage:

> One day a Malay knocked at my door. What business a Malay could have to transact amongst English mountains, I cannot conjecture; but possibly he was on his road to a seaport about forty miles distant . . .

As all who have read *Confessions of an English Opium-Eater* know, the exotic caller at the door was (or seemed to be) *real*–and well-disposed, even though De Quincey refers to him, even on that first encounter, as "the ferocious-looking Malay"–but he was to return, in far less friendly guise:

> . . . [T]his Malay (partly . . . from the anxiety I connected with his image for some days) fastened afterwards upon my dreams, and brought other Malays with him worse than himself, that ran "a-muck" at me, and led me into a world of troubles. . . . The Malay has been a fearful enemy for months.

Malays came into Conan Doyle's reading in the 'eighties from a different direction. Great Britain, alarmed at the progress that the resurgent French were making in their efforts to gain possession of Indo-China, determined to put a barrier-colony between French Indo-China and British India by annexing Burma. Boys' books and magazines (as with modern comic strips) are always highly topical, and the leading *Boy's Own Paper,* for which Doyle himself wrote, ran several serials based on adventures in Burma and in a rather shadowily conceived "Far East," which included what are now called Indonesia and Malaysia.

Jungle and Stream; or, The Adventures of Two Boys in Siam by George Manville Fenn may serve as a typical example of this class of writing, which shifted its interest to Egypt and the Soudan after Burma was annexed in 1886, and the plans to avenge Gordon's murder by the Khalifa formed the principal theme of stories for the British boys' market.

This is really a word-association exercise–Conan Doyle would have delighted any psychiatrist who sets store by this system of analysis. For, having checked the meaning of "crease" as "a Malay dagger with a wavy blade," Doyle now examined the semantic content of "wavy blade," and must have come up with this from *Nuttall's:*

> **Blade:** . . . a dashing, rakish fellow . . .
>
> **Wavy:** . . . playing to and fro . . .
>
> **Wave,** *v.n.:* To play loosely . . . to waver . . .
>
> **Wave,** *v.a.:* . . . to move one way and the other; to brandish . . . to beckon; to cast away; to reject; to quit; to to depart from; to put off; to relinquish, as a right or privilege: usually written *waive* . . .

Well, now, Conan Doyle must have reflected, we have all the elements which go into the making of that most uncertain of all lovers, Arthur Brierley, dyer and laundryman, of 22 Mount Vernon Road, Liverpool, with his place of business in *Java* Street, Burlington Street, Liverpool–and Java, as any map will show, is the big island to the east of, and practically touching, Sumatra. (And Doyle did not miss the echo of the murderous "Dyaks"–a people of Borneo with the reputation of "thugs"–in that trade-name *dyer;* nor the exact echo of the name of the murderous Mrs. Dyer, the notorious–and later hanged–"baby-farmer.")

To the *preux chevalier* Conan Doyle, the two prime villains of the Maybrick case were the treacherous confidante, Mrs. Matilda Briggs, and the cowardly lover, Arthur Brierley, who left his mistress as the prey of others. Doyle was very much of a prude (he quarrelled with his brother-in-law over Hornung's "modern" broad-mindedness), but though, to Doyle, sexual irregularity was no commendable thing, disloyalty–and cowardly disloyalty at that–was worse.

Shocked as he undoubtedly was by the clear evidence of Mrs. Briggs's treachery, as set out so plainly in his friend Irving's detailed account of the Maybrick trial, it can only have been with a most disturbing sense of *déja vu* that he found himself encountering, *for the second time,* the not-all-that-common name of "Matilda Briggs"–and more, he had first encountered that name in what, to the young and still-struggling Conan Doyle, were circumstances of the greatest importance in his striving to establish a literary career.

Conan Doyle's first important story, as it was his first truly successful one, was "J. Habakuk Jephson's Statement," written at Southsea in, probably, 1883 and published in the *Cornhill* magazine for January 1884. "Habakuk" is described by the late John Dickson Carr as "a highly fanciful tale, based on the derelict mystery-ship, *Mary Celeste*"; an adequate description of a tale which, as Carr adds correctly, "had repercussions beyond critical praise"—a fact into which we need not enter here.

What is truly relevant here is that the real *Mary Celeste,* found derelict in the Atlantic without a soul on board, had sailed under the command of Captain Briggs...and Captain Briggs's daughter, who sailed with her father in the ill-fated barque, was named *Matilda.* All this years before Conan Doyle was to meet the name again in the account of the Maybrick murder trial.

In that reference to the "unreported" case, the *Matilda Briggs* is the name of a ship—but here, "ship" merely symbolizes "Liverpool" and Thomas Briggs's martime business. Doyle had found "crease" and "blade" and "wavy" and "wave"—and now he was to turn to what was nearest to the name "Brierley" in the dictionary, to see what *Nuttall's* had to say about "the dashing, rakish fellow, playing to and fro." This is what Conan Doyle found that *Nuttall's* had to tell him...

There was—and is—no such *word* as "brierley"; though there is, of course, "brier" ("A prickly plant or shrub; the bramble; a wild species of the rose") and "briered" ("Set with briers"). In fact, the nearest word in the dictionary to "Brierley" is "briery," which is followed immediately afterward by what must have struck Conan Doyle (as it did me) with something of a sense of shock:

> **Briery,** *bri'-er-e, a.* Full of briers; rough, thorny.
>
> **Briery,** *s.* A place where briers grow.
>
> **Brig,** *brig, s.* A small vessel with two masts, square-rigged...

So here, in *Nuttall's,* almost by chance, as it were, Doyle found, cheek-by-jowl, the near-enough names of the two arch-villains (as Doyle saw them) in the Maybrick tragedy. No wonder that the evil Mrs. Briggs was memorialized, in Conan Doyle's most cryptic code, as a small trading vessel working the pirate-infested waters of the Far East.

For by this time, the original names and words had sprouted and re-sprouted like a bunch of undisciplined Japanese water-flowers. And there was even further reinforcement for the trend toward the "orientalizing" of the Maybrick–Brierley–Briggs word-play. Here is the relevant entry in *Gore's Street Directory of Liverpool,* 1889:

> Briggs, Thomas, flax and jute merchant, Oriel Chambers, 14, Water Street, Liverpool.

The Liverpool jute was imported direct from *Burma.*

One thing only needs to be explained now that we have accounted for the "Far Eastern" element which originated in the simple recognition, by Conan Doyle, that the mysterious second half of the house-name "Battlecrease" could only mean "a Malay dagger with a wavy blade." That the commodity in which Mr. Briggs dealt–*jute*–and the name of the street where Brierley had his dyeing and laundry depôt–*Java*–had the strongest associations with the Far East was purely fortuitous but still served to reinforce Doyle's fanciful creation of an "Oriental" atmosphere from that half-word, or half-name, "crease."

The juxtaposition of the words "briery" and "brig" in *Nuttall's* must have seemed to Conan Doyle an almost mysterious affirmation of his suspicion that the real reason why Mrs. Matilda Briggs betrayed her best friend was a base desire to supplant Mrs. Maybrick in the "wavy" affections of Arthur Brierley, that "blade"; that (as *Nuttall's* explains) "dashing, rakish fellow."

How did Mrs. Maybrick first meet him? In connection with some dyeing? In connection with the "sent-out" laundry at Battlecrease House? Did Mrs. Maybrick feel a sentimental pang in hearing Brierley's private address, not only American, but very grandly American: Mount Vernon Road? That he was a weak-principled philanderer is not to be denied, and that Mrs. Maybrick was not his only conquest could explain much of what happened in the "select" Liverpool suburb of Aigburth, where they all had their comfortably large houses.

Small-minded he may have been, but he was not small physically. He was indeed well-named by Conan Doyle the "Giant Rat"–not of Sumatra, but of Java Street: named from the next island to Sumatra as one goes east. . .

Sumatra and Formosa: A Giant Rat and a Certain Corruption

The so-far-unexplained mention of two Far Eastern islands in the Canon–Sumatra and Formosa–has puzzled many a Sherlockian exegetist; and not in spite of, but because of, the fact that the names are mentioned in two adventures of quite unrelated plot, and those separated by a time interval of eleven years (*The Dying Detective,* 1913, and *The Sussex Vampire,* 1924). What then is the explanation of this mention of the two large East Indian islands; and are they, as mentioned, though occurring in two stories of different plot and date, linked in any way?

Yes: they are linked. . .but not, as the advertising men say, "plot-wise"; they are linked only in Conan Doyle's word-play, and both originate in his unhappy reflections on the tragedy of Mrs. Maybrick, in which, to the always gallant woman-championing Doyle, the treachery of her friends was almost more shocking than her condemnation at the hands of the insane, woman-hating judge. And of these treacherous friends, the most treacherous—as she was to prove herself the most dangerous—was Mrs. Matilda Briggs.

Now it is more or less commonly accepted that Conan Doyle was less than happy during his schooldays at Stonyhurst; but this does not mean that what he was taught—and well taught—at that renowned Jesuit academy did not mould his character in such a way that it reflected his Jesuit training in all that he was to think and do for all the years of his life. And, like most human beings, as he grew older his memory concerned itself more and more with a constantly receding past: and very important in that past were the Classical tongues to which all the educationalists of the last century attached such prime importance. Conan Doyle never forgot the Latin which had taken up so many hours of class- and "prep"-time at school, but which was a compulsory subject in *all* British universities until nearly the middle of the present century, and which, further, entered so largely into the education of a physician or surgeon in that better-educated epoch (all prescriptions in the *British Pharmacopoeia* were given in Latin).

I am not a Witness for Jehovah, nor yet a Fundamentalist of the Morristown persuasion, but it is my innocent habit to read the Bible frequently—both in the Authorized (the American's "King James") version and in the French equivalent (my wife's copy). Now, in my browsing through the pages of that unique Book, a thought—at first encounter, seemingly somewhat fanciful; perhaps a little too fanciful—entered my head: could the name—word, rather—"Sumatra" have "happened" in Conan Doyle's "playing around" with the Vulgate (Latin text) original of *The Song of Songs*, where the unnamed lover proclaims herself proudly as being "black but comely"?

Latin, a language rich in words, has, as does English, a number of ways of expressing the idea, "the opposite of white"; of all these the two most important are the words *niger* (feminine *nigra*) and *ater* (feminine *atra*), where *nigra*, the choice of the Vulgate, means "shining black," whilst *atra*, "dead black"—and, by extension, "dark, gloomy, boding ill," and, even further, "malicious, poisonous, accursed."

It did occur to me that Conan Doyle, not only a Jesuit-trained Latinist but one familiar (at least in boyhood) with Holy Writ, may well have, thinking of *The Song of Songs*, substituted *atra sum* ("I am darkest black-as-night") for the correct Vulgate *nigra sum* (merely, as the English version has it, "I am black . . .").

In contemplating this possibility—and at that time I could not feel justified in advancing it as anything like probability—I still had a curious persuasion that there might be something in it. Not for several days–indeed, not for many days, as it happened–did I realize that, were I to complete the *Latin* sentence which, in English begins, "I am black. . ." I should have the most convincing, as well as the most startling, confirmation of the accuracy of my intuition–wild as the supposition might have seemed, even to myself.

First of all, it is of importance to note a fact which, even in the most carefully detailed accounts of the Maybrick trial, has been completely ignored: that Mrs. Matilda Briggs was, like her betrayed friend, Florence Maybrick, a remarkably attractive woman: handsome of face, elegant of dress, and extremely conscious of her attractiveness, especially of its influence on the ordinarily susceptible male.

So that, given the close "friendship" of two women of not merely comparable physical attractiveness but of *competing* physical attractiveness, we need seek nothing more recondite than ordinary sexual jealousy sufficiently to explain the betrayal of one woman by the other. (Weak, cowardly Mr. Brierley, whatever his imperfections of spirit, must have had considerable physical attractions for married women with well-to-do husbands far too much engrossed in business or other affairs not to neglect their womenfolk. The simple truth, not apparently detected by even so astute a criminologist as H. B. Irving or Edgar Lustgarten or Nigel Morland, when each came to write–and all passionately "pro-Maybrick"–on the trial, is that both Florence Maybrick and Matilda Briggs were actively competing for the favours of Arthur Brierley. It really is–was–as simple as that.)

We shall not, I think, ever know why, of all the world's erotic literary compositions, *The Song of Songs* became associated in Conan Doyle's mind with the tragic Maybrick affair–but there is, perhaps, a clue to that association in an echo of a cry from *The Song of Songs* in one of Florence Maybrick's more guarded but not less passion-inspired letters.

Mindless with the erotomania of the *furor femineus,* the Woman of the Song cries:

> Stay me with flagons; comfort me with apples; for I am *sick of love.*

And the passion-racked Florence Maybrick writes to her lover (about the grievously ill Mr. Maybrick):

> *He is sick unto death.* [Her emphasis]

Perhaps, as Conan Doyle read this, the curiously Biblical phrasing of Mrs. Maybrick's sentence may, in his mind, have echoed that cry from *The Song of Songs.* But whatever the reason for his associating Mrs.

Maybrick with *The Song of Songs,* the nexus was established and, as I shall now show, is undeniable.

Thus, to Conan Doyle's way of thinking, Mrs. Briggs could be made to say quite correctly of herself (quoting *The Song of Songs* 1:5), "I am black (-hearted, that is) but comely . . ." But Doyle, reflecting that the "black" of the Vulgate–*nigra*–hardly did justice to the blackness of Mrs. Briggs's heart, substituted for *nigra* the Latin word for "dense black, black-as-night, malicious, poisonous, accursed": *atra.*

So that, instead of the Vulgate's *nigra sum* . . . Doyle substituted *atra sum.*

But now, see how the completed Latin sentence runs. When *I* completed it, I couldn't imagine why I hadn't seen at once what was so clearly to be seen. Look!

> Authorized (King James) version: *I am black but comely* . . .
> Vulgate (Latin) version: *Nigra sum sed* . . . (wait for it!) . . .
> *FORMOSA* . . .

One may say, in English, either "I am black" or "black I am"; and the Latin is even more tolerant of such inversions, so that one may say *Nigra sum* or *Sum nigra.* (And Doyle, remember, put *atra* for *nigra* . . .)

I thought it possible that "Sumatra" *might* have resulted accidentally from the inverting of *atra sum* into *sum atra,* but no such inversion need be postulated in the case of the Latin word for "comely," *formosa.* And thus to find that (a highly probable) "Sumatra" is found in the closest apposition to a *certain* "Formosa" would seem, in my opinion, to certify the correctness of my proposed derivation of "Sumatra" from the inversion of *atra sum.* And, furthermore, the background of the Maybrick case surely now explains that hitherto mysterious "black Formosa corruption" as (in the view of Conan Doyle, no mean prude in sexual matters!) "the moral corruption which so often, and so tragically, proceeds from physical beauty."

The reference to the "Formosa corruption" (which may be read as "the corruption that the beautiful–*formosa*–often breeds") occurs in the adventure of *The Dying Detective,* which appeared in *Collier's* in late November and in the *Strand* in December 1913–and so would have been written shortly after Conan Doyle would have read his friend H. B. Irving's account of the Maybrick trial, which had been published in the previous year. Eleven years later, returning to the theme of the Maybrick tragedy in *The Sussex Vampire* (1924), Conan Doyle *almost* emerges from the cryptic in using the full and correct names of the Maybrick traitress, though still hesitating at a complete revelation, and, though naming Matilda Briggs *en clair,* maintains the cryptic in his reference to the "giant rat of Sumatra"–a reference which, since its first appearance in 1924, has successfully defied all the ingenuity of two full generations of Sherlexegetists to explain.

Here, then–and for the first time–is the explanation, the interpretation, of those cryptic references to the case of the *Matilda Briggs*, the "giant rat of Sumatra," and the "Formosa corruption."

Originating in Conan Doyle's "improving" on a well-known quotation from *The Song of Songs;* in his substituting *atra sum* (developing into *sum atra*) for the Vulgate's *nigra sum*, the changed initial words became Doyle's cryptic name for Mrs. Briggs: "Sum atra"–"I am black-hearted, malicious, treacherous, ruthless (but comely, of course: for Beauty is my stock-in-trade. . .)" So the altered phrase *sum atra*–"Sumatra"–fits black-hearted Mrs. Briggs well indeed. We shall read "Matilda Briggs" for "Sumatra." What, then, does "Matilda Briggs and the Giant Rat of Sumatra" mean?

Simply this: "Matilda Briggs and 'Sumatra's' Giant Rat"–or, even more plainly, "Matilda Briggs and her Giant Rat"–that very tall, immoral, cowardly Mr. Arthur Brierley whom Matilda Briggs had captured for herself through the most black-hearted treachery. . .

Envoi

Conan Doyle never forgot what he had read in *The Exeter Flying Post*, to which he had gone for the details of the Oliver–Galley trial; and there were many items outside the report of that (for Conan Doyle) seminal trial which seem to have impressed him even more strongly. Mrs. Elizabeth Bird, for instance, and the false accusation respecting her "blue-stone". . .

In one of Doyle's medical tales, "The Third Generation," a young baronet, stricken with a fatal hereditary disease (and due, after he has been given the terrifying prognosis by the fashionable doctor, to commit suicide), sits waiting, in the doctor's consulting-room, for the Great Man.

To take his mind, even momentarily, off his fear, young, unjustly-doomed Sir Francis looked around the room–"nothing was too slight to arrest his attention." And, as Conan Doyle describes all the items which catch the stricken patient's eye, it need not surprise us that, amongst those articles, "There was one [bottle] with a broad neck, just above him, containing bluestone. . ." So that, far beyond the wide limits of the Canon, the memory of Mrs. Bird and her "blue-stone" was ever-present in Conan Doyle's mind. . .

INDEX